By the same

The Manor House Stories

A series of beautifully produced traditional books for children
and the young at heart. These stories, charmingly illustrated by
the author, recount the daily adventures of a family of birds who
live at the house, recalling the values and traditions of a gentler
way of life that disappeared long ago ...
Foreword by Julian Fellowes

www.themanorhousestories.com

A Greek Island Nature Diary

A lavish journal of watercolours and pencil drawings of the flora,
fauna and natural objects seen and collected during the author's
years living in Corfu and sailing the Ionian. The book includes
descriptions of the medicinal, olfactory and culinary uses of
the wild plants, as well as personal observations, smatterings of
related Greek Mythology, folklore and quotations.
Foreword by John Seymour, Duke of Somerset
Introduction by Dr Lee Durrell MBE

(To be published shortly by Unicorn Press)
www.janitullychaplin.com/books

I dared to swop *swapping* for *swopping*,
I even swopped *swapped* for *swopped*;
Swop is tip-top and looks better than *swap*,
But I wouldn't try messing with *crop*.

Jeremy Just Chaplin

Jani Tully Chaplin

The Butterflies Fly Backwards

To travel is to live.
Hans Christian Anderson

Cover image: *View across the Corfu Straits from Agni*
Jani Tully Chaplin, © 2001

Enquiries to: jani@janitullychaplin.com
www.janitullychaplin.com/books
www.themanorhousestories.com

Printed and bound in the UK by Gomer Press Ltd, Ceredigion

Typesetting and design by JS Typesetting Ltd, Porthcawl, Mid Glamorgan
jstype@btconnect.com

Cover layout by Rory James Christopher Chaplin,
RJCC Events, Oxfordshire
rjccevents.com

FSC logo here

Author's note

I wish all my Corfiot, English and cosmopolitan friends could have found their way into these pages; they all played and continue to play their much valued parts in the lives of my family.

Several of the characters in this book have been disguised to protect both the innocent and the guilty alike; the innocent who do appear have been described with much affection.

This all began as a diary for my family. I make no apology for any similarities to other books about families in Corfu, for this is exactly how it happened.

This book is dedicated to Jeremy, my long suffering husband of 40 years at the time of writing. He has been our family's Captain in so many ways, carefully steering his crew of Rory, Miranda, me and our Cavalier King Charles spaniels over calm and stormy seas, navigating us through so many unchartered waters. He has been our anchor and found us safe harbours with unparalleled skill and fortitude. He has been at the helm of our little ship, steering us steadfastly through life's gales, on the right course according to his instinctive compass of what was best for us. He has sailed us through the eddies of education, the typhoons of teenagers, the hurricanes of house building and the whirlpools of wanderlust. Whether to port or starboard he has guided us fore and aft, hoisted the mainsail and used his sextant to measure the progress of our passage. He is our port in a storm, the first one we turn to for direction and help. He has climbed from the yardarm to the top of the mast to call 'Land Ahoy!' if we lost our way. He has surfed the tidal waves of misfortune and brought us through the roaring forties safely back to shore. With his family aboard, all sail set and spinnaker billowing, he has taken us where we might never have gone, usually with a liferaft at the ready.

Without him this marvellous adventure would never have happened.

With love and gratitude from his First Mate.

Contents

Chapter One
Serendipity

Travelling leaves you speechless, then turns you into a storyteller.

Ibn Battuta, 14th century Moroccan explorer

Italy disappeared over the horizon as night fell, the thin ribbon of Calabrian shoreline replaced by menacing clouds and a stiffening wind. Thunder cracked and rumbled overhead as a curtain of rain bit at our heels and lashed into the rough seas just yards astern. Alone on my watch at the helm, I strained my watering eyes beyond the red glow of the compass into endless darkness, pierced at intervals by dazzling shards of lightning. Knowing there would be no landfall before dawn, I wondered for the umpteenth time why I had come on this journey; yet I knew if I stuck to the set course it would take us to our final destination, the magical island of Corfu.

Eventually the storm gave up its chase and by the time the soft silhouette of Corfu showed itself, crouching low against the first glimmer of eastern twilight, we were once again sailing beneath moon and stars. Too excited to sleep I found myself recalling Gerald Durrell's poetic words from *My Family and Other Animals*, so fondly and perfectly remembered since the day I had first read them:

> *The tiny ship throbbed away from the heel of Italy out into the twilit sea and ... somewhere in that tract of moon-polished water we passed the invisible dividing line and entered the bright, looking-glass world of Greece.*

* * *

I was just thirteen, sitting on a creaking wooden chair confined amidst the jaded elegance of my school library. Ancient cast iron radiators gurgled gently, giving off their low metallic warmth into an atmosphere already heavy with the drowsy mustiness of damp woollen blazers and dog-eared books; the ornate Adam fireplace beside me had long since been consigned to decorative purposes and housed a dusty arrangement of faded dried flowers. Tall Georgian windows were being lashed by stinging rain driven straight from the tors of Dartmoor, which lay swathed in heavy mist on that cold November afternoon. My set book was *My Family and Other Animals* by Gerald Durrell and little did I know then, as I began reading, how much this book would influence me; I must have read it a dozen times, yet it still conjures the same magic today as it did all those years ago.

Buried in the heart of the soggy Devonshire countryside I longed to visit this warm and colourful island set in a sparkling sea, about which the book was written. Corfu seemed a million miles away from the regimented life in an English boarding school during the late 'sixties; I could never have dreamt it would one day become my home. The vivid portrayal of the island remained locked within my head for years; I continued to dream of visiting Corfu one day, but life seemed to lead me in other directions. Exams, horses, finishing school, career, marriage to Jeremy, starting a family, a year's sabbatical in Spain and finally the serious business of educating our son and daughter had all conspired to frustrate that ambition. It was quite by chance, in the summer after Jeremy's mother had so very unexpectedly died, that a friend suggested we join them for a short holiday in Corfu. Unwittingly she had reopened the book.

"We're all going at the end of July," Bridget announced at the end of a particularly tedious Red Cross Committee meeting.

"You must come! You need to get away and there'll be loads of young for Rory and Miranda ... We're all renting villas in the North East of the island around Kassiopi."

It seems so strange now to think that I actually had to write down the name of the quaint, erstwhile fishing village that would become so very familiar to us.

"It's simply gorgeous!" she waxed lyrical, eyes glazing over. "Warm sea, wonderful countryside, delicious food … The Tennysons, Robertsons, and Cliftons are all coming; with you there'll be fourteen adults and twenty teenagers. Book today darling, it's exactly what you need!"

Looking out of the window of the drably depressing Devon Branch headquarters at the incessant drizzle and leaden sky I thought, 'Yes, Corfu. Sun, sea and Greeks – perfect for us all'. I drove straight to a travel agent and booked the only remaining property, the top floor of a fisherman's house overlooking the entrance to Kassiopi harbour.

Wherever you go, go with all your heart.

Confucius

The smart villas had gone, every last one reserved in the autumn of the previous year by those in the know; my family, the new kids on the block, would have to make do with whatever was left. Actually, although it was positively the only accommodation available, the little house turned out to be charming. It was central, clean if decidedly spartan, with French windows in each bedroom that opened onto a long balcony from where one could lob an olive pitt into the shimmering sea, beyond which the parched foothills of Albania rose beneath distant mountains. Our apartment soon became the envy of all and my husband was quietly delighted it had cost a quarter the price of our friends' luxury villas up in the hills above Kassiopi, where the swimming pools were constantly patrolled by hordes of angry wasps that year. The heat also seemed to collect in parts of the countryside where the evening sea breeze did not blow home, sometimes persisting well into the night. Cocktail parties up in the hills could be uncomfortably hot, the mercury on a shaded terrace still obstinately stuck at a debilitating thirty-five degrees at eight in the evening.

Despite coinciding with a fierce heatwave we enjoyed a wonderful week, swimming and lazing on white pebble coves just two minutes walk around the headland from our house. At sunset we would amble back to shower and change before meeting our party of friends at a taverna for supper. With three courses followed by coffee, and a score of us at two tables, the meal would take most of the evening; sometimes we would drift to one of the harbourside bars for nightcaps – a Greek brandy or an exotic cocktail. Jeremy and I rarely visited pubs in England, but the prospect of drinks served by a friendly and attentive waiter at a waterside table beneath the stars, where children were not only welcome but expected, was difficult to resist. As the nights were almost as hot as the days my family often returned along the rough path to the beach where, by the light of a brilliant moon, we would cool ourselves in milk soft sea; it was so clear we could study the texture of every pebble beneath our feet, marvelling at the phosphorescence sparkling around us like glitter as we disturbed the sleeping water.

Corfu was beginning to cast its gentle spell.

* * *

I knew when I met you an adventure was going to happen.

Winnie the Pooh, A.A. Milne

During these few days fond memories of our two years living amongst Greeks in Cyprus came flooding back. Jeremy and I had bought our first catamaran less than a month after our March engagement; it was as if she had been waiting for us. I was modelling in London when Jeremy telephoned to tell me about her; the first thing I asked him – by far the most pertinent in my expert opinion – was her colour. I choose my cars in very much the same way and have rarely been disappointed.

"Her hulls are dark chocolate and the decks are cream," he replied with a tinge of disapproval.

That just happened to be my favourite colour scheme at the time and was very much in vogue. Then I asked her name.

"Aries," he answered.

"Buy her!" I said without a moment's hesitation.

"Are you sure? You haven't even seen her yet."

But I was so certain she was meant for us, both being Arians; moreover she was lying close by in Plymouth and was a rare, much sought after example of a brand new design.

The first time I saw her I fell in love; she looked so elegant and distinctive with her spacious decks and tinted windows. Below decks I marvelled at the roomy accommodation and well equipped modern galley, its long windows giving a panoramic view of the water outside; at least I would have interesting views as I did the washing up. But I began to feel decidedly seasick, despite being securely moored to the jetty in a flat clam. This was slightly worrying, but we were not yet married and I couldn't possibly let on to Jeremy.

We had married in May, giving my poor mother just six weeks to organise the wedding; but as my future husband explained, we needed to catch the weather window for the journey to Cyprus. I had originally intended to fly out to join Jeremy and Aries in Larnaca, having never sailed before in my life; I preferred my horses to boats and would even feel seasick on the Dartmouth ferry. However, all the rest of my family had been keen sailors, so when Jeremy showed my parents the route he had planned on the charts I began to be tempted by the wonderful places he would be visiting on the three thousand mile voyage, not to mention the countless shopping opportunities. Since I was a very tiny girl I have always loved buying things – any little souvenir – whenever I visit somewhere. I am even satisfied with a handful of postcards, as long as I have bought *something*. The traders of Gibraltar were renowned for silk pyjamas; in Spain and her islands there would be beautiful leather handbags and belts; Sardinia would be awash with fabulous shoes and silk scarves. I could buy lace in Malta and Crete would offer delectable Byzantine style jewellery, while Rhodes would be stacked with convincing copies of designer umbrellas and high end fashions at astonishingly reasonable prices, as there was no tax on luxury goods on Greek soil. My resolve was starting to slip.

Mummy made it plain she would think me very feeble if I did not accompany Jeremy all the way; it would be our honeymoon after all. In truth my parents' encouragement was extraordinarily selfless; they had lost their only son, my older brother Christopher, when he was drowned in Torbay at the age of fifteen. His body was never found, but his sailing canoe had been washed up in a cove near Brixham a year later. I'm sure she must have regretted her words when we were crossing the Bay of Biscay, out of contact for five days until reaching a telephone in La Coruňa. During our third afternoon at sea a Nimrod long range reconnaissance aircraft had swooped low over us, a figure in the cockpit waving enthusiastically. Jeremy remained convinced it was my mother.

We had set sail from Salcombe in July 1980, taking just six weeks to reach Larnaca. Could it have been a premonition of this journey that I had dreamt one night when, as a young teenager, I had stayed at Jeremy's family home near Salcombe? My schoolfriend Denise and I both lived twenty miles away in Torbay, so Jeremy's mother had invited us to stay after a party in one of the farm's barns, rather than have our parents collect us after midnight. Denise and I shared a beautiful Regency four-poster bed in one of the spare bedrooms; the large Georgian window next to the bed enjoyed uninterrupted views over the fields to the estuary below. That night I had dreamt most vividly (five years before the Disney film *Bedknobs and Broomsticks*) that the bed had magically flown out of the open window with me in it, landing on the estuary and slowly sailing away towards the sea … Fifteen years later Jeremy and I sailed away from the very same spot below our land; in all the 3,000 miles to Cyprus I never felt seasick.

We had loved the way of life in Cyprus for its climate, the friendliness of the Greek Cypriots and the variety of its food; but most of all we had enjoyed the freedom afforded by living on a boat. From early spring to late autumn we could cast off for days at a time on trips to deserted bays where, surrounded by everything we possessed, including our wedding presents which had been geared to life afloat, we were utterly self-contained and self-sufficient. I had succeeded in getting quite a lot of modelling work in the thriving Cypriot fashion industry and Jeremy had taken various skippering jobs. Thus we lived extremely well on a fairly meagre income, only returning to England two years later for Rory's imminent arrival.

Being on Greek soil once more in Corfu after fifteen years was like awakening from a long sleep, reaffirming our love for this corner of the world and its people; the remoter parts of Corfu resembled the Cyprus we had loved so much before its idyllic coastline was blighted by the march of reinforced concrete. The sight of the boats in Kassiopi harbour and the yachts at anchor in neighbouring bays and coves reminded us how much we missed Aries, especially as we had not owned a boat since our year's sabbatical in Spain. Back then, in the late 1980's, we had bought a forty-foot motorboat of the tinted patio door variety – much against all our instincts – which nevertheless was an eminently practical craft for a family with a small child and a baby on board.

"No wonder Jani likes her," my father had remarked to Jeremy when he first saw *Seahawk*. "She looks just like Hoopers!" (in those days a luxurious department store on The Strand in Torquay).

For a challenge Jeremy had taken Seahawk straight across the Bay of Biscay and around Cape St Vincent in mid-November – setting something of a record in the process – while I flew with the children, my parents, a young nanny and eighteen pieces of luggage, to meet him in Moraira for Christmas. Sitting in bed on Boxing Day, reading the local newspaper, Jeremy spotted an advertisement for a house for sale a few kilometres inland from Javea; a million miles from the dozens of homogenous urbanisations stuffed with expats, it sounded perfect for us. A picturesque 200 year-old finca nestling in two acres of tranquil isolation amidst a patchwork of orange and almond groves, *La Abubilla* was also astonishingly cheap – in fact almost too good to be true. Nevertheless it was ours within the week.

Some of our furniture soon arrived from Devon, including the Georgian 4-poster bed in which I had sailed away to sea in my dreams so many years earlier; Jeremy's mother had given it to us as a wedding present and it had to be hauled through our bedroom balcony at the finca, being far too large to carry up the dogleg staircase. We quickly congratulated ourselves as we settled into life under the warm spring sunshine; at weekends we would potter around the coast and during the summer months we would take off to Ibiza. Seahawk's main advantage was speed; from Ibiza Town we could reach the unspoilt island of Espalmador in minutes, spend the whole day swimming and be back in Ibiza in good time for supper. Five year-old Rory had been too young to be able to help with the boat, despite his most gallant efforts, while nine month-old Miranda had spent most of the day in her lobster-pot playpen safe in the shade of the deep cockpit. We missed the whole ethos of sailing, but sailing boats are difficult with young children and we knew we would have to bide our time.

When the time came for Rory to take his place at prep school we disposed of Seahawk, having already sold our little farmhouse that nestled in the fertile valley beneath the village of Jesús Pobre, or Poor Jesus. *La Abubilla* should have provided an idyllic setting and home for a young family – were it not for the robbers. The first burglary happened while friends from Devon were staying with us with their three year-old son James. We had all been for supper in the nearby town of Denia and it was pitch dark when we returned home to find we were treading on broken glass. The *reja* bars protecting the French doors of the garden entrance had been wrenched out of the walls and the glass panes smashed. Inside was a scene of havoc and destruction; chairs had been overturned and every cupboard and chest of drawers had been opened and searched, the contents scattered all over the stone floors. Upstairs the same turmoil greeted us; my few pieces of jewellery were missing, as well as some electrical equipment and a briefcase containing important documents. Rory's eyes were like saucers as he clutched my hand tightly; we were all speechless until little James, a great fan of cowboy cartoons, broke the silence.

"Do you think it was Indians, Mummy?" he announced to Denise in a high, clear voice.

We reported the incident to the local Guardia Civil in Javea the following morning. There was much shrugging of shoulders and puffing of cigarette smoke, but they couldn't care less because we were foreigners and they had seen it all so many times before. A couple of weeks later we returned from a shopping trip to Altea to find the doors to the small courtyard had been broken down, the heavy front door within forced open. Once again the burglars had been back in action and stolen whatever they could lay their sticky fingers on, although there was little of value in the house as most of our personal belongings were in store in England. This time we didn't bother to inform the Javea plod and of course there was no insurance company to notify.

Less than month later friends from Munich had come to stay. On arrival they left their luggage in the guest *casita,* which stood on the far side of the swimming pool only fifty yards from the main house. Halfway through lunch Vanessa asked Stefan to fetch her camera; he ran back within seconds with the news that all their suitcases had been opened and rifled, their cash, cameras and Vanessa's handbag all gone. We hadn't heard a thing and realised the thieves must have climbed through a back window of the casita.

Every time we came home after that, even if we had only been out for a few minutes, Jeremy would lock us in the car while he crept into the house armed with a crowbar, hoping to catch the burglars red-handed. In fact it was very fortunate that he never did manage to catch the intruders in the house, as several foreign home owners had been shot and killed by burglars who they had disturbed mid-crime. By the sixth burglary the robbers had resorted to taking our clothes and even the children's toys.

"A house near Jesús Pobre, for heaven's sake!" I had furiously exclaimed to Jeremy as we cleared up yet more broken glass. "No wonder

Jesús was poor! He probably got robbed silly too!"

Enough was enough: we moved onto Seahawk and put the finca up for sale, having occupied it for less than five months. The boat was air-conditioned, spacious and comfortable; moreover the marina had twenty-four hour security and the children would feel safe again.

Before our summer visit to England at the end of June we took Seahawk to Ibiza for a week's holiday; there I bought Rory and Miranda some beautiful children's clothes and swimwear, as well as summer wear for Jeremy and me as replacements for our stolen clothes. Back in Moraira we packed all our new clothes, rolls of unde-veloped film and everything else needed for our journey by car back to England the following day. We were intending to stay with my parents in Devon for a couple of weeks, then on to Sussex to stay with Jeremy's parents before returning to Spain for Rory's final term of Spanish school. During our absence in Ibiza our remaining furni-ture had been collected and sent home to England; the finca was now empty apart from a few clothes of Jeremy's, which the robbers had obviously decided were too unfashionable to touch.

Our car was going to be full to bursting when all the accumulated luggage was eventually stuffed in; the children would have to squeeze in amongst the cases and bags at the last moment. So, just before we set off for England, we left these remaining possessions at the finca for twenty minutes while we dashed out for some fresh snacks and drinks for the journey. Surely the little house was impenetrable now; the doors and windows had all been heavily reinforced in turn after each burglary. But we had not counted on the zeal of our burglars, who had somehow got in again and made off with the lot.

French doors in the children's bedroom led onto a tiny semi-circular balcony which was enclosed by a cage of iron bars; two centuries ear-lier when the finca was built, these impenetrable little balconies were designed to prevent ardent Spanish Romeos from climbing into the maidens' bedrooms. We had always reassured Rory, who was getting more and more nervous with each robbery, that no burglars could ever break into his room because of the iron bars. However there was also a tiny ventilation window, no larger than a box of Cornflakes, high on a wall in the bedroom. Rory had been the first to look upstairs, where to his horror he found a large carving knife lying on the floor where Miranda's cot had once been; the wire mesh on the little window above had been slashed open, allowing a small child the size of Rory to squeeze through the opening. When Jeremy looked amongst the vines in the garden he found the fully extended pool cleaning net lying near the foot of the wall below. Obviously the thieves had hoisted a little urchin up to the window inside the frame of the the long handled net; the miniature acrobat had then cut his way through the netting, climbed in and unlocked a door from the inside.

This time the burglars had cleared our luggage, which contained everything we needed for the long journey back to England, including clean clothes for us all. I shot into the local market in Moraira and tried to find some clothes that were not beachwear. It would be several degrees cooler in Santander and even cooler on the ferry; in England it could be positively arctic even in mid summer. In desperation I found a lurid purple track suit which would fit Rory. Then I found an identical, tiny one for Miranda. But what about me? Jeremy could manage very well with his usual shirt and jeans but I had only the strappy sundress I was wearing. In desperation I looked at the very back of the rail for a larger suit that might fit me; and there in all its violet glory, (or violent gory, as Rory described it), was another suit to match the children's, clearly marked *Age 14*.

Three days later we arrived home in England, left with nothing else to wear except the matching purple track suits, although I was probably more upset about all the photographs we would never see. More importantly Rory was traumatised, haunted by images of a Captain Hook lookalike scaling the wall and climbing into his bedroom with a carving knife between his teeth. It was more than three years before Rory would go upstairs alone in any house – until Miranda learnt to walk, that is, when he would bribe her to climb the stairs in front

of him with the promise of a sweet at the top. Coincidentally we
abandoned Spain for good exactly one year after we had arrived the
previous December.

We eventually heard from the retired English couple to whom we
had sold the finca. They were grateful that we had warned them about
our string of burglaries, but assured us they knew how to cope with
such things having lived in Spain for many years. They had immediately erected two rows of ten-foot high wire fencing around the entire
property to discourage further thefts. Such fences were common in
Spain and every one of these enclosed properties resembled a giant,
floodlit tennis court; the narrow gap between the two netting fences,
the 'killing zone', was usually patrolled by large, very vicious guard
dogs. The new owners had a handsome golden retriever who gamely
patrolled the fences whenever his owners went out; but tragically,
less than two months after moving in, the burglars returned to the
blighted property and shot the pet dead before ransacking the house
again.

It made our blood run cold.

* * *

*It takes a lifetime for someone to discover Greece, but it only takes an instant to
fall in love with her.*

Henry Miller

The years had flown by and now Rory was fifteen and a competent
sailor, while Miranda was almost ten and a very confident swimmer;
suddenly the time had come when we might contemplate buying a
sailing boat again. Being confirmed warm weather sailors who had
been thoroughly spoilt by so much time afloat in the Mediterranean
and the West Indies, we could only entertain the idea of keeping a boat
in an equable, oilskin-free climate. The idea of returning to Corfu on
a regular basis had dawned on us both, but plans were forming in our
minds without either of us daring to voice them.

During that week of extreme heat we had taken a tourist caique from Kassiopi to Corfu Town one evening. We docked at seven in the evening but the temperature was still in the high eighties as we walked from the port, up through the narrow streets to the top of the town, where the aromas of fresh coffee, baking pastry, leather and expensive perfume wafted from the shops to mingle beneath festoons of fresh washing suspended high above the narrow side streets. Eventually we emerged onto the verdant expanse of the Espianada, pleasantly surprised and relieved to find slightly fresher air; turning around we were entranced by the sight of the Liston, the magnificent French colonial, five-storey arcaded building now home to a dozen restaurants; the perfect proportions of its façade were further enhanced by the patinated splendour of weathered plaster and paint, which glowed under the brilliant evening sky.

The four of us wandered along the promenade in search of an air-conditioned restaurant for supper before our return boat trip to Kassiopi, unaware of the cool shade offered by the acacia trees above the many outside tables. As we passed a jewellery shop that stood in isolation between the many restaurants, a rush of icy cold air wafted out of its open doors.

"Come on," I said. "Let's go in here to cool off for a minute."

"You can't, Mummy. They'll think you want to buy something!" insisted Miranda, who was still thinking like an English girl.

But I knew the Greeks better than she did. We stepped over the threshold to be greeted by the astonishing sight of handsome identical twins dressed in matching pale blue shirts and navy trousers; they welcomed us warmly and immediately offered us cold drinks.

"Oh no thank you; we won't be buying any jewellery, I'm afraid," I said apologetically. "We are just so hot! Do you mind if we cool off for a minute in your wonderful air-conditioning?"

"But of course you are most welcome," said one of the twins in impeccable English. "Take a seat and stay as long as you like. Where do you come from?"

"Oh, a tiny village in England, you won't have heard of it," I said.

"What part of England?"

"The West Country, South Devon actually," I replied, certain he would not know anywhere in Devon.

"Do you know Kingswear, by any chance?" inquired Christos, the chattier of the twins.

Miranda gasped.

"Very well indeed! Several of our friends live there; it's not far from our home," I replied in amazement.

"My mother-in-law's house is called Nethway, a great big Queen Annie mansion. You know it?" enquired Christos.

"That once belonged to a friend from school!" I exclaimed, hardly believing my ears.

As we chatted about Nethway and some mutual acquaintances in South Devon, we realised we had met Christos' mother-in-law and her Italian husband at our closest friends' wedding in Kingswear in 1983. I called Jeremy and Rory into the shop and made our formal introductions. Cold drinks arrived as if by magic and a table was spirited up for us at Aegli Restaurant next door; thus a potentially disastrous evening had been transformed into the most memorable night of our holiday. When Jeremy asked for the supper bill he was assured it had already been settled by our new friends, despite all protestation. We could not have known at the time that we would never be allowed to pay any such bill when the twins were with us, or even nearby: 'I can't take your money, sir; it's more than my job's worth!' the waiters would invariably reply.

Later, as our caique puttered up the coast through deliciously refreshing sea air, passing a handful of unspoilt capes and headlands on the way back to Kassiopi under a star filled sky, I thought it was high time to sow the seed.

"Wouldn't it be super to come back next year? It must be wonderful at Easter ... I must find out if our little house will be available."

"We need some sort of base here," Jeremy replied. "Somewhere we could come for most school holidays. We could probably get about eighteen weeks' use each year, if we put our minds to it."

Had I noticed the dreamy look in his eyes as he gazed at the shadowy shapes of indented coastline from the bow of the caique, I could have guessed what he had in mind; it was not the fisherman's house, nor yet a beachside apartment or luxury villa. His holiday home would have to incorporate a mast, sails and engines.

On the final day of our holiday we rented a small car for the day and went to explore. I had envisaged a day driving into the hills, marvelling at views of mountains and fertile valleys, enjoying the slightly cooler air, taking lunch at some rustic taverna before buying local honey and olive wood souvenirs on the way home. Jeremy, however, drove us determinedly in the opposite direction from the beckoning foothills, interrupting my daydreams.

"Why are we going this way?" I asked disappointedly.

"Well, there's this marina......"

"*Oh no!*" groaned the children and I in unison, realising we had been caught up in another pointless reconnaissance mission. We were all too well aware of Jeremy's total fascination with boats and his unhealthy interest in marinas and chandleries.

"It'll take hours," wailed Miranda, "I want to go swimming."

"It will be nice to see something different," cajoled Jeremy, "and there's bound to be a café serving croissants."

"Chocolate ones?" asked Miranda, perking up.

"I'm quite sure of it," retorted Jeremy, rather unconvincingly.

In our long experience of Mediterranean marinas we had seldom found any that offered drinkable coffee, let alone fresh croissants. Most ablution blocks were so appalling that you would be loath to bath a dog in them, certainly not yourself or your children: dirty floors, unlockable doors, smelly drains and enough hungry mosquitoes to deter even the staunchest yachtsman. Generally marinas are constructed in the most inhospitable areas, either where no breeze ever penetrates or where perpetual gales produce ragged nerves; favourite sites seemed to be chosen either for their proximity to industrial zones, or for their remoteness from any vaguely pleasant beach, civilization and shopping facilities; often they were cleverly carved directly out of a cliff face so that maximum reflected heat and swirling dust storms could smother you and your craft.

Rory, although slightly more sanguine about the visit, was feeling carsick in the back of the car, thanks to the hairpin bends of the coast road from Kassiopi. I swopped places with him, then felt carsick as well; consequently the children and I were irritably hot by the time we arrived at Gouvia an hour later. Jeremy was still exuding cheerful optimism, unusual for him except of course when matters nautical came into the equation. At first glance we could see this marina was different. Behind the car park was a luxuriantly green cricket pitch around which saplings had been planted; mimosa bushes decorated the grass verges and pink and white oleanders surrounded the buildings. The marina offices, shops and restaurants were built in deference to Corfiot style with a multitude of archways, shutters and balconies, the whole painted in a profusion of toning pastel colours. Of course we were still in Corfu, so the occasional quaintly attractive anomaly was only to be expected: a colossal pile of rusting chain and tangled cable at the centre of an immaculately planted flowerbed, or a rotting wooden yacht balanced at an alarming angle atop a hillock of freshly quarried boulders to resemble some studio back-lot reconstruction of a disastrous shipwreck.

We settled ourselves in one of the quayside cafes, having made use of the gleaming facilities, and ordered freshly squeezed orange juice and the elusive chocolate croissants while we waited for Jeremy to complete his enquiries at the office. The orange juice was ice-cool and served in long, frosted glasses with gaudy miniature paper parasols, which nine-year-old Miranda thought the height of sophistication; the sensuous pains-au-chocolat were hot and crisp on the outside with soft, warm chocolate oozing from within. Sitting on comfortably upholstered cane chairs in the shade of canvas awnings, we absorbed the view beyond the neat rows of shining yachts directly in front of us. The natural harbour of Gouvia, arguably once the most important in the Venetian Empire, has a spectacular setting; the view beyond the entrance stretches over the straits to the distant hills on the Greek-Albanian border, flanked to the north by the majestic presence of Pantokrator Mountain. It was a stunningly beautiful outlook, by far the best I had seen from any marina in the Mediterranean. Across the bay stood a tiny, picture postcard white church, sitting at the end of a narrow causeway like a sugar lump; the nearer promontory provided thickly wooded shelter to a cluster of ramshackle fishermen's cottages, fronted by rickety wooden piers bedecked with nets drying in the sun. In the majority of marinas your berth faces a singularly unattractive concrete seawall or an even uglier stone breakwater; unless you climb to the top of your mast you will never gain sight of the open sea.

The sun was at its zenith as Jeremy emerged from the air-conditioned office, looking rather smug and clutching a glossy brochure. We spent the rest of that day back on the beach at Kassiopi, the children and I in the water, Jeremy under an umbrella engrossed in his brochure and undoubtedly choosing his future berth. Unable to get any sense out of him about our plans for dinner, I gave up and resigned myself to the inevitable. One look at his glazed expression told me all I needed to know: from now on we would be seriously on the lookout for the third boat in our married life.

On the final evening of our holiday our group of friends had arranged to meet at a taverna at the very top of the village, overlooking the beach at Imerolia. I had spent the late afternoon packing our luggage ready for a very early morning departure the following day; the heat was intense in the apartment, having built up during the day with doors and windows closed while we were on the beach. I left it until the last minute to take a shower and wash my hair, but Jeremy, Rory and Miranda were ready before me and were anxious to start walking to the taverna.

"Go on ahead, I won't be long. You can order for me if you like." I suggested.

I still had to blow dry my hair, which would make the apartment even hotter and I knew there would be complaints unless I sat on the balcony with the hairdryer. I was admiring the wonderful view of the sea and distant Albania when an enormous white motor yacht appeared around the headland and glided towards the entrance to the harbour. With her name emblazoned in large letters on her flanks, *Opari* was the biggest superyacht we had seen all week and I idly wondered if perhaps she belonged to a pop star or a film director. Her captain seemed to be unsure where to drop anchor near the harbour, but after several manoeuvres I heard the clanking of heavy anchor chain as it rumbled its way down to the sea bed. The commotion eventually ceased and the harbour was at peace again, although its entrance was now dominated by the overhanging reach of the superyacht's high bow.

I finished my toilette and walked down the thirty shallow steps towards the harbour. As I passed Limani Bar, I noticed a group of three young men sitting at one of the harbourside tables. They were the only customers; at that time of the evening the town was always devoid of tourists who would all be indoors getting ready for a night out. I glanced at them and immediately noticed how different they looked to most holidaymakers; two were dressed in immaculate black polo shirts and trousers, with walkie-talkies and holsters on belts around their waists. They looked exactly like the villain's lackeys from a Bond film, or at least security guards from a London night club. The young man in between them looked vaguely familiar; I walked on a few paces trying to think who he resembled. Suntanned and handsome, he was wearing a navy blue polo shirt with white chinos and expensive white deck shoes, but infuriatingly I couldn't identify him. As casually as I could, I ambled back towards the bar and stopped at the neighbouring gift shop, where I pretended to be engrossed with the range of sun hats on display. The racks were only separated from the bar by a clear plastic screen, so I could peer closely between the rows of hats at the group of men, now only four feet away, without being noticed. Or so I thought. Then I heard the handsome one speak in a soft American accent to one of his companions.

"What should I order here?" he asked as he studied the drinks menu.

"Well Sir, at this time of day in Greece it's usual to have a cocktail," suggested one of the lackeys.

As I stared, the handsome youthful face suddenly looked up from the menu straight into my eyes and smiled. It was only then that the penny dropped with a clang: I was gazing into the beautiful blue eyes of Leonardo di Caprio. Blushing the colour of a beetroot, I turned on my heel and quickly retraced my steps towards the town. In hindsight I have never forgiven myself for being such a coward. If only I had gone over to him and asked for his autograph for Miranda; had I been twenty years younger I would not have hesitated – Miranda has never forgiven me either. Hurrying through the village to the taverna where we were meeting, barely able to breathe from the exertion in such heat, I finally found our table.

"Leonardo di Caprio is at Limani!" I blurted out to my family, who were still waiting for the rest of our party to arrive.

The children looked astonished and Rory immediately started texting his young English friends.

"Don't be silly, it was probably just someone who looked like him," Jeremy said. "Why on earth would he be in Kassiopi?"

"Well it was him and what's more he arrived on an enormous yacht which is now anchored beside the entrance to the harbour!" I retaliated.

"Come on Miranda, let's go!" said Rory, racing out of the taverna before Jeremy could object. By the time our starters arrived they were back.

"We just missed him at Limani," Rory said. "But we did see him being taken back to his yacht in the tender."

"Yes, it was *definitely* him," said his very excited nine year-old sister assertively. "I recognised his back from *Titanic*!"

There was a great deal of animated chatter from the teenagers at our table that evening, all of them wolfing their meals so they could get down to the harbour for a glimpse of the famous Hollywood film star. We walked back later and lingered on the quayside to admire the illuminated yacht, whose tender was ferrying small groups of young people to the far side of the harbour to disembark. After a few trips back and forth I finally spotted the young man in the blue polo shirt and white trousers again, with the same two attendants sitting either side of him in the tender. A group of about twenty young English girls had gathered and were waiting on the spit of sand and rocks beside the harbour wall. Suddenly, as the tender drew within a few yards of the shore, female shrieks of *Leonardo! Leonardo!* rang out across the harbour. Instantly the tender turned around and headed back to the yacht. I felt decidedly guilty at having started the whole episode by blowing Mr. di Caprio's cover and making it impossible for him to come ashore with his guests. I voiced my feelings to Jeremy.

"If it really was him, his skipper should have dropped anchor out of sight beyond the headland; then her tender could have slipped into Kassiopi unnoticed, instead of all that wilful attention seeking," Jeremy muttered. "But I still think you were mistaken."

However I was eventually proved right. The following year when we were in Thailand for a week, en route to Australia, our Thai friends had taken us to a particular spot on the southern tip of Phuket, popular with the locals for watching the sunset over the sea. As we wound our way along the high coast road I glanced at the sea below and there, resplendently at anchor in Chalong Bay, was the unmistakeably distinctive outline of Opari. Leonardo was living on her while filming *The Beach,* which was released the following year.

This episode has a post script: a year later we were at anchor in Voutoumi Bay and found ourselves just a few hundred yards from Opari. Now was my chance to redeem myself in Miranda's eyes and get Leonardo's autograph, I thought. Without saying a word to the family, I donned my lucky white swimsuit, slipped into the water and swam over to Opari, where I tried to look entirely nonchalant as I trod water a few feet astern of her vast boarding platform. A large man was just stepping onto a powerful jet ski; it certainly wasn't Leo – this man was built like an all-in wrestler, tanned the colour of polished teak and sported a blonde crew cut. In fact he was a double for Auric Goldfinger, the illusion becoming complete when he spoke to me with exactly the same German accent:

"Hallo, can I help you?" he asked huskily.

"Hello, I saw this yacht last year in Thailand" splash, splash, "and I wondered if Leonardo di Caprio still owned her?" splash, splash – it's quite difficult to tread choppy water and hold a conversation at the same time.

"Nein, I have just bought her. Vhere have you come from?"

"Our catamaran," I pointed to her, nearly going under in the process.

"You vould like a lift back?" he asked.

"Oh yes please!" I answered without hesitation, having never been on a jet ski but always secretly wanting to have a go.

This was highly hypocritical as Jeremy and I loathed jet skis buzzing about the coastal anchorages like hornets. I climbed on behind Goldfinger and put my arms around his bulky middle; he had no waist and I wasn't at all sure my hands would maintain their grip on his slippery, hairy, well oiled body. Jeremy and the children stood on our catamaran's aft deck with open mouths as Goldfinger drew up alongside. I climbed off the jet ski as gracefully as I could and thanked my new friend.

"Anytime! Auf weidersehen!" he called as he roared off.

"Can I have a ride?" asked Rory hopefully.

"Me too!" said Miranda.

"Certainly not!" said Jeremy.

"Why not?" the children chorused.

"Because *you* don't have white swimsuits!" answered my husband, with just the merest tinge of disapproval in his voice.

* * *

Choice, not chance, determines your destiny.

Aristotle

A year or so before that first holiday in Corfu, Jeremy had seen a brokerage advertisement in one of the yachting magazines for a catamaran he had dreamed of owning one day. Quite a sizeable cruising yacht for British waters, most of the half-dozen examples of this particular design were based in the Caribbean or Pacific; this one had been available for viewing in Gibraltar, but as it was not the right time for us to buy, Jeremy had simply filed the particulars away for future reference. As soon as we returned from our holiday in Corfu he dug out the file and contacted the brokers, but they had unaccountably lost touch with the owners and had no idea where the boat might be, although rumour had it she had been spotted in Majorca. By the end of the week we were on a flight to Palma, thereafter spending four fruitless days scouring every marina and cove on the island where the elusive boat could have been hiding We had also briefly considered Majorca as a temporary base for our future boat, but if the haughty waiters and arrogant shopkeepers did not finally discourage us, the thriving cockroach population on Palma's *paseo* soon did the trick.

Instead Jeremy had finally been reconciled to looking for something similar to Aries – the much smaller catamaran bought for our honeymoon – a fine example of which duly came on the market in southern Spain. He answered the advertisement and by a quirk of fate instantly found himself caught up in a moral dilemma. This boat, *Seaspice*, belonged to an old sailing chum who he had not seen for many years; now suffering with great fortitude from an inoperable brain tumor, Richard was in the very last days of his life. He had been a bank manager who, fortuitously as fate would decree, had taken early retirement to spend most of his final years afloat in the Mediterranean. With the diligence of his profession he was desperate to leave a tidy estate for his more landlubberly family; Seaspice was the one loose end remaining. To Richard's evident distress the sharks had begun to close in for the kill, so when he named his price Jeremy was overcome by a righteous obligation to buy Seaspice, subject – more pragmatically – to a hastily arranged viewing. Four days later Jeremy phoned from Spain to say he had arrived safely, although the trip had begun in disarray and ended in farce. This is how he later described his journey ...

As invariably happens on such occasions when a schedule is particularly tight, my early morning flight to Madrid was delayed; consequently the connecting flight to Almeria was missed and I eventually found myself at Malaga, well over one hundred miles from my destination. I had been travelling for nearly forty hours when I finally arrived at Aguadulce, exhausted and suffering with the volcanic consequences of a delicately curled airport sandwich, as well as from the racking debilitations of the accompanying migraine and fever. At the entrance to the little marina the taxi driver delivered me perfunctorily into the grip of an unseasonably filthy night; this was all I needed, having already lost a day and a half from my brief visit. I had been given a key to Seaspice, but had neither the enthusiasm nor the strength to climb aboard and sort out my billet on an unfamiliar boat in complete darkness. Besides, a hotel somewhere within the marina complex had been highly recommended.

Peering through the driving rain I could just discern the illuminated sign of a hotel beyond the Club Nautico; my trembling legs eventually carried me into the foyer, where I found the desk unmanned. Nursing my splitting head in both hands, elbows planted firmly on the counter, I gently tapped the reception bell. A moment or two later the night porter, curiously dressed in a high-collared tunic, appeared from the office beyond; he seemed a little perplexed by the picture of abject misery before him, but asked me politely how he might assist. My grasp of Spanish was still respectably fluent – subtle nuances excepted – and I dismissed the mild astonishment evident in the man's tone.

"Just a single room please, but I'll take your best suite if I have to," I groaned, elbows still planted akimbo on the counter. "Money's no object now ... I've never felt closer to death."

"Dare I ask how long you expect to be with us, señor?" inquired the hapless porter in very correct Castilian, his face a study in deferential compassion.

"I only have a couple of days at most now, but my time will probably be up tomorrow," I murmured with half-closed eyes and an involuntary wince, as another blow from the cranial piledriver knocked me sideways.

"So soon! *Qué tragedia*! It's a little unusual as we were not expecting you, but of course we can accommodate you," sympathised our man. Seeing my debilitated state he picked up my overnight case, took me gently by the arm and led me to my room.

"We will complete the formalities tomorrow after a doctor has seen you. Now, can I help you with your clothes, or anything else at all?", he asked, rather too familiarly for my liking.

I thanked him for his unnecessary concern and collapsed gratefully onto the bed as he quietly closed the door behind him. Opening my eyes next morning I felt almost human again, quickly registering that I had been given one of the hotel's rooms for the disabled, for it was liberally furnished with alarm cords and grab rails; moreover the bed had been supremely comfortable, its mattress possessing a peculiar life of its own. I was the first customer in the dining room, a leafy conservatory overlooking the marina; the French windows had been thrown open to the brilliant morning sunshine beyond, where a distant curtain of storm clouds were receding over the farthest rim of the horizon. Gradually my fellow guests appeared for breakfast; without exception they were all extremely frail, some even having nurses in attendance. One poor soul was wheeled to her table still attached to a cluster of drips suspended above her chair, from where she smiled at me toothlessly and crossed herself.

Perhaps, I considered, the hotel specialised in coach parties for the elderly and the disabled, a Super-Saga club for the over nineties; or maybe an outbreak of legionnaires' disease had struck the area. Either way I was beginning to feel uneasy, more so when I became aware of some barely concealed tittering at the reception desk behind me. Finishing the meagre breakfast with undue haste I collected my bag, paid the very reasonable bill and left. Glancing back in the direction of sudden guffaws of unrestrained laughter I could now see the sign above the entrance. In four languages it read: *Welcome to the Hospice of Aguadulce.*

The catamaran turned out to be in immaculate condition; however, Jeremy was slightly reticent and I noticed a hesitance in his voice.

"What is it?" I asked.

"Well," he began guardedly, "you'll never guess what else is here."

It was of course the elusive fifty-foot catamaran, *Sarava*. Jeremy flew home the following day and we discussed the possibility of buying her instead of the smaller catamaran.

"How much more is she?" I asked, innocently expecting a difference of a few thousand pounds at most.

"She can't be worth three times the price, surely." I gulped, genuinely shocked by his answer.

"Oh how she is!" was his wistful reply.

"Well, I think Seaspice will be fine for us; she's only for the holidays after all."

We toyed briefly with extravagance, but in truth we had unintentionally become players in the final act of a tragedy that allowed no improvisation. Richard had deteriorated fast during the intervening days, but Jeremy was able to speak to him and assure him the money had been transferred.

Richard died a few hours later.

* * *

One of the greatest things in human life is the ability to make plans. Even if they never come true – the joy of anticipating is irrevocably yours. That way one can live many more than just one life.

Maria Von Trapp

At half-term in May we flew to Almeria to take possession of Seaspice and to enjoy a week's holiday in the sun. With all four of us on board and substantial quantities of luggage there was hardly room to move; it was desperately hot and stuffy.

"Oh crumbs! She seems so much smaller than Aries," I said.

"Actually she's slightly bigger, but there were only two of us then and we were probably slightly smaller," explained Jeremy.

That evening we walked to one of the restaurants for dinner.

"Sarava's down there," remarked Jeremy casually, pointing to the end of the pontoon where the larger yachts were moored. Looking very regal and absolutely enormous in comparison with our humbler boat lay the beautiful cream and royal blue catamaran that Jeremy had set his heart on two years earlier. He rejected my suggestion to go and introduce ourselves to the owners. But I was longing to see the boat at close quarters, so I walked on along the pontoon with the children and hailed the lady who was relaxing in the cockpit with a book.

"Hello," I began. "My husband and I have been looking for this boat since last October."

The lady seemed puzzled and called to her husband, who appeared from inside and explained in a delicious French accent that his wife did not speak a great deal of English. I apologised to her in French, and repeated myself to him. He was astonished and immediately invited us aboard, grinning with glee.

I summoned Jeremy, who was still hanging back and clutching his wallet ever more defensively as we introduced ourselves. We sat down to drinks around the cockpit table as Jeremy related the story of his long and fruitless search for Sarava; her Belgian owners Philippe and Christine could not believe how their brokers had not contacted them; they even had a fax machine on board. With her beam that would spill into the third lane of a motorway, her four en-suite double cabins and cottage size saloon Sarava seemed simply vast; she was an extremely comfortable home as well as a fine oceangoing yacht.

Back on what was thereafter referred to somewhat sniffily as the *little boat* we spent the night feeling hot, cramped and talking about what might be done. Just before falling asleep we came to the conclusion that we had made a huge mistake; having now seen Sarava in the flesh I could see why she was so very much more expensive and how perfectly she would suit us. As Jeremy had so often tried to explain to me, the living space in a boat increases exponentially with each foot in length – as does the price.

Philippe and Christine mixed Gallic charm with an infectious sense of humour; after a long dinner with them the following evening,we felt we had known each other for years. On our last evening in Spain they suggested a trip to an elaborate restaurant set somewhat unpromisingly in the caves of an old quarry. Jeremy and I were still in a quandary and debating our options. If we wanted Sarava, which we certainly did, we would have to put our smaller catamaran on the market first; it could take months to sell her, by which time we could lose Sarava. The alternative prospect of owning two sizeable craft at the same time, however briefly, was quite out of the question. I sat next to Philippe at dinner and, between the main course and pudding, and after several glasses of wine, I casually suggested that if they could consider a part exchange for Sarava we could come to a mutually satisfactory arrangement which would enable us to buy her straight away.

"Ha, ha! Your English sense of 'umour!" he laughed. But by the time we were sipping liqueurs I could see his resolve weakening.

"Are you serious? I don't know what to say," he said looking completely nonplussed.

"Just say yes," I whispered in his ear.

"What are you talking about?" asked Jeremy.

"Oh nothing," I replied.

"OK, yes!" agreed Philippe finally.

I shrieked and hugged him, almost knocking him off his chair.

Philippe and Christine were planning to have another even larger catamaran custom built to incorporate a music studio, as Philippe, who had retired in his forties, was now a keen and accomplished musician. The exchange also suited them very well, not wishing to move ashore while their new boat was being built. In due course the arrangement was finalised and we agreed to 'swop' boats as soon as the children had broken up for the summer holidays.

On 4th July we flew to Almeria with the children and Sam, a chum of Rory's who was joining us for the trip to Corfu. We spent almost a week transferring belongings from one boat to another but by midnight on the sixth day we were finally ready to leave. Poor Philippe was so fond of Sarava he was loath to let her go, holding on grimly to the stern line and being pulled along the quayside as we edged our way slowly out of the marina.

"Are you sure you will be okay?" he shouted. "Jeremy, do you want me to come with you?"

"We're okay, Philippe; we will be just fine!", Jeremy reassured him.

"You 'ave to let go now," cried Christine, tugging at Philippe's arm.

"No! I 'ave changed my mind with Sarava!" wailed Philippe, straining all the harder.

"Philippe, LET 'ER GO!" Christine implored.

Very reluctantly he threw the rope to us, only inches from the end of the jetty; there they stood together arm in arm, waving forlornly, a picture of dejection. Somehow they must have had some premonition that parting with Sarava would turn out to be a decision they would come to regret. We watched and waved back as they grew smaller and smaller, until they disappeared into the twinkling necklace of coastal lights. We headed out into the darkness of the the open sea in an unfamiliar vessel with three children in our charge, our next port of call Ibiza some two days away. For me it was a slightly sobering prospect, for Jeremy a routine beginning to another long awaited adventure.

Chapter Two
Landfall

Come fly with me where dreams are born, and time is never planned, just think of happy things, and your heart will fly on wings, forever, in Never Never Land.

These magical words from J M Barrie's *Peter Pan* describe my feelings whenever we set sail for a distant shore.

Sarava handled like a dream, cruising smoothly and easily to Ibiza, where we called the port authorities to request a berth for the night but were told nothing was available for a boat of Sarava's beam, the marinas all stuffed with the smart motor yachts that congregate there in high season. We were fairly tired after two nights at sea, so we decided to try and bluff our way in anyway; besides, the wind was increasing and the boys were anxious to sample Ibiza's legendary club scene. As we edged towards the fuelling pontoon, which was on the point of closing for the night, Rory had a brilliant idea.

"Let Mummy go and speak to the chap on duty as if she is skippering the boat," he suggested. "You can take the inside helm, Daddy."

So with Rory ostensibly at the wheel in the cockpit, I leaned over the railings as we came alongside and pleaded, in rusty Spanish, to be allowed into the marina as the children and I were so tired and it was getting *muy agitado*, out at sea.

"*Vale Señora,*" he agreed, flashing me a charming, if gap-toothed grin. "You can stay here for the night, *sí*, right here, until morning; but you will have to leave before seven when I open again for business."

Delightedly I told the boys to make fast and went inside to tell Jeremy it was safe to come out. My Spanish hero sauntered off for his supper, chewing a wooden toothpick and giving us a cheery wave. We had bagged a prime spot in the harbour, close to the restaurants and facilities, with a fabulous view of the Old Town, high on a hill overlooking the sea and illuminated like a fairy castle. Better still our overnight berth was free of charge.

"How *on earth* did you manage that?" Jeremy asked as he reappeared from below decks. I shrugged it off, "Easy," I said.

"It was her white swimsuit," said Rory casually. "Does it every time; poor chap didn't stand a chance."

"Hmph," said Jeremy dismissively. But I noticed each time we were approaching a new port he would suggest I put on the same costume, just in case.

From Ibiza we sailed to Menorca, spending the night in the pretty harbour of Mahon, refreshingly unchanged, if somewhat busier since our last visit. The rest of our journey fell into a pleasant routine of sailing in perfect conditions, constantly escorted by schools of dolphins, flying fish and encouragingly large numbers of green turtles basking lazily on the surface.

Life at sea generally enhances the appetite and certainly sharpens the taste buds. For lunch we would sit in the shady cockpit and eat mozzarella, ripe vine tomatoes sliced into juicy chunks, fresh basil leaves torn roughly and scattered on top and dressed – *drizzling* is banished in our family – with virgin olive oil, and hunks of crusty bread. We would sometimes enjoy wonderfully sweet melon slices covered with wafer thin, almost transparent prosciutto, salty Parmesan shavings, freshly ground black pepper and balsamic vinegar. Tea was always at four and served with home made cake, usually brownies, which Miranda cooked to perfection in our gently swaying gas oven. While we read, slept or just sunbathed on deck Jeremy would study the Admiralty Pilot, choosing a suitable harbour or anchorage for our next landfall.

Summer nights at sea in the Mediterranean are magical. In common with most seafarers, our family tradition whilst sailing is to have a glass of wine, or two, as the sun goes down. Sunsets at sea are spectacular, the water changing from the deep indigo of the sunlit hours to milky turquoise striped with pink and lilac. Just as you are eating supper in the cockpit the moon might appear, sometimes the rich colour of a pomegranate, fading to gold then platinum as it rises, casting a shimmering trail of mercury on the water. With no light from land the stars hang low over the sea, so numerous and bright that the sky looks like a swathe of black velvet studded with a million sparkling diamonds. Shooting stars are a constant feature in these latitudes, particularly in the season of the Perseids; they never fail to bewitch and thrill, so numerous that one can almost run out of wishes to send into the firmament. The only sound is the whispering of the warm, gentle breeze in the sails and the lap and flow of water past the hulls. Over the side, or in the wash behind us, luminous green-gold plates of phosphorescence flashed in the foamy water, leaving a trail of liquid fire in our wake.

Arriving at San Pietro, the small island off the south-western tip of Sardinia, we found a berth in the harbour of Carloforte. This was another return visit for Jeremy and I, as we had been here on our last catamaran during our honeymoon nearly twenty years earlier. The small town and its long promenade are very picturesque, fronted by imposing houses decorated in the scrumptious shades of Italian ice-cream, many with intricate wrought iron balconies; large shutters frame elegant French windows and dark green umbrella pines cast cool shadows over the cobbles. We had tied up before dawn, but I was badly in need of dry land, the scents of trees and flowers, a real cappuccino, a serious shop for ship's rations and some retail therapy – this was Italian soil after all and there would be *shoe shops*. The smell of freshly baked bread wafted into my cabin and I dressed with lightning speed. The glorious thing about these warm climes is the ease of choosing an outfit; when not in a swimsuit one only needs a sundress, large straw hat, sunglasses and sandals.

The others were all catching up on sleep; night watches can be quite exhausting, even when taken in turns. Jeremy and I were on duty for four hours each, accompanied by one or other of the boys who usually fell asleep within the first minutes of duty. My watch was often a lonely vigil during which the only aid to keep me awake was my trusty Walkman: Abba, Mozart and The Beatles. So I was glad of the chance to potter off on my own on this beautiful morning; I took my largest shopping basket and, sandals in hand, tiptoed barefoot along the passerelle onto the quay, trying not to disturb the others. On the freshly washed promenade a handful of locals were busying themselves with early morning tasks; laying tables at the cafes, emptying rubbish bins, tidying chairs, sweeping and cleaning. I was greeted effusively by everyone I passed. *Buongiorno* is such a cheerful word.

I took some photographs and soon found a charming café with extravagant white umbrellas, choosing a table with views of the harbour as well as the bustling activity in the narrow streets opposite. I thoroughly enjoyed two coffees and some delicious home made biscuits flavoured with almond; I bought postcards, stamps and some local pottery before setting off to explore. It was heavenly to have my own time and space. I loved Sarava dearly but after a couple of weeks at sea, with five on board, I missed the solitude to think my own thoughts and dream my own dreams. I found a tiny doorway where a wizened old fisherman, gnarled as a sun-dried prune, sat on a low stool busily weaving fish traps out of thin strips of cane. The design was so intricate it looked like beige lace.

"Can I buy one?" I asked.

"You want one? What for?" he replied, bright blue eyes twinkling deep in his walnut brown face.

"Oh, just decoration," I said, hoping he would understand. He handed one to me and I paid the equivalent of two pounds.

"*È pazza, crazy woman!*" I heard him mutter to himself, as I walked away with this very awkward cone-shaped object dangling from my hand.

The supermarket was at the farthest end of the long promenade. I took a trolley and enjoyed exploring aisles full of unfamiliar items and brands. Before long my trolley was full to overflowing; spices in pretty jars, a basil plant with vast emerald leaves, parmesan, mozzarella, salami, ripe melons, tomatoes as big as grapefruit, fresh prosciutto as thinly sliced as tissue paper, crusty bread, Italian biscuits, drinks, ripe nectarines, juicy white peaches, bottled water and washing powder called *Aids*. I chose a magnificent selection of pasta in all shapes and colours, adding jars of sun-dried tomatoes, pesto, extra virgin olive oil and balsamic vinegar from Modena. My best find was real chocolate vermicelli, so hard to find at home. As I reached the checkout I realised I could not possibly carry all this back to the boat; the temperature outside was about 35 degrees centigrade by now, so I asked if my shopping could be delivered.

"Si signora, he will take it for you," the assistant jerked a thumb at a lanky young man standing behind him. I watched the boy pile his Vespa high with my shopping before wobbling precariously down the road. I had a long hot walk ahead of me, yet I needed to get there in time for my helper's arrival, or the precious supplies would be dumped on the jetty in the full sun. I spotted a minute *Ape*, the ubiquitous three-wheeled van that buzzes and splutters so angrily in the hands of Italian farmers, shopkeepers and fishermen alike; an elderly man and an assortment of young children were piling in. I asked him if he could possibly give me a lift to the marina and gesticulated at the blazing sun and my heavy basket of souvenirs. He beamed, unceremoniously dragged a couple of infants out of the little cab and told them to climb into the open back. With much chugging and bumping we arrived at the pontoon in a cloud of oily fumes just as the heavily laden scooter pulled up, whereupon grandpa and infants eagerly lent a hand to unload the shopping and carry it on board. The boat was strangely empty and I wondered where the family had gone. Soon Jeremy appeared looking hot and irate, Miranda wearing a suitably similar expression behind him.

"Where *have* you been? We've been worried sick! Rory and Sam have gone off to look for you; they're doing a grid search, street by street. It's been over four hours. Why didn't you answer your phone?"

"It was in my basket under the shopping, so I guess I couldn't hear it," I said, not realising what all the fuss was about. "Why on earth were you worried? I only went shopping."

"You have no idea of the danger you were in. Look at this!" he snapped, thrusting one of the pilot books in front of me, open at the page describing San Pietro and its harbours:

> *In recent times several incidents of kidnapping have occurred on San Pietro. Although these have usually involved wealthy Italian families it is only prudent to show extra vigilance when at anchor.*

"They can't be serious ... everyone was so friendly!" I laughed.

"Well, next time keep your phone handy and leave a note saying where you've gone," he grumbled, stomping into the saloon.

Rory and Sam returned half-an-hour later looking even hotter than Jeremy and I received another admonishment from my son. What I did not tell them – having reflected upon the last weeks on the boat in high temperatures, endlessly washing clothes, rinsing towels and cooking for five people – was that the prospect of being abducted by a gang of dashing Italian kidnappers and held captive in a five-star, air-conditioned hotel with a bath, hair salon and room-service did not seem altogether unappealing; naturally my abductors would all resemble George Clooney, reek of Chanel aftershave and be dressed in Armani suits and Gucci shoes. In retaliation, at our next port of call, Villasimius, on the south-eastern tip of Sardinia, I scribbled a note on the table before I left: *'Have not been kidnapped – just shopping, with phone, Love Mummy.'*

It was there I bought a sketch book for Miranda; she whiled away the hours as we sailed along the North coast of Sicily and turned south through the Straits of Messina, lying flat on her tummy on deck drawing everything she saw and writing poems.

> *Dolphins high in the sky*
> *Only I can see them fly*

Leaping for joy
Or playing with a drifting buoy
Having fun in a cave
And in the rolling ocean wave.

Late in July we arrived at our final port of call on the journey to
Corfu. The marina development at Rocella Ionica had been built as a
money laundering wheeze by the Mafia, but something had obviously
gone wrong and the harbour lay abandoned; the charming, dusty
little town next to it clings to the very sole of the 'boot' of Italy. We
were by now running behind schedule owing to unforeseen difficul-
ties in obtaining diesel in Southern Italy, where fuel pumps and their
attendants never seemed to appear in conjunction. However Jeremy
spotted a taxi on the otherwise deserted quayside and, disturbing the
driver from his siesta, urgently communicated our need for diesel.
Ilario turned out to be a treasure, first taking Jeremy to collect jerry
cans from a dozen relatives around the countryside before driving to
and fro the nearest fuel station some miles distant. Determined not
let anyone touch the leaking cans he donned a full set of heavy red
overalls and insisted on filling Sarava's tanks singlehanded. He would
take no payment for his considerable labours, so Jeremy asked him
and his family to join us for supper that night at a restaurant of his
choice. Washed and scrubbed Ilario arrived alone at eight sharp and
we piled into his little taxi.

"Donde eínai votre familia?" Jeremy asked in an innovative mixture
of four languages. Ilario waved an arm towards the seats and held up
his ten fingers to demonstrate that there would not be room for us all
in his taxi.

The restaurant specialised in fish and was obviously favoured by
the Italian holidaymakers who monopolised this corner of the country. During an excellent supper we chatted with Ilario and his young
family in a mixture of our best French and Spanish, as he spoke no
English and our command of Italian ran only to pleasantries. On the

way back to Sarava we took a detour up a winding track to the imposing 13th century Swabian castle that stands neglected high above the town; after a brief tour conducted by the light of Ilario's fading torch we finally returned on board and fell into our beds. Bright and early next morning as we were preparing to leave, we heard someone hailing us from the quayside. It was Ilario; he seemed reluctant to say goodbye and invited us to go into the town for ice-creams. This, he told us, was his favourite food and he took us to a pretty café in a leafy piazza, where we sat beside a grandly ornate stone fountain and enjoyed the best ice-cream we had ever tasted.

That afternoon, fully victualled and ice-creamed, Sarava struck out from the sole of Italy for Corfu and her new base at Gouvia, some 250 miles away. Chased by a storm from the Gulf of Squillace that never quite overtook us, our final night at sea was filled with the delicious anticipation of arrival. I took the first watch of the night and tried to block out the sounds of thunder and wind by listening to my Walkman. A few hours later as Jeremy took over the watch we were once again sailing beneath moon and stars.

> *You enter Greece as one might enter a dark crystal; the form of things becomes irregular, refracted. Other countries may offer you discoveries in manners or love or landscape; Greece offers you something harder —the discovery of yourself.*
>
> Lawrence Durrell, *Prospero's Cell*

In the hazy, early morning light this sliver of land on the horizon was slowly reeled in until shimmering olive trees were discernible amongst the general mass of greenery; slim cypresses stood tall in pleasing clusters and random avenues, patrolling the hillside groves between water's edge and the distant treeless heights that gradually appeared through a thin veil of mist. I had never seen such a verdant island in these waters or indeed anywhere in the Mediterranean; this lushness had certainly not revealed itself so easily during our holiday a year earlier, but then again all coasts show themselves most favourably from the sea.

Rudyard Kipling knew what he was talking about when he said the first condition of understanding a foreign land is to smell it. Mingling scents of pine, wild thyme and aromas of freshly baked bread and charcoal ovens carried across the sea on a raft of earthy island breath, while patches of vivid turquoise appeared under the ultramarine water as we glided over tracts of white sand on the seabed. Close to shore the water turned into a strip of pure emerald edged with white foam as waves broke against rocks. Excitedly we vied for the binoculars and picked out beachside tavernas and tranquil anchorages, or exotic cliff top villas, looking as if they might at any moment lose their precarious grip and tumble into the sea.

At last we glided gently into the bay of Gouvia and its bustling marina. An inflatable came speeding towards us, nose in the air, with its driver, a uniformed marinero, waving wildly; ducking beneath our stern he reappeared at our bow and beckoned us to follow. He then proceeded at a slow and stately pace, majestically escorting us to our berth, reserved in advance by Jeremy as soon as we had bought Sarava. But as we reached the space allocated for us I realised it would not do at all; we were expected to dock alongside, which meant every time we wanted to disembark we would have to climb over the two rows of railings on the boat and jump a full five feet onto the pontoon, scrambling up again for the reverse procedure. Fine for a long-legged chap in shorts and deck shoes, not fine for a petite lady with a skirt and mules. Summoning my few Greek words I took issue with the hunky marinero.

"*Se paracalo, kalós ánthropos mou,*" I ventured, in appalling Greek that translated 'Excuse me, my good human being'.

"I cannot possibly manage this big jump, in a skirt, for heaven's sake! Can't we go on the other side over there?"

"But of course, Madame," he crooned, oozing charm, "I did not realise there were two ladies on board".

Miranda giggled, at eleven she had not been honoured with this grown-up title before. And before Jeremy had finished saying, 'No, we can't possibly move, this has been reserved for us and we've already paid up for five years,' the marinero had sped around to the berth I had spotted and was hovering, his outboard engine buzzing like a hornet, ready to help us dock. This way we came in stern-to and were therefore able to lower the passerelle directly on to the pontoon and walk gracefully ashore with our dignity and our skirts intact. The white swimsuit, bought at great expense in Harrods, had once more earned its keep.

We had finally arrived in Corfu three hours before our first friends were due to land at the airport; not bad timing considering we had just travelled more than 1200 nautical miles. Jeremy attended to the customs formalities ashore, while I raced about like a headless chicken making up the double beds in the guest cabins, which had been used as extra stowage during our passage; on deck the children washed the accumulated layers of salt from Sarava's topsides and by the time our friends arrived everything was ship-shape and Bristol fashion.

My friend Julie and her husband had arrived to spend a week with us on Sarava. Julie and I had become instant best friends from the time we met when we were both in our late teens and fledgling fashion models. After leaving school Julie had trained at Lucie Clayton and I had been with the Cherry Marshall model agency; Cherry miraculously maintained her twenty-two inch waist even after giving birth to three children and held the record for London's smallest waist. One of her first model 'discoveries' was Ruth Ellis, the last woman to be hanged in Britain, so I was in good company. Julie and I had both been working as models in London at the same time, but had never met until we returned home to South Devon. I had admired her enormously, not only for her beauty and poise, but far more for her sweet, generous nature and hugely infectious sense of humour. I was also in awe of the fact that she was already married by the age of nineteen and would be expecting her first child less than a year later; I had not even acquired a steady boyfriend by that time. Julie quickly became my mentor, adviser, confidante and the sister I had never been blessed with; she was the natural choice of godmother when Miranda was born in 1987.

One of my own goddaughters, Natasha, was Miranda's guest for the week Julie and Alan came to stay; the boat echoed with giggles and squeals of laughter from the two young girls and the two slightly older girls. One evening we were anchored in Agni Bay and decided to take the RIB tender to the neighbouring, deserted cove for a barbecue supper on the beach. The August night was warm, humid, moonless and still; it was the perfect night to try out our new portable barbecue. Much like my father, Rory has always loved camp fires, picnics and barbecues, whereas Jeremy had never come to terms with the inevitable proximity of food to grass or sand; nevertheless he gamely went along with the preparations with patience and good humour, despite his reservations about the wisdom of inviting guests so promptly after our long trip from Spain. We were all very tired and disorganised, moreover Sarava still had a few teething problems to be dealt with.

Julie and the girls helped me make a variety of salads and we packed some baskets with plates, cutlery, glasses, wine, Mythos beer and soft drinks. The men loaded everything into the tender and put in some rugs for us to sit on. We skimmed across the little bay leaving a trail of sparkling flashes of green-gold phosphorescence as we disturbed the calm, dark water. As the outboard engine fell silent two scops owls piped melodically to each other from either side of the cove; apart from their calls there was not another sound to be heard other than the crunch of shingle and sand underfoot as our picnic was carried up the empty beach.

It was much darker onshore than we had expected, which made it difficult for the men to cook the marinaded chicken breasts and sausages. One held a torch for the other and the curses grew ever more unsavoury as yet another chicken breast fell off the grill onto the sand, or a sausage fell spitting through the grill onto the red hot charcoal where it burst into angry flames. Julie had recently qualified as a yoga teacher and suggested we girls had a calming session on the sand at the water's edge where we could escape from the choking smoke of the barbecue and increasingly bad language from the chaps. We laid out a large rug on the damp sand and the girls and I arranged ourselves in the lotus position opposite Julie. This was a little more tricky than it sounds, owing to the gentle slope of the beach and the ample quantity of chilled rosé Julie and I had drunk since the sun had slipped over the yardarm. Hard as we tried to sit gracefully straight and composed, we would list either to port or to starboard as the soft sand shifted beneath us. This would start us giggling like schoolgirls until we lost our balance completely and toppled over on our sides in convulsions of helpless laughter. Julie tried valiantly to maintain her composure, but we could see her shoulders shaking. After a few false starts we settled into our lesson and Julie suggested we start by slowly exhaling, making a hissing noise with pursed lips as we did so. The four of us managed to accomplish this simple task in perfect unison and out came a loud continuous hissing, worthy of steam venting from the boiler of the Flying Scotsman. Suddenly Jeremy flew past us, barking his shin on the cast iron barbecue and almost knocking me over as he raced towards the tender, which was bobbing gently in the shallows.

"Damn it all!" he shouted, "Now the dinghy's got a puncture! It must have been an ember from that bloody barbecue! Quick! Rory, bring the torch."

Jeremy darted from one side to the other, pressing an ear close to the taut rubber tubes as he examined the boat for a hole. His anguish sent us ladies into paroxysms of giggles once again, knowing full well it was the hissing of our little yoga group which had caused my husband's panic. When we eventually managed to stop laughing, I explained this to him and he came out with an expletive which I hoped the girls and our guests had not heard. Joining the others to eat our chargrilled burnt offerings in total darkness, our teeth grated on the coating of fine Corfiot sand.

Returning to the boat, we girls decided to have a last swim before bed. The phosphorescence sparkled and glittered around our bodies as we lazily drifted around in the lukewarm water. Back on deck Julie and I were drying ourselves with towels before going below to our cabins when we heard a shout.

"Ooh, Jani, quick, come and look at this, my loo's alight!" shrieked Tasha from inside the boat. We all rushed into her bathroom where she was pointing to the loo, where the bowl was glowing eerily in the darkness, filled with sparkling phosphorescence drawn in with the flush of fresh sea water.

* * *

So began our first summer aboard Sarava in Corfu, marking a turning point in our lives; from that moment on we would have a base on this wonderful island where friends and relatives could join us. For the next eight years Sarava became our second home, cruising around the Ionian, discovering the hundreds of anchorages on dozens of different islands, or simply revisiting our favourite haunts in Corfu. Like foraging butterflies we would roam about our new territory, sometimes moving to the next bay a mile down the coast, sometimes travelling one hundred miles in a day; wherever we found ourselves, the view from Sarava's decks was constantly changing. Every school holidays we would return to Sarava, often hotfoot from speech days or parents' meetings directly to the airport; school uniforms would be discarded in the boot in favour of casual wear, none of us wanting to waste a single second. Most holidays we invited a succession of friends and relatives to stay, some for the children and some for us; the majority of these visits were very successful and mutually rewarding. Occasionally our passion for all things Greek and nautical was not to everyone's taste and a few found life afloat rather too taxing. We philhellenes however, made more Greek friends with each visit and soon felt more at home in Corfu than in England. Every time our plane took off from Corfu airport I would find myself crying involuntarily, while Jeremy and the children would sink into depression as the island disappeared from view.

The most difficult departure always came at the end of the nine-week summer holiday. As another English winter stretched out ahead of us, its cold, dark, rainy school terms looming for Rory and Miranda, we dreaded our return to reality despite the promise of a snatched week on Sarava for the October half-term.

"Why are we doing this?" Jeremy asked impatiently at the end of our second barefoot summer.

"Education," I replied.

"Shame there isn't an international school here," he said.

"Why don't we open one?" I suggested.

"That really would be ridiculous, we're not teachers and I'm no businessman; I just want to live here."

"Me too," I said, "We should look for some land before it gets too expensive".

The idea had been in both our minds for some time. It had jumped up and hit us in the face two days earlier as we prepared to leave Kassiopi harbour for the final time that summer. Sadly we made the rounds of friends and acquaintances in the town, embracing, kissing or shaking hands with heavy hearts. We left until last the staff at our favourite harbourside restaurant. Whenever in the village we would always meet there for early morning Nescafé Frappés, a tradition we had taught and instigated; the waiters became so used to me writing my numerous postcards and shopping lists, always at the same table next to the venerable elm tree, that they nicknamed the restaurant 'Jani's office.' They would even serve us before they were open for business, politely turning away any perplexed holidaymaker who ventured to sit down, adding in case of further argument that we were the owners of the restaurant. In the evenings we would often return for dinner and, with our guests, sometimes filling a long table with a dozen or more; Sarava was always safely at anchor across the harbour where we could keep a watchful eye on her.

On this occasion a sombre group of staff surrounded us. It felt like a funeral. We shook hands solemnly with each waiter and lastly with

Bambas, literally a giant amongst men; six foot four and built like an Olympian, he hugged us both with strong arms around us in a bear-like grip. As I said goodbye to him, my eyes brimming with tears, I looked up to see his eyes were also full.

"When you are leaving I knows the summer is over," he would always say.

At that moment I knew, I think Jeremy and I both knew, that somehow we had to live there.

* * *

Judge your success by what you have had to give up in order to get it.

The Dalai Lama

Devon pulled out all the stops on the first morning of our return, as if trying to dissuade us from leaving. Basking in an Indian summer the rolling countryside was a patchwork quilt of autumnal colours; balmy air gently ruffled leaves, which had just started to take on the reds and golds of the season. Along overgrown lanes the improbably high hedges displayed a riot of jewel coloured berries, old-man's-beard, crab apples and brambles heavy with shining black fruit, all contending for the last rays of summer sun; after the long, dry summer in Corfu the sweet scent of dew-damp grass was unfamiliar and overpowering. The gardens of our rambling seventeenth-century manor house were full of roses, dahlias, gladioli, clematis and a late flowering Dutch honey-suckle I had planted to climb over the wooden archway leading to the croquet lawn. At the farthest end of the formal gardens, enclosed by high hedges, thatched outhouses and a heavy wrought iron gate, the swimming pool beckoned. The rockery to one side was still a sea of brilliant busy-lizzies cascading over mossy granite boulders; mature dark green conifers formed a semi-circle behind it, producing a mi-croclimate and sheltering the pool from the prevailing westerly wind.

My little white beach-hut, with its Harrods green stable-door, stood sleepily in one corner of this secret garden, unused now but loyally waiting like an old friend for us to come home. It had belonged to my parents and after their deaths I had persuaded Jeremy to retrieve it from Goodrington Beach, where it had been since I was a toddler; my children and I had enjoyed many happy days at the beach with their grandparents, mirroring the carefree days of my own childhood; miraculously my mother would often cook a complete supper on the tiny cooker within, the delicious aromas of roasting lamb and potatoes sending holidaymakers and locals alike racing for home. My father had taught Rory to fish there and bought him a rod and fully equipped tackle box for his seventh birthday; I can still see the two of them like peas in a pod, standing side by side, leaning over iron railings on the promenade staring patiently into the water, with the sun setting a over cold, Prussian blue sea.

Next to the pool garden stretched the paddocks where Miranda's ponies had grazed and cavorted, their sizes increasing as she grew, from Gingerpops, the shaggy nine-hand chestnut Shetland better known as GP, to Priestwood Orlando, nicknamed 'Billy', a stunning, thirteen hand, Welsh Section B chestnut with a white blaze and one white sock. There were happy memories of times spent mucking around in the stable, and even more spent mucking out. I would walk with Miranda for miles around the narrow lanes while she rode, at first on the leading rein and later with my hand ready to grab the reins at the first sign of trouble. When Billy arrived one Christmas Day, GP fell instantly in love with him and decided he could not be parted from him for a second. As soon as he lost sight of Billy, he would career around his paddock at a miniature Shetland's version of a flat out gallop, whinnying loudly and frantically for his new chum; his shrill screams of panic could be heard all over the valley. This behaviour forced us to lead him alongside Billy on every outing. Sometimes Jeremy joined us, walking our three Blenheim King Charles Cavalier Spaniels, Bramble, Briar and Burberry, in front of the ponies like an advance guard; our cavalcade of ginger and white animals must have made an amusing spectacle, for we often had our photograph taken by passing motorists.

The house had been a wonderful home for us during the children's school days, offering acres of room for parties and barbecues. Rory's friends often camped out like boy scouts in tents on the lawns, while Miranda preferred swimming parties or giggly sleepovers; one way and another we never seemed to stop entertaining. Jeremy and I had moved several times during our marriage and only by good fortune and rather less judgement had we found ourselves owning this wonderful, rather quirky house for the last eight years. A late Georgian wing had been added to the main seventeenth-century building, so the house was a mixture of cosy rooms with beams, archways, open hearths and flagstone floors that led into elegant, airy accommodation with the fine proportions and style of the later period. But we had inherited all its charms and vices together: faded, velvet soft carpets, lustrous paintwork as thick as Jersey cream, float glass window panes that added ripples and shimmies to the views beyond, but also nail-sick roofs, death watch beetle, dry rot, temperamental drains, six chimney stacks on life support and a winter heating bill that would service a cathedral.

Old country houses require constant maintenance, and Jeremy – who could never bring himself to pay for work he could carry out himself – would repaint a dozen of the rambling property's thirty-six windows each year, first repairing rotten wood in the ancient frames in scant hope they would see out another winter. The swimming pool, built during the sixties when it appeared on the estate's tax returns as an emergency reservoir for fire engines, had to be emptied and re-painted every spring; larger than many hotel pools it alone accounted for a full three weeks' work each year for Jeremy. In its heyday the house had two permanent indoor staff and two full-time gardeners; in our tenure the work was divided between the two of us with further help from Margaret, our stalwart housekeeper who had worked at the house since she was a girl.

I would miss the space, the graceful rooms with their extravagant fireplaces and the outrageously elaborate Smallbone bathroom adjoining our bedroom, installed by a previous owner at huge expense, which my mother-in-law had cruelly labelled a 'Torquay tart's bathroom' when first she saw it. I would miss our large bedroom with its bay windows looking out over a rolling patchwork of fields; in summer I would throw them wide open and the scent of new-mown hay filled the room, while in spring we would awaken to the bleating of new born lambs. Most of all I would miss walking out of the kitchen door into the garden at dawn, while the rest of the household slept, to sit amongst the lavender on the low stone wall of the east terrace in my dressing gown with my first cup of Earl Grey; there I would watch the sun rise over the distant hills and listen to the gulls call as they headed for the fishing grounds off Brixham.

Reflecting more objectively it was not the sort of place we could lock up and leave for extended periods; nor could we trust its fickle structure to behave itself if we were to lease it in our absence. Moreover since the arrival of Sarava we had suddenly realised there were corners of the grounds that we never set foot in for six months at a time; equally there were rooms in the house that remained semi-permanently mothballed. During the summer term when the pool was filled with visiting children and their parents every weekend, Jeremy and I felt as if our home had become a Butlins camp – we the ever cheerful Redcoats. Rory and Miranda had almost outgrown their days of playing in the gardens and fields, preferring to spend their holidays aboard Sarava where sun, warm sea and new sailing adventures awaited them; their love of Corfu was also taking hold as new friends were made and new anchorages discovered on each visit.

But there was another lure, one that Jeremy and I had experienced years earlier in Cyprus, an invisible magnetism drawing them towards Greek waters. Almost subconsciously they had both become aware of a genuine affection shown to them by the locals, young and old alike; a warmth, generosity and friendliness so perfectly described in the Greek word *philoxenia* – friend to strangers – which surrounded and embraced them. It was a feeling they had never experienced during their childhood in England. Miranda hit the nail on the head during our first visit to Corfu when she asked me, with the innocence of a ten year old, why the Corfiots were so nice to her.

In most Mediterranean countries children are cherished and welcomed everywhere; in shops they are plied with sweets or biscuits, in restaurants some cushions will automatically be brought to raise little hands to table height and chairs will be pushed together at the end of a meal, so a child can sleep while parents linger over coffee; their small heads are patted and hair tousled affectionately, no quarter given to the creep of stifling political correctness. When Miranda was about ten months old we were still living in Spain; with her fair skin and white-blonde curls she grew accustomed to the attentions of every passing Spaniard. Her favourite admirers were the handsome young waiters in their smart uniforms, she loved their glossy, jet black hair, spaniel brown eyes, dazzling white teeth and overpowering colognes. At restaurants she would sit up in her pram beside us, cutting her teeth on pitted olives and drinking fresh orange juice from a plastic beaker. Totally at home in café society by that age she was pampered and fêted wherever she went.

One evening we took her out to a favourite restaurant which nestled on the slopes of the Montgó Massif, the Elephant Mountain which dominates that part of the coast. Miranda was enjoying every moment of this unexpected escape from bedtime; the fairy lights twinkled, the soft strains from three Spanish guitars filled the warm evening air, people laughed and chatted and she evidently felt in very high spirits. She was in love with everyone that evening, particularly the waiters in their crisp white shirts and shiny, tight black trousers. Our waiter always smiled, clucked and gently pinched her cheek as he passed. Delighted by this custom Miranda decided to reciprocate at the first opportunity. Waiting until the perfect moment when the waiter's back was turned, as he lent over to pour Jeremy's wine, she reached out and grabbed his shiny bottom firmly in her little fist, giving it an affectionate squeeze. The waiter skipped sideways, slopping wine into

Jeremy's lap and turned to look directly at me. Realising what was in his mind I blushed profusely and muttered something about *la niña*, the baby, which only served to confirm the waiter's worst suspicions; he went off to get a cloth, relating the incident to all his compatriots in the kitchen, who then peered out, incredulous at the audacity of this brazen, foreign hussy.

Rory was also afforded a great deal of attention in Spain, which he soon expected as his due. His order for food was always taken first and if nothing on the menu took his fancy he was whisked off to the kitchens by a concerned waiter to inspect the specialities for himself. One evening in Ibiza he had noticed blackboards advertising *Crêpes Suzette* outside many of the restaurants. We were winding our way up through the narrow, cobbled streets of the Old Town, Jeremy pushing Miranda in her pram as I held Rory's hand, as we made our way towards the citadel and our favourite restaurant, 'Las Ventanas'. The only thing Rory wanted, despite having no clue what it might be, was a Crêpe Suzette. The waiter was most apologetic and said it was not on their menu.

"Why don't you have some onion rings?" we had suggested, this being our name for squid or octopus where Rory was concerned.

He was a finicky eater at the age of five on our arrival in Spain and we struggled to tempt his appetite; no baked beans, fish fingers, boiled eggs, sausages, spaghetti Bolognese or other nursery favourites were available in those blissful days before fast-food or 'full English breakfasts' loomed on his horizon. Hard Spanish cheese, crusty bread, or chewy Serrano ham hurt his wobbly teeth and he detested the Spanish milk, for which my mother sent regular supplies of strawberry flavoured *Nesquick* from England to take the taste away. One day I had ordered some calamari frito and he looked interested.

"Try one of mine," I offered.

"What is it?" he asked suspiciously, taking one fried squid ring on his fork and studying it minutely with the intense scrutiny of a five year-old.

"Onion rings, deep fried … mmm … quite delicious!" suggested Jeremy, jumping in quickly. Rory put it in his mouth, began to chew and nodded like a seasoned gourmet.

"Mmm, it's nice, I like these Spanish onion rings."

From then on 'onion rings', salad and chips were his favourite food, the only concession we made to his juvenile palate was the addition of tomato ketchup.

"I don't want onion rings tonight," he insisted. "I would like a Crêpe Suzette please."

I was just explaining that this must be the only restaurant in Ibiza that did not serve them, when the waiter butted in.

"One moment please," he said, dashing off towards the kitchens. Moments later he returned with news that the chef would be delighted to make Crêpes Suzette for Rory, adding that if he would care to visit the kitchens he could watch them being cooked. Rory was highly impressed and went off hand in hand with the waiter, throwing us a backward glance and a cheeky grin that said *See!* The chef, a statuesque Dane with a mop of thick blonde hair and co-ordinating beard, followed Rory back to our table carrying a plate of sizzling crêpes flambées and ceremoniously presented them with great panache in front of the delighted little boy. Rory finished every mouthful and promptly fell asleep on three chairs and a pile of cushions provided by the waiter.

Sadly our experiences of dining out with children in England have been less successful. When our children were toddlers my girlfriends and I would meet for coffee or lunch, often in the cold and pouring rain, only to be greeted by welcoming signs on doors stating *No pushchairs.* In country pubs we were looked upon with disdain for daring to have children with us and were quickly herded into the 'Children's Room' – without exception the coldest, most dismal place with lino floors and cheap furniture – usually set adjacent to the lavatories, so the lingering aroma of disinfectant and worse could cling to our unimaginative food. We had been spoilt during our short time in Corfu;

the years of being made to feel unwelcome and invisible in our own country had hit home and none of us wanted to spend another school holiday there. Disenchantment with England had crystallised into a determination to change our lives; although we loved our home we could not justify keeping it if we wanted to spend more time abroad. Sentimentality would have to give way to practicality. The verdicts of our friends fell into two distinct camps: some considered us foolhardy in the extreme, while others thought us rather daring. All, however, were eagerly looking forward to holidaying with us.

The agonising decision was finally made to sell our cherished manor house and at the end of the summer we moved to a chocolate box thatched cottage in a rural hamlet in Somerset, close to Miranda's prep school. With Albertines around the front door and wisteria covering the walls, Rose Cottage was Miranda's idea of heaven, revelling in the small rooms and proximity of her own bedroom to ours, she settled in to this cosy home easily. Always nervous of the rambling passages at the manor as a three year old, she had counted the number of her tiny paces from her bedroom to ours and was always disgruntled that her brother's room was closer to us. We on the other hand found it very trying, particularly as most of our furniture would not fit and Jeremy kept cracking his head on the Lilliputian doorways. Rory chose to remain as a full boarder at Millfield, only a few miles distant, where there was more room for his sound equipment, deigning to visit us occasionally but never staying very long. The cottage was a stopgap, somewhere to live while we were in England, a base for us until we had bought some land and built a house in Corfu.

Chapter Three

Greek Easter

As Brits, we love a do, don't we? I adore our national celebrations. If I see a gold coach, you almost need to put me in a straightjacket, I get so excited.

Joanna Lumley

The autumn term fell into a depressing routine for all of us, already missing our summer life aboard Sarava. We were in an unfamiliar county where we knew nobody and felt we were merely biding our time until we could get back to Corfu. Somerset chose to deepen our gloom by providing one hundred days of rain in succession. Opening my eyes each dark, wet morning the words *Now is the winter of our discontent* sprang to mind, adding to my depression; I certainly wasn't banking on any Son of York ever appearing to make it glorious summer. In the surrounding villages the Bloody Assizes seemed to have cast a pervading, icy shadow over the entire county; every other square or crossroad displayed a plaque with an uplifting message such as *'At this place in 1685 eleven villagers were hung, drawn and quartered by order of Judge Jeffries and the King'*.

Miranda, however, was very happy at Millfield Prep, making new friends easily and remaining blissfully unaware of our misery. Somerset must have many good qualities, but to us it was charmless and drab, its dreary vistas of flood plains and ditches uninspiring, the majority of its shopkeepers shockingly unfriendly. It just wasn't Devon. As we sloshed through the muddy puddles on our daily walks with our three Cavaliers we consoled each other through chattering teeth.

"It's only until Miranda finishes school, it will soon pass," I said bravely, trying to keep our spirits up. 'Not soon enough,' was the unspoken response.

So the winter gradually dragged past and by the time the daffodils appeared and new buds were forming on the trees we had already booked our flights for Corfu. Apart from the long summer holidays when Sarava was our home for nine weeks, we increasingly longed for these few weeks' respite in the spring. The first trip each year for the family would be taken during the Easter holidays, which generally co-incided with the Greek Orthodox celebrations. Corfu attracts Greeks from all over the world at Easter; joyfully converging on the island they almost double the island's population of one hundred thousand.

On the last day of each spring term we would pack our bags into the car ready for our trip to Heathrow, where an overnight flight to Athens awaited us. Our indomitable house-sitter Jacky would arrive with her Jack Russell – usually coinciding with a flurry of snow or a clinging Somerset fog – trailing dog blankets, dog food and treats, bowls, leads and an assortment of canine toys to keep all four dogs happy during our absence. Bramble, Briar and Burberry would bark wildly, chasing around Jacky's feet in a frenzy of excitement at the prospect of the weeks ahead of them. They knew as soon as Jacky arrived that they would be *properly* looked after: three long walks each day over hill and dale, through woods and fields. Unlike us, Jacky was intrepid and adventurous; belying her small stature and arthritic hip, no fence or gate could delay her progress through the countryside. The dogs would form a patient queue every morning for their groom-ing session and be rewarded with doggie treats at every opportunity. They must have thought Jacky really knew how to care for them; each evening promptly at five they would be fed generously, then Jacky would collapse on the sofa in the sitting room to watch a succession of soaps, surrounded by the four of them snoring contentedly.

With feather pillows on the back seats, the children would sleep peacefully as we drove through the night to the airport, waking briefly to board the Olympic Airways flight and immediately dozing off again with enviable ease for the duration of the flight. A delicious Greek breakfast of creamy natural yoghurt with nuts, fresh fruit and Cretan mountain honey would bring them to life before we disembarked in

Athens to catch our dawn connection to Corfu. Finally, at eight in the morning, we would kick off our shoes on Sarava's aft deck and tumble into our beds for an hour's sleep to recuperate from the night's journey.

I had slept so soundly after our very first arrival that I could not remember where I was when the high-pitched peeping had awoken me; caught halfway between dream and reality, I opened my eyes to see Sarava's mast glinting in the sun, high above the hatch. Sighing with relief to be back in Corfu after such a miserable winter, I fumbled for my alarm clock and quickly realised I had not set it. Then I recognised the sound: it was a kingfisher, directly over my head on the railing above my cabin window; his shrill, piping call went on long enough for me to get me out of bed and creep upstairs into the saloon. As I peered, bleary-eyed, out of the windows I was just in time to catch a tantalising flash of brilliant turquoise as I disturbed him. He streaked away from Sarava, increasing the tempo of his call as he skimmed low over the water towards the shore, obviously annoyed that his morning fishing routine had been interrupted by my presence.

Our first Easter on the island was typically frenetic and memorable; no sooner had we set foot on Greek soil than we were caught up in the whirlwind of ceremonies, festivities and social events that follow in rapid succession and seem to continue for ten days or more. We hardly had time to draw breath, my mobile telephone rang incessantly with various invitations from our new Corfiot friends.

"HELLO!" a voice would instruct. "You must come to ..." followed by details of where and when we would be expected. These calls never took the form of requests, they were more like commands and brooked no argument. Naturally we were thrilled; the only problems arose when two invitations clashed. Tact and diplomacy were called for and occasionally, when no other solution could be found, we ended up eating two lunches on the same day to avoid upsetting any of our generous hosts.

The sky was electric blue on Good Friday; I was so pleased for all the people in Corfu that the first day of the Easter celebrations would be perfect. If the weather held, the processions through the streets on Saturday morning, in Corfu Town and the remotest mountain villages, would also be blessed with warm, spring sunshine. The brass instruments of the town bands would gleam and the gold braid and embroidery on the robes of the bishops and papas would sparkle in the brilliant April light.

Miranda and I decided to go into town for a little shopping, coffee, then lunch among the locals and Greeks visiting from the mainland and other Ionian islands. We left rather later than usual, having unpacked our cases and generally re-organised Sarava. Clean towels were pulled out of cupboards, still smelling of washing powder and fresh air from the last time they were laundered in October; winter woollies, socks and warm pyjamas, used when Jeremy and I had stayed for a bitterly cold week in January, were stowed away under bunks until the next winter, which we hoped would be far less extreme.

Corfu had been blasted by icy Siberian winds during that week; the walk from the airport taxi along the pontoon to Sarava was turned into a gruelling expedition as we battled against a blizzard, our wheeled suitcases intent on hurling themselves into the water behind us. We had found Sarava's cockpit inches deep in snow and hail, but below decks she was warm and cosy as an Austrian ski chalet. That evening we had decided to eat at a little taverna within walking distance of the marina, which we knew would be welcoming with its open log fire and home cooked fare. I wrapped myself in every warm thing I could find on board and followed Jeremy out into the cockpit. He turned around to give me a helping hand along the icy passerelle.

"What on earth are you wearing?" he shouted above the howling wind.

"Well, my eyes will water and my mascara will run without it!" I shouted back.

"I'm not going out for supper with you dressed like Jacques Cousteau! Take it off!"

Reluctantly I had done as I was bid and tossed my diving mask, complete with snorkel, back into the cockpit.

Beneath the warm April sun Miranda and I wound our way towards the market, but the traffic was crawling at a snail's pace and it was soon apparent that every parking space in the town was already taken. Everywhere we looked the shop windows were full of chocolate Easter eggs in gaudy cellophane wrapping, toy bunnies of all shapes and sizes and long candles – far too pretty to burn – in all colours of the rainbow; ribbons, lace, net, silk flowers, charms and miniature religious icons adorning every one. We decided to buy the most tasteful candle we could find for the boat; the one we had been given had been left in the sun and was already beginning to curve like the sword of a Turk in the spring heat.

"Look out, Mummy!" Miranda suddenly squealed. "Those cars have right of way."

At such a tender age I was amazed at her road sense. I was not feeling comfortable driving a left-hand drive hire car for the first time; being left-handed I found it very awkward to change gear with my right hand.

" You drive just like a Greek! Let me do the gears for you."

"Oh thank you so much!" I replied, taking it as a distinct compliment and immediately feeling very much part of the local scene.

Funnily enough Rory had reassured me I would be perfectly at home driving in Corfu; according to him I always drove in the middle of the road and parked like an Italian. For some obscure reason my family always worried about my driving abilities, never letting me forget one particular incident in Devon. Reversing out of the courtyard one day – a routine manoeuvre I could perform with my eyes closed – I had forgotten it was dustbin day; so when the battered rump of the Land Rover struck something metallic I cursed the dustmen for leaving the empty bins in the middle of our drive. I pulled forward and took a far more spirited backwards charge at the offending bins, only to discover that I had completely destroyed the side of my beautiful

Jaguar convertible, which now resembled a shiny, if crumpled steel boomerang. Earlier in the day Jeremy had moved it from the garage into the drive, so naturally the whole thing was entirely my husband's fault. He in turn reminded me that I was never slow to pass the blame whenever dents appeared in any of our cars, citing the time I had reversed into a police car – don't ask, it's a wing mirror allergy. I quickly decided attack was the best form of defence and rebuked the startled copper, demanding 'How dare you creep up behind me like that!' The poor young policeman was particularly upset as it was the very first time he had been allowed to drive on his own.

So for the rest of the way around the park and cricket pitch, past the former Summer Palace of the King of Greece and under the magnificent archway, the Gate of St. George, Miranda changed gear for me while I looked fruitlessly for a space.

"Listen to this music, it's really cool." Without waiting for a response she poked one of the earphones from her CD player into my right ear. Recognising a song I liked, I joined her in singing along, jigging to the music in unison. With the windows fully open, we pulled up at the traffic lights and I realised we were being stared at by a group of traffic police standing in a huddle around their motorbikes. We must have looked and sounded ridiculous, joined ear to ear by black wire, gyrating and singing with gay abandon to the strains of *I Love Rock and Roll*; but with typical Greek good humour the smartly uniformed officers all started gyrating in time with us ... Just try that in England sometime and see how many different varieties of tickets and fines you can collect.

Eventually we found a space in the car park at the Old Port, back where we had started. Miranda asked me why I had gone all that way around the town when we could have parked here in the first place. She was already impatient to return to the boat for some serious sunbathing, grimly determined to go back to school with a respectable tan. Most of her chums holidayed in tropical locations over the Easter break and returned the colour of polished conkers. Miranda was concerned that the reputation of Corfu would be tarnished if her colour did not match the tan on the pupils who had spent their weeks in Mauritius or the West Indies.

Sweet scents of aniseed, mahlab and vanilla were everywhere, seeping out of doorways as the special *Tsoureki* Easter bread and cakes were baked. The atmosphere of anticipation and excitement was palpable. Small earthenware pots stood at the entrance to every shop, a gift to the shopkeepers from the town council, ready to be smashed in the streets on Easter Saturday morning at eleven sharp in order to expel malevolent spirits. We walked past tourist gift shops near the port, their gaudy souvenirs, worry beads, sunglasses, cheap jewellery and tee-shirts overflowing onto the pavements; their cluttered displays contrasting incongruously with the chic uptown boutiques selling designer clothes, the exclusive furriers with coats made from luxurious Canadian skins and the glitzy, be-mirrored jewellery shops; their proprietors stood expectantly in the doorways, like smiling predators ready to entice potential customers into their twinkling, air-conditioned lairs.

A whiff of freshly brewed Greek coffee hit me, surely one of the most tantalising aromas, so we headed for our favourite restaurant and chose a table next to the cricket pitch. Shaded by elegant cream parasols the area felt quite colonial; I could imagine a scene from the nineteenth century, with customers in wide brimmed hats sipping the ginger beer introduced by the English and locally called, *tsin-tsin birra*. The area where we were sitting is called the Liston; there are many theories as to the origin of the name. I have been given several explanations of variable credibility. The first, quaint but improbable, dated from when Corfu became a British protectorate after the fall of Napoleon; the duty roster for the British officers was posted each day on the wall under the arcade, thus becoming the wall with the *list on*. Another more probable explanation derives from the Italian word *lista*, meaning a long, narrow strip of ground, a place where Venetian officers and their ladies could promenade; a similar area in front of the Piazza San Marco in Venice also bears this name. However I have it on good authority from a Corfiot friend that, during Venetian rule, one side of the structure was for the use of the *panton*, the ordinary people; the other side, the *liston*, was reserved solely for the nobility whose names were in the *Libro d'Oro*, which listed aristocrats of the Republic of Venice – the Serenissima. The dividing line was the space between these two arcaded buildings, which were modelled on the Rue de Rivoli in Paris, itself designed by Matthieu de Lesseps, whose son Ferdinand initiated the building of the Suez Canal. Whatever its heritage, it was Edward Lear who described the Liston as the most beautiful esplanade in the world.

As I drank my frothy cappuccino and Miranda sipped her sweet fresh orange juice, I was reminded of the perfect description of such a delightful moment on the Liston.

> *...to gaze at the trees, at the sea, at the arches with their massive and beautiful lanterns, and at the towering old houses – at a whole world rooted somewhere in the past, as if casting its mind back and meditating – to gaze upon everything with a carefree eye and to feel the fatigue seeping away with each sip of my drink and a new soul entering into me.*

These words, written by I. M. Panagiotopoulos in the last century, perfectly express the elation I feel whenever I am in this gorgeous place; often I am alone here, but having my lovely teenage daughter sitting opposite me made the pleasure all the more intense. Small boys were playing football on the cricket pitch, casually watched by their mothers as they chatted and drank coffee, while doting fathers drank ouzo beneath a haze of cigarette smoke. The youngest children, decked in their Easter finery, played on the polished flagstones of the esplanade, some with balls, others with tiny scooters, tricycles or push-along toys with bells and rattles, each one attended by a gaggle of besotted parents, aunts and grandmothers. Two little girls rumbled past the toddlers in a battery-operated four-by-four, looking as smug and hoity-toity as Sloane mothers delivering their offspring to an exclusive nursery school.

Miranda and I watched with fascination as a miniature 'Rambo' of about four, complete with hefty boots, began harassing a tiny girl of three; her ringlets were tied in a pink silk bow and she was clinging to a large beach ball for dear life. The mothers were oblivious as he tried to remove it from her vice-like grasp, attacking from every angle but always out-manoeuvred by her tenacity. He walked away, feigning loss of interest, then came back at a charge, baring his little milk teeth at her like a rabid dog. To her great credit she didn't bat an eyelid but stood her ground and clasped the ball all the more firmly to her chest, until eventually her aggressor found a better grip on the ball. Letting out a wail worthy of a banshee she finally burst into tears, as all the mothers swivelled round at once. 'Spiro, leave her alone!' they shouted in unison, at which point little Spiro started to sob quietly with down-cast eyes. His victim, obviously moved by such a display of dejection, gently handed him the precious ball and they toddled off together hand in hand, Spiro gazing at her adoringly through tear filled eyes. If you sit here for long enough, they say, the entire world will pass by.

Early that evening Jeremy drove us back into town to watch the Epitaphios Procession. The town was already full of cars, coaches and a throng of people as we abandoned the hire car by the waterfront in Garitsa Bay. Over a glass smooth sea the setting sun hemmed distant clouds with rose gold as we walked through the park amongst the crowd towards the Liston. Tens of thousands already lined the streets, waiting patiently in subdued, respectful hush. As the light faded the rows of Venetian lanterns on the Espianada's arcade glowed eerily, their bulbs covered with purple cellophane as a sign of mourning. Suddenly all talking stopped. You could have heard a pin drop – a miracle when so many Greeks were assembled in the town. Not a child cried and even the stray dogs fell silent. Then the slightly discordant notes of the town bands struck up, drums beating out the rhythm of a slow dirge, the smaller brass instruments struggling to be heard above the doleful bellowing of the tubas. Small groups of bishops and priests escorted ornately framed icons of saints and the Madonna; tasselled pennants and elaborate gonfalons billowed gently in the evening air, the spectators crossing themselves several times in rapid succession as the procession passed by. It was deeply moving to see such faith, devotion and respect in this modern world.

When the procession seemed to be thinning out and the music began to fade as the bands left the Espianada for other parts of the town, we realised we were rather hungry. Threading our way through the melée into our favourite Aegli Restaurant, we asked for a table. An apologetic waiter, who knew us as regular customers, explained that tables in the evening were booked months in advance for the Easter period. It was the same story everywhere; we would have to try further afield. As politely as possible we pushed and squeezed our way through the unrelenting sea of bodies, intending to turn down the street by the Pentaphanero; this well-known landmark, a graceful, wrought iron street lamp with five lanterns, stands at the southern end of the Liston.

"It should be called Triaphanero," I quipped, as two of the lamps were permanently broken, but nobody was listening to my joke as we reached the crossroads. Another band was rocking slowly past, playing a different funeral march. Hot on their heels was a seemingly end-less following of priests, church dignitaries and groups of Scouts and school children.

"We won't get across here," Jeremy explained, "We'll have to back-track through the side streets."

At every junction we met another procession. Jeremy, never at his best in a crowd, was exasperated by now and we were all tired, irritable and hungry.

"It's all one blessed procession and it's encircled us ... probably goes on all night, we'll never get back to the car ... who's idea was this?" Jeremy continued, striding off determinedly as the rest of us trotted to keep up. "There's only one thing for it, we'll have to head them off, go down by the port, up the other way past the market, through Sa'Rocco Square and down to the seafront that way."

Miranda and I stopped in our tracks.

"No," she said firmly, "I can't walk that far and I'm starving."

In daylight, wearing flat shoes, Jeremy's suggested detour would have amounted to a walk of forty-five minutes, involving several steep hills and uneven pavements; I was wearing court shoes and a skirt, in deference to the occasion. The heels were low but after an English winter in wellies my feet were already hurting.

"I think I know somewhere down there," I said in desperation. "Let's try it." We struggled down a flight of uneven steps and found a tiny restaurant with its iron tables and chairs neatly arranged in the middle of a narrow, cobbled street; the roof tiles of the tall, crumbling buildings at either side almost touched overhead.

"We can't eat in the middle of an alley!" Jeremy protested, quickly backed up by Rory, both noting with distaste the proximity of two large drains.

"There's nobody else eating here," Rory noted. "That's never a good sign!"

But Miranda and I were already seated at a table, where two attentive waiters were fussing over us. It was bliss to sit at last and within seconds a bottle of ice-cold mineral water, a dish of local olives and a basket of crusty bread were before us. Jeremy and Rory capitulated warily.

The food, a vegetarian meze, was of course freshly cooked and delicious. Greeks do not eat meat for forty days before the Resurrection; the fast ends at midnight on Easter Saturday when priests call out *Christos Anesti*, Christ is risen, echoed by the worshippers' response, *Alithos Anesti*, truly he is risen. With lighted candles in hand, everyone then returns home to eat the special soup, *maghiritsa*, made from unappetising entrails of the lambs to be spit-roasted on Easter Sunday. It is considered very lucky to keep the candles alight until reaching home, then allowing the smoke to leave a mark on the lintel above the door frame. As we were finishing our meal a few weary young bandsmen, with shiny, plumed helmets tucked under their arms, strode past us towards the Old Port and their buses home. Fortified by our supper the walk back to the car was easy. The streets were almost empty; just a few groups of young people lingered on, planning where to go next. Eventually we found the car and drove back to the marina under a sky thick with stars.

"It feels like a very holy night, doesn't it?" I asked, glancing over my shoulder when neither of our children replied. They were curled up like two cats on the back seat, fast asleep.

On the morning of Easter Saturday it would have been impossible to park in town, as the police habitually close the roads leading into the centre until lunchtime. Jeremy drove us into town and dropped us off at Mantouki, where coaches and buses were disgorging their cargoes of smartly dressed passengers from all corners of the island; we walked together in a jolly, chattering throng along the seafront towards the town. Miranda and I were wearing jackets, as a fine mist had hung over the marina early that morning; by the time we reached the Mourayia, the cloudless sky had turned a vibrant blue and hot sun beat down on our heads. Once again a Corfiot spring day had caught me without a hat. Removing our jackets we sought any available segment of shade.

"Oh no, Mummy, you can't do that!" Miranda exclaimed in horror as I reached in my bag for my small black umbrella. "You'll look just like a Greek Granny!" Teenage girls can be so self-conscious.

By the time we reached St. George's Gate we were both sweltering and I desperately needed to dive into the nearest 'ladies' to whip off my tights. Thankfully we found a spot in the shade of the Palace's magnificent Doric colonnade to watch the beginning of the procession. Crowds filled the Espianada, the cricket pitch and as far as the eye could see to the park beyond. The first of the town's bands had already reached our friends' jewellery shop, halfway down the Liston, and we had arrived in time to see the Guides, Scouts and Sea Cadets marching sedately past. I assured Miranda we hadn't missed St. Spyridon, who was just being carried towards the Liston, when dozens of video recorders and cameras were suddenly raised in front of us, blocking our view.

Grabbing her hand and pulling her after me, we threaded our way to a better vantage point, where only a thin rope divided us from the procession. Always fascinated by Corfu's patron saint, partly because of my own firm belief in his powers, Miranda had never managed to get a really good look at him. The camera we had bought for her birthday, the size of a matchbox, was certainly discreet and I felt sure the venerable saint could not possibly object to a close-up. The parade had come to a sudden standstill and we found ourselves cheek to cheek with the bandsmen, surrounded by a strong smell of mothballs and cheap cologne. In their dashing royal blue and gold livery, sweat trickling from beneath their sparkling brass helmets, they waited in the full sun, the flashes of light thrown from their instruments dazzling the onlookers.

"They must be boiling in those heavy uniforms," I said to Miranda.

"Sshh!" she replied curtly.

I noticed one handsome young trumpeter was giving her a shy, sideways glance. Smiling coyly back, it was evident that Miranda did not want him to know she even *had* a mother, let alone that she was standing beside her. Watching this would-be Romeo carefully as the band struck up again, I wondered how he could possibly play a note with his mouth so firmly set in a grin. The legacy of Casanova – who served in Corfu as a sub-lieutenant in the Venetian navy – obviously persists.

A collection of priests and bishops rounded the bend, resplendent in jewel coloured or white vestments heavily embossed with gold and silver embroidery. Obliviously crushing the scattered flowers beneath their feet, they seemed to roll in unison from side to side, as if on the deck of a ship in heavy seas. The pungent scent of incense filled the air as a silver brazier, smoke gushing, was swung wildly on its chains in time with the rocking priests. A hush descended on the crowd surrounding us as everyone made the sign of the cross.

"Get your camera ready, here he comes." I whispered to Miranda.

Preceded by a silver-bearded bishop, impressive with his ivory and gold mitre and robes, four white-robed priests with black stove-pipe hats carried the upright golden casket, a sort of sedan chair containing the saint's mummified remains; in the early days of the Protectorate he would have been carried by four British colonels. St. Spyridon has four official outings each year, as well as countless clandestine, ethereal sorties on his own.

Glass panels revealed the shrivelled, ashen head of St. Spyridon lolling, open-mouthed, to one side. This saint, born around 260 AD, became Bishop of Trimythous in Cyprus; years after burial, when the Arabs invaded Cyprus, his uncorrupted body was taken to Constantinople, whence in 1453, now fully sanctified, he was smuggled to the safety of Corfu strapped to the back of a donkey. Considering his great antiquity and his very uncomfortable last mode of transport, it is perfectly understandable that he looks more than a trifle jaded. Corfiot friends assure us that the saint's dainty, hand-made, embroidered slippers have to be replaced every few months; apparently they are worn out by his nocturnal wanderings around the island as he works his miracles. The wear and tear could also be attributed to the multitude of kisses the slippers receive from devout worshippers. A flap at the bottom of the ornate silver sarcophagus, which resides in its own crypt in St. Spyridon's church, is opened at regular intervals to reveal the feet of the saint. By law no building in the town must stand above the terracotta-domed campanile of the church. It is reassuring to spot this landmark from the plane as it swoops low over the town when approaching the airport from the north, particularly when regular travellers to the island are preoccupied with images of the tricky landing ahead on the short, peninsular runway.

"I feel like a tourist," Miranda hissed under her breath, aiming the minute viewfinder at the casket, taking her photograph and quickly returning the camera to her shoulder bag.

Fragrant smoke from the burning myrrh billowed from the filigree holes of the braziers and swirled around us. Petals had been strewn on the road along the processional route, the scent as they were crushed underfoot mingling with the incense until we were enveloped in a haze of transcendental fragrance. Eventually the column petered out to a trickle and we followed behind the stragglers at the back.

"I must have a coffee," I said.

"And I need a cold drink," Miranda added. "But look at the cafés, every seat's taken and we'll never get served."

Then she had a brainwave, "Let's go to the jewellers, they always want to give us a drink and last time you refused because we were in a hurry."

"Good idea. I need to speak to them about something anyway." I said, quickening my pace until we could dive into the cool of the little shop.

"Ah, *Kalo Paska,* Happy Easter," chorused the twins. "What would you like to drink?"

Gratefully we sank onto dainty ormolu chairs and within minutes Christos returned with a cappuccino and a fresh orange juice.

"How on earth did you get those so quickly? It's so nice to have friends with influence isn't it!"

Miranda nodded in silent agreement as she sipped from her straw. Christos then offered us hand-made chocolates, from a specialist chocolaterie in the town, which their mother had brought in for them that morning, as she did every Easter Saturday.

We chatted for a while, exchanged family news, discussed the weather in England, the winter in Corfu and the state of tourism, which had been badly affected by the disastrous introduction of the euro, so cynically engineered by Brussels and Goldman Sachs, when a small bottle of water had doubled in price overnight.

"The Germans are not coming any more, they used to buy a lot of jewellery," Christos said wistfully.

"Now we have to rely on the cruise ships to bring customers," added Andreas, "but the passengers don't spend as much as they used to when we had the drachma."

We began to discuss the gold signet ring Christos would be making for Rory's birthday; I had already drawn our family crest for the engraver in Athens to copy. Back in the 1830's this particular Swan With Two Necks insignia was known throughout the land as the crest of William Chaplin's colossal coaching empire.* But when Christos had first seen its rather intricate design he advised us to choose a ring with a large escutcheon, otherwise, as he had laughingly explained, 'Your swan will look like a scrawny goddam chicken!' How we loved the plain speaking irreverence of the Greeks!

Suddenly whistles started blowing outside and the twins' gloomy expressions vanished.

"Quick, we must go to the other side!" they cried out, beaming like gleeful children at a party.

Each grabbing a small earthenware pot, they chivvied us across the promenade through the line of policemen into the assembled crowd, leaving millions of pounds worth of jewellery unprotected. They arranged us in line in the front row, checking their expensive wrist watches every few moments.

"Two minutes to go! Get your cameras ready and mind your legs!"

They held their pots aloft and kept a watchful eye on the policemen for the signal. A group had gathered in every window and on every balcony of the six storey Venetian buildings facing us. Over each sill hung a gold-fringed crimson cloth, some vividly brand new, others worn and washed out to the colour of a dusty rose.

---

* Shrewd William sold his coaching empire at its zenith in 1837, reinvesting the proceeds and his acumen in the railways to make an even larger fortune in the process. Turning down a string of titles from a Baronetcy upwards – being unwilling to settle the lion's share of his colossal estate on the eldest of his six sons – he vowed to accept nothing less than an Earldom for his many services to the nation; sadly for him that one never turned up before his untimely death. As the lineage has shaken down, my father-in-law would eventually have had a coronet to accompany his aloof manner; equally I might never have met Jeremy.

"Look up there, Mummy," Miranda pointed out a high window where a wizened, grey-haired old lady was shaking out her cloth, carefully smoothing it over the window ledge. The cloth was so faded it must have been used every Easter Saturday since she was a little girl, lifted up no doubt by her father to watch the excitement far below. On each windowsill or balcony a pot was balanced, held in place by a member of the household. They varied in size and we had fun trying to spot the largest, but every time we found a winner another even larger pot would be unveiled.

"Look at that one on the corner," Miranda said. "It's absolutely enormous!"

"What a waste," I replied, "it seems such a shame to think what's going to happen to them, I would love some of those for our garden."

There was a sudden gasp from the crowd. Exactly opposite us a gargantuan pot appeared on the balustrade of the highest rooftop balcony; it was so huge that its owner was completely obscured by its mass. Slowly it wriggled and wobbled forward, seemingly unaided by human hand, tilting from side to side, inch by inch until it had reached the point of balance. As it teetered on the ledge, ready for the grand finale, I kept my camera trained on it, fervently hoping no careless policeman would pass underneath. The police whistles blew in unison and, to a great roar from the crowd, the pots were released, falling through the air and smashing deafeningly on the esplanade. Bits of broken pottery ricocheted everywhere; despite the pots containing water to prevent the pieces flying too far, I felt a small shard hit my ankle. Christos and Andreas threw their pots into the melée as the elated crowd clapped and cheered.

Finally a great roar went up from the onlookers as the largest pot was nudged over the edge to its ultimate doom. I clicked my camera frantically as the pot toppled, water flying out in a sparkling cascade as the pot fell, finally hitting the ground with an explosive crash as it shattered into a thousand pieces. The crowd surged onto the streets to retrieve shards of pottery for luck, a hazardous business as the smooth paving stones were slippery with a bright ochre soup of clay dust and water.

The roots of the pot throwing ceremony lie deep in history. Everyone knows the purpose is to rid house and family of bad luck and to bring general good fortune for the year ahead; some say its origins stem from biblical times, the pots representing the one in which Judas' thirty pieces of silver were placed in payment for his betrayal of Jesus. I have read somewhere that Judas was from Corfu, in which case the action of smashing the pots is the Corfiots' way of showing their abhorrence. However the trees that grace Corfu in springtime with their beautiful purple blossoms are known as Judas trees, as it is believed that Judas hung himself from such a tree in shame.

Tiptoeing over the rubble, Miranda and I picked our way carefully along the Liston, there was little room to manoeuvre as we were being crushed on all sides by jubilant Greeks and our progress was an inch at a time. We were meeting English friends for lunch and frantically trying to reach our rendezvous, but once again the brass bands blocked our path and there was nothing to do but stand and wait. I held tightly to Miranda's hand, lest we were parted in this sea of humanity and would never find each other again.

"We're going to be late now," grumbled Miranda who was looking forward to her lunch.

"There's nothing I can do except to send Susan a message."

"What shall I say?"Miranda asked, pulling her phone out of her bag, thumbs poised over the keys.

"Held up by tubas, c u asap,"I said, trying to be succinct.

"I've got a message from George." Miranda announced, "He says he's here and coming to see us."

"He'll never find us in this," I warned, but I had underestimated her young Greek friend's ingenuity and determination. No sooner had I spoken than George popped up behind Miranda, grinning from ear to ear.

"How on earth did you find us?" I asked in astonishment, for you could not fit a playing card between the seething mass of people on the Espianada.

"She's tall," he replied simply, in his clipped no-nonsense way. "And blonde!"

He was right. As I looked around I could see only dark hair, whereas Miranda stood head and shoulders above most of the crowd, her long hair glinting in the sun. She smiled, evidently pleased by George's explanation as he took her hand. However, he had a way of making sure she would never become conceited.

"Come on, Feta Cheese!" George teased, using his nickname for her which alluded to her pale English Rose complexion.

We eventually met Susan and her family, who had flown from England to celebrate Greek Easter. We lunched indoors at Aegli as all the tables under the Volta – the local name for the arcade – as well as the umbrella-shaded tables next to the cricket pitch were occupied. There were special vegetarian dishes on the menu as the Lenten fast still had a few hours to run; we chose fresh artichokes, served with a home made egg and lemon sauce, buttered French beans and tall glasses of ice-cold Mythos beer.

Back at the marina the sun was strong, a warm breeze blowing off the land beneath skies the clear, brilliant blue of spring; the colour becomes less intense later in the year when the sky is so full of light. Miranda and I could not resist a siesta on Sarava's foredeck; after only an hour she was thrilled to discover white marks where her bikini had been. We showered and changed, had an early supper of bacon and eggs and drove along the coast road north to Kassiopi. The sun was sinking behind the hills and in the distance, across the sea, Corfu Town had turned powder pink in its glow. At each side of the road thick curtains of lilac wisteria cascaded over walls and balconies and climbed in spirals up telegraph poles and, amazingly, to the very tips of mature cypress trees; the heady scent of their prolific blooms wafted through the open windows of our car as we passed.

"Are you sure you've got the right evening?" Jeremy asked, surprised to find Kassiopi dark and deserted, its streets empty.

"Of course. There's only one Easter Saturday," I replied as we parked beside the harbour, feeling rather self-conscious in our isolation.

"Now what?" asked Jeremy rather irritably, concluding the trip had been a wild goose chase and already anticipating the long, tortuous drive home in the dark.

"Let's get out and wander around for a bit until everyone arrives," I said, rather more optimistically than I felt. Perhaps everything had been cancelled or moved to another village; this was Greece and anything could happen, only the locals would know what was going on. After all I had only heard rumours that Kassiopi was *the* place to be on this holy night; it was not mentioned in the paper or on advertising posters in town.

"I bet nobody's coming," said Rory, picking up his father's ingrained negativity, "I think you've got it wrong and everybody's gone somewhere else!"

"I'm tired," groaned Miranda. "Why did we have to come all this way?"

I tried to ignore these gloomy pussies by my side and focused instead on the beauty of the evening. It was like a mid-summer's night, the air so warm it felt like being wrapped in a soft cashmere shawl; there was no breeze and the exotic scent of jasmine was everywhere. The cobbled path leading to the church was lit by two strings of tungsten light bulbs illuminating a canopy of wisteria, the extravagant blossoms hanging like bunches of lilac grapes and exhaling their heady perfume into the balmy air. Dressed in black from head to foot an elderly couple shuffled past us like a pair of tiny jackdaws and disappeared into a doorway.

"You see, they were carrying a candle!" I said cheerfully, "I'm sure something's going to happen."

"They're probably going to a funeral," Jeremy retorted. "You can see there's not a sign of life anywhere."

I had to admit it did not look promising. As we sat in solitary splendour in the unlit car park my hopes of an Easter celebration were dwindling. Then to my immense relief a few people wandered into the road in front of the church, a few more gathering in the car park. One car arrived, then another; after ten minutes every space was taken, the harbourside full of local men, women, children and babies all holding candles. We joined the crowd, greeting familiar faces and wishing them *Kalo Pasxa*. Miranda's face suddenly lit up as he spotted Jon; she and Rory threaded their way through the crowd to find their chum. 'Phew, now they're all happy,' I muttered to myself. Even Jeremy had perked up, chatting to Jon's father as Rory eyed up the local girls. Young children, clutching outsize candles, glowed with as much excitement as English children on Christmas Eve. No doubt the prospect of eating their chocolate eggs outweighed the imminent resurrection of Jesus.

As the church bell tolled Papa Makis appeared from the church and wove his way through the congregation towards the quayside, where a small dais had been erected beneath a decorative archway, covered with greenery and flowers. With cross and microphone to hand he took his position behind the lectern, framed against a backdrop of the harbour, which was empty except for a couple of small fishing boats. Amid a deafening squeal of feedback from the loudspeakers the priest began to recite the litany at great speed, racing the second hand to the first stroke of midnight. But before he could finish his address with the uplifting and long awaited words, *Christos anesti*, a series of violent explosions rent the air as a dozen flares and firecrackers were simultaneously lit directly behind the dais. Papa Makis made a frantic grab for his stovepipe hat, keeping his hand firmly planted on top of it as he competed with the pandemonium to finish the devotions. A crimson wall of flame had shot up behind him, silhouetting him like a black-cloaked apparition from the underworld as a choking smoke-screen obliterated the dais, the arch, the harbour and the twinkling lights of distant Albania, leaving the hapless priest apparently suspended in mid air above the cauldron.

"It looks like a floor show from Las Vegas!" Jon said.

The 'cabaret' priest seemed unperturbed as the first mortars shook the ground and soared into the night sky, each one exploding in a shock of colour high above the sea. Eventually he gave up the struggle to be heard and wisely vacated the dais, still clutching his hat as he ran back, vestments flapping, to the relative safety of the crowd to watch the fireworks.

The display was magnificent, vast globes of coloured stars exploding overhead and illuminating the still water in the harbour. The noise of the detonations was equally overwhelming, sound effects always as important as the visual in Greece. Everyone 'oohd and aahd' with appreciation as they do the world over, the children shrieking at every bang. Ten minutes later the grand finale was a colossal rocket that screamed up into the sky and exploded into three shells, each one sending out a different coloured starburst. With the sounds of clapping, cheering and the cries of *Christos Anesti* and the response, *Alithos Anesti* ringing in ears already humming from the mortars, we picked our way back to the car through a tide of flickering candles and smiling, elated faces. Christ had risen and all was right with the world. The assembled crowd began to disperse, walking slowly, sheltering candle flames with their hand. It is considered very lucky to keep the candles alight between altar and home, then allowing the smoke to leave a mark on the lintel above the door frame. The first time I had attempted this was with my Greek friends in Cyprus ... Costas was not impressed with the scorch mark my candle indelibly seared into the cream roof lining of his smart Mercedes.

"Jon's asked us to go for a drink," Miranda said. "Do you mind waiting for a bit?"

Before Jeremy could object I kicked him smartly on the ankle.

"Of course not," I answered, not wanting to be a wet blanket and spoil her fun; this was her last chance to see Jon before he returned to England the following day. Jeremy and I were secretly longing to return to Sarava and our comfortable bed. Enviously watching the over-forties returning to their houses with their flickering candles for a meal of hot Easter soup and crusty bread, we got into the car as Miranda, Jon and Rory joined the horde of local youth heading for the only bar that had opened for the occasion. My trusty Thermos flask to the rescue, I poured hot chocolate for both of us and silenced Jeremy's grumbling with a tin of Scottish shortbread. After what we thought was a reasonable time, about three quarters of an hour, Jeremy went to extricate our children from the young revellers who seemed intent on staying out all night. There were a few mutterings about how *early* it was to go home, how in the summer nobody even *goes out* until this time, how they were not *at all* tired; but once on the back seat of the car they instantly fell fast asleep.

Jeremy and I were staying for another week to deal with Sarava's annual trip to the slipway, but Miranda and Rory had to fly back to England before us for the start of the summer term. During our holiday I had tried to discipline myself to clean and organise cabins, lockers and cupboards in preparation for the summer holidays, when a long list of friends would be arriving in quick succession. Early every morning I closeted myself below decks, but I could feel my resolve slipping with every breath of warm air and call of the seagulls. Like Mole in *Wind in the Willows,* I knew I would give up as soon as the first rays of the morning sun penetrated below decks, instead scampering out into the sunlight shouting *Bother spring-cleaning!* Rory and Miranda were understandably reluctant to leave Corfu at the end of their Easter holidays. Things were literally beginning to hot up; night clubs and music bars were opening for the season, the sun was already fiercer than the hottest rays of an English summer, shops were displaying new ranges of swimwear, the sea warming by a degree or two every week and George and his friends were once more terrorising the island on their motorbikes.

Corfu's gentle spring was bursting into vibrant summer, colours were changing overnight, delicate spring blossoms were being ousted by the rampant, flamboyant blooms of high season. At the airport

Rory and Miranda looked enviously at the winter-white tourists filtering into the arrivals hall, replacing the suntanned, sandalled holiday-makers queuing at the check-in desks.

"Never mind, darlings, you'll soon be back again," I said, putting my arms around their brown shoulders and giving them a squeeze.

"Not until half-term," Miranda replied miserably, "and after that it's back to exams."

"It will go really quickly," I said. " By July there'll be no more school for nine weeks!"

I always hated watching them wave and smile bravely as they disappeared from sight into the departure lounge.

On Sarava later that morning I received a text message from George. 'R U LIVING 2MORO?'

"Tell him we certainly hope so!" quipped Jeremy.

"NO. WE LEAVE ON MONDAY MORNING." I replied.

Considering our friends are writing in a different language *and* in a different alphabet these minor errors are inevitable. I dread to think what faux-pas I will make if I ever learn to write Greek, having already made quite a few using the spoken word. Years before in Cyprus I had to welcome the audience at a fashion show I was arranging at the Nicosia Hilton. As most of the guests were Greek Cypriots I decided to attempt my speech in Greek; I simply had to greet the President of Cyprus' wife, then the lesser mortals. But I was puzzled when the audience started giggling; I thought I had done quite well, considering it was spoken from memory. I left the stage quickly and returned to the changing room, where my Cypriot friend Angela explained. Failing to stifle a laugh she told me that I had actually said 'Ladies, gentlemen, young ladies and homosexuals'. I was mortified, flatly refusing to appear on stage at the end of the show to receive the customary bouquet of flowers.

More recently I had visited the butcher in Corfu Town for the first time. I wanted to buy ten chicken breasts; we had six friends arriving from England that day and I was going to marinade the chicken in preparation for a barbecue supper. I knew a little Greek but, having mentally composed my sentence, I was still having difficulty with the word for *breast*, knowing it was definitely not *vysiá,* the indelicate Greek for boobs. I looked it up in my trusty phrase book without success; it was not in my small dictionary, neither did it appear in the '*Visiting the Doctor'* section, which listed every part of the human anatomy except breasts; even penis merited an entry. Rory and I went into the tiny shop and offered the usual greetings of *kalimera sas, ti kanete* to the butcher and his staff. Believing we were obviously fluent in their language we were assailed by a torrent of greetings and enquiries about our state of health, our country of origin and where we were staying; the latter I always dread as it is difficult to answer. 'We are staying on our yacht' sounds too pretentious for words and conjures up images of the huge, white 'gin-palaces' of the glitterati. There is no general word in Greek for boat, which is how we always referred to Sarava, although most people called her a yacht; occasionally I reverted to 'our catamaran,' an international word understood by most people, although it covered anything from enormous oceangoing ferry to highly dangerous dinghy. The shop was run by one family consisting of father, three sons and a corpulent grandfather who was sitting on a large tree-stump in one corner. This block of wood was obviously used for dismembering the larger joints of meat, judging by the bloodstained bark. Summoning my memorised sentence I asked for, *Deka fresco kotopoulo* ... before getting stuck.

"Ah, you want ten fresh chickens!" the father said in Greek, grinning widely.

"*Oxi, oxi, thelo deka fresco kotopoulo* – No, no, I want ten fresh chicken ..." I replied, adding *breasts* in English.

The three strapping sons came forward to try to help, but they were equally perplexed. Each one brought various gory portions of chicken for my inspection including half-chickens, thighs, and legs. When one of them produced a clutch of pimply, white necks dangling limply from his hand I began to feel faint and grabbed Rory's arm for support, my knees turning to jelly. I have never liked butchers' shops; as a small child I always refused to go in with my mother, finding the smell of blood and sawdust quite bad enough outside the door where I had to stand and wait for her. I was getting nowhere and the heat of the summer morning was increasing by the minute; I longed to leave the shop and get out into the fresh air. In desperation I repeated my request slowly and clearly, this time miming the unknown word for *breasts* by outlining a voluptuous bosom protruding, Mae West style, from my own slighter figure. All the butchers burst out laughing, repeating the correct word, *stithos*, literally *chests*, loudly to each other. Grandpa fell off his stump, doubled-up with laughter and holding his ample sides as he rolled onto the floor. The lady from a gift shop across the narrow street asked what was the cause of so much mirth and was soon passing it on, cackling hoarsely, to her neighbouring shopkeepers.

"God, Mummy, how could you!" hissed Rory over his shoulder as he shot out of the door.

As we reached the end of the street we could still hear laughter.

"It'll be all over town in twenty minutes, in fact it's probably reached St. Spyridon's already ... You won't be able to show your face in there again!" muttered Rory furiously under his breath.

My next few visits to town were spent avoiding the butchers' gaze, but unfortunately my hairdresser was almost next door. Despite sidling past, my face turned away in the opposite direction, they would always spot me, chuckling as they called out gaily 'Good morning, Madame, would you like some chests today?' I buy from them regularly now, having studied the correct Greek for almost every part of a carcass and daring them, with my eyes fixed on theirs, to laugh.

Chapter Four

Corfiot Kindness

Leave every place you go, everything you touch, a little better for your having been there.

Julie Andrews

Before leaving England in those early days I would always book our favourite taxi to collect us all from the airport. This spotless blue Audi, which the children had nicknamed 'Canine' – the phonetic of the letter and number on the car's roof – belonged to Christos and his handsome younger brother, Yiannis, who took turns to operate the taxi. Christos would usually do the late afternoon and evening runs while Yiannis ran the family bakery in Corfu Town, where his long nocturnal baking hours only allowed him to drive in the morning and early afternoon. However Christos, as the older brother, felt it was his sole responsibility to collect and deliver us to and from the airport. Sometimes Christos' fares continued well into the night; he would never go home to bed at all if we were on the dawn flight. During the winter months getting to Corfu meant driving from South Devon to Heathrow, then catching a plane to Athens, waiting around for a few exhausting hours, then taking the 6am flight to Corfu in a much lighter aircraft. It was always such a comforting thought that Christos and his shiny taxi would be waiting to welcome us.

We had come across K9 purely by chance and, much as we had met Ilario and his little Fiat in Roccella Ionica, each encounter had enriched our lives in their own way. On one occasion our plane had been delayed by fog at Heathrow, yet Christos had waited at the airport all night, just in case. At the end of our second summer in Corfu, when I had got to know him better, I asked Christos about the miniature photographs of two young men, framed in gold and positioned close to his eye level on the dashboard; I had noticed there was always a scarlet rose bud or dianthus tucked between the frames.

"They were my sons," he said, kissing the tip of his forefinger and touching each picture in turn.

"Were?" I questioned, unsure whether his slight command of English had failed him and he had used the wrong tense.

"They died of Leukaemia, both of them, two years apart."

I had no words. What can you say at such a time? I put my hand over his and told him I was so very sorry, but it seemed completely inadequate. Christos had started to build a substantial house in his garden for the boys, but after they died he never had the heart to finish it; he would often take a detour on our way back to the marina from town, so he could proudly show me his vegetable garden and pick a basketful of fresh produce for me to take back to Sarava. It was heartbreaking to see the brick shell standing there deserted and empty opposite his own house, its vacant windows staring blindly towards the home that had once heard the happy laughter of two young boys.

A few weeks later on a return trip from town, Christos asked Jeremy and me if we would accompany him to see the graves of his sons, which he visited every single day. We felt very honoured as we drove up the narrow track and arrived at the wrought iron gates of the cemetery, which stood at the top of a hill in the village of Kombitsi. Christos made the sign of the cross as we walked into the tranquility of the hallowed ground, leading us to the monuments he had erected side by side for each boy, two exquisitely carved marble angels completely surrounded by neat globes of fragrant, small-leaved basil plants. It was the saddest of moments to watch Christos murmuring Greek prayers for his beloved sons, all the while subconsciously plucking the flower buds off the basil plants to prevent them going to seed. There was something propitious in his action, as if the thriving plants would keep his sons' memory alive and fresh in his broken heart.

Returning down the hill from the cemetery, Christos had stopped again to show us the remains of his childhood home. From the verge we looked down on a tiny single storey building with a rampant fig tree growing through its roof; it was no larger than three parking spaces outside a supermarket, yet within its crumbling stone walls Christos and his ten siblings had somehow been raised. It was impossible to imagine their long struggle to the more prosperous lives they now enjoyed.

Like Venetian lions these two endearing brothers took us under the shelter of their wings from our first serendipitous meeting. They shepherded us protectively around their island as if we were long lost relatives. There was no shop, craftsman or tradesman in the town they did not know by name; whatever peculiar or elusive item Jeremy needed for Sarava was found almost instantly. When I wanted to make a necklace out of some beautiful shells I had found, I was patiently escorted by Yiannis to a minute jewellery workshop, in what used to be the Jewish quarter* of Corfu Town, to buy silver wire as fine and sparkling as unicorn's hair.

As soon as we had arrived on Sarava for the first time in Corfu, I needed to fit out the cabins to suit our needs. Yiannis knew where to take me to buy customised, pocket-sprung mattresses padded with horse hair – the comfiest we had ever used – fluffy, bouncy pillows stuffed with natural sheep's wool, or mirrors cut to size for all the

---

* It is heart rending to see the statue which stands in a pretty square in this area. Christos had pointed it out to me on my very first visit to town and told me the tragic story of the Jews in Corfu. The statue depicts a desperate mother and father with two young children in hand. It is a memorial to the Corfiot Jews who were rounded up by the Nazis and deported to concentration camps during the second world war. Like so many others, the sign on the front of the memorial reads 'NEVER AGAIN'. The Vecchia synagogue was destroyed by the German bombing in September 1942. Young Jewish men had fought in all the wars which threatened Corfu and prosperous families donated great sums to aid the struggle of the Greek nation. All Jews on the island, men women, children and babies were arrested and deported to concentration camps. Two hundred Jews escaped and fled the island but the remainder were sent to Auschwitz via Athens after the Nazi soldiers had looted their homes and shops. Of the 1900 Jews of Corfu less than ten percent survived the Holocaust. Today there are just 65 members of the Jewish Community living on the island.

cabins. The interior designers of yachts being predominantly male in those days, there were never enough mirrors in my opinion – certainly no full length ones in the right places. But I have since discovered that the amazingly sumptuous interiors of some of the Sunseeker gin palaces are designed by a woman; having been given the tour of one of these great white giants at the Southampton Boat Show, Miranda and I decided we would quite like one of those next time – if ever Jeremy or I inherit an oil company to supply the colossal engines.

With his film star looks, Yiannis would trail around after me, like an obedient Labrador, from shop to fascinating shop in the town, insisting on carrying everything I had bought, patiently asking me what else I wanted, when I could only just hear him with his face almost hidden behind the pile of bags and boxes which reached the tip of his aquiline nose. On my very first shopping trip I had been guided by Yiannis to *Kastamonitis & Sons*, a wonderful miniature emporium gleaming with vintage mahogany cupboards, drawers and shelves filled from polished marble floor to ornate plasterwork ceiling with sumptuous linens, fabrics, tablecloths, fluffy towels in every shade possible, embroidered napkins and hand towels and other accoutrements required by the refined and genteel Corfiot household. A sign above the door proudly boasted that it had been established in the 1890's. I immediately decided Sarava needed a quantity of everything the shop had to offer, including a large tray with a beautiful design of blue shells which fitted Sarava's colour scheme perfectly. The owner of the shop spoke perfect English, as did most of the shopkeepers and restaurateurs in town; he politely enquired where I was from and whether I owned a house or apartment on the island. Yiannis jumped in belligerently before I could answer:

"My Lady is *English*, can't you tell? *And* she does come to live in Corfu, but not just in a house, she has a *YACHT!*" He thrust out his chin at these last words, as if to challenge anything but an appropriately respectful and grovelling response. His wish was granted; to my embarrassment and before you could say 'Acropolis' an antique bentwood chair had been eased beneath me and the latest Laura Ashley catalogue had been plonked on my lap, as a yell went out to the unseen ladies in the stock room to bring refreshments for their esteemed customer. A glass of fresh orange juice and some little cinnamon cakes arrived as if by magic, with much bowing and kow-towing by the be-slippered, black clad matrons who were obviously kept in the back rooms of the establishment for just such a purpose. I was told with great pride by the shopkeeper that Mrs. Durrell had been a regular customer. Did I know her? (How *old* did he think I was!) Louisa Durrell lived with Gerald and her three other children in Corfu from 1935 until they left in 1939 at the outbreak of war. To be fair Mrs. Durrell died in 1964, so it was entirely possible that, as a young child, I could theoretically have met her during her last years when she lived with Gerry at Les Augrès Manor, the setting for Jersey Zoo. Sadly I did not.

After so many years in Blighty I was unaccustomed to this welcoming treatment, but my family and I soon learnt that such affection and generosity was nothing unusual. It always came as a surprise to our friends from other parts of the world, this unconditional love of the English. Perhaps it was all down to Lord Guilford and his drains, or Lord Byron and his philhellenism, Lord Palmerston and the return of the Ionian Islands to Greece, or even to the Cheddar cheese. Rory's cynical comment included in a school essay following our first year in Corfu belied his age: 'The Greeks smile at my mother as they take her money'. He was wrong of course: they always smiled at me even when I wasn't buying anything.

On the way back to the marina, Yiannis had pulled off the main road and drove the taxi down a dusty track to an equally dusty warehouse, announcing, 'Here you will find your mirrors'. He opened my door and ushered me into the gloomy interior with the suave efficiency of a doorman at the Ritz. It was a veritable Aladdin's cave of mirrors and glass of all shapes and sizes. Yiannis turned to me as the elderly proprietor approached us.

"Let me do the talking, you just tell me what you want. This man isn't educated like me; he has no English."

There followed a long torrent of bullet whistlingly staccato Greek which I found impossible to follow. Occasionally Yiannis would ask me for a dimension or two then repeat it in Greek to the glass cutter.

"When you wanting them?" he almost barked at me, forgetting to moderate his tone as well as the language for what he imagined to be my fragile, English lady sensibilities. I told him I needed them by Monday as our guests were arriving on Tuesday. Another tirade followed and the glass cutter shuffled off towards the workshops.

"OK, all done," he said, and led me back through the dust and mirrors to the taxi.

The following Monday morning Yiannis collected me from the marina and we drove back to the glass works. I followed him inside and the dust covered proprietor started talking to Yiannis, waving his arms about in an extravagant expression of regret. What issued from the mouth of my hitherto gallant, gentlemanly guide can only be described as obscene. Of course I didn't recognise any of the Greek words that spewed from Yiannis' mouth like molten lava from an erupting volcano, but I got the gist. The glass cutter was visibly shaken by the blast and seemed to shrink as I watched in horror. He whispered something inaudible in my direction but Yiannis turned on his perfectly polished heel, grabbing my arm as he did so, and firmly propelled me towards the door.

"What on earth was that all about?" I asked him.

"The bastard say your mirrors not ready," he fumed. "I told him he was a disgrace to his mother, his children, Corfu, and the Greek nation."

"What happens now?"

"They will be ready this afternoon and he will deliver them to your yacht, IN HIS PERSON!" he added for effect, staring at me to see my reaction.

"It's a boat, Yiannis," I corrected him, forgetting that Yiannis knew about nautical terminology from his time in the Greek Navy.

"No, Mrs. Jani, she's over fifty feet so is a yacht." There was no arguing with my hero of the mirrors.

* * *

In hospitality, the chief thing is the good will.

Greek proverb

"*Kalimera, kalos sas irthate!*" Good morning, welcome to you both. "You are just in times for the very big episode in my village this weekend, on the Sundays after Easter. You are alone?" asked a swarthy little figure hopefully.

Andreas was one of Jeremy's handy helpers at the marina, a painter known as Andreas the Antifouling to distinguish him from countless others of the same name we knew on Corfu.

"Yes, the children have just gone home," Jeremy began. "But I have a lot of work to do and Sarava is due on the slipway this evening and ...".

"Of course," Andreas interrupted. "But on Sunday you must make day away and comes with me for the best village episode. I arrange everything." It was a fait accompli; this time we were obliged to go. We had no idea what this 'episode' would be, only suspecting it might involve a procession and a church service.

"I really can't spare a whole day," grumbled Jeremy after Andreas had trotted off so happily, his mission finally accomplished. The week we had remaining was hardly long enough to finish preparing the boat for the summer holidays; a day lost to a social outing would be a considerable setback.

"Well we *must* go, Andreas will be so hurt if we don't," I insisted, already anxious that I had seriously misjudged the situation.

The journey would take well over an hour each way, moreover this was Greece and rushing would certainly not be on the agenda for such an important episode.

"Perhaps we could just go for an hour or two, watch the procession and skip the service, then we could be back by lunchtime," I suggested.

Andreas was a diminutive but dynamic member of the marina workforce; he operated out of a battered van that could once have been white, but a glance at the caked paintwork and burgeoning rust revealed it was well past its sell-by date. Andreas, in contrast to his antiquated transport, was always immaculately turned out in his own livery of snugly fitting royal blue overalls, zipped up to the neck even in the hottest weather. Perspiration glittered on his pixie-like brown face, his permanent grin and twinkling eyes giving him the appearance of a stout, freshly painted garden gnome. In his spare time he was a local historian who was inordinately proud of his village, which nestled in a fold high on the slopes beyond Agioi Deka, a settlement in the ridge of hills running down the southern spine of the island. As a founder member of a committee dedicated to the preservation and beautification of his village and its surrounding countryside, he had plans to restore the many remote footpaths in hope of promoting them for tourists whose interests lay in botany, entomology and ornithology, rather than beaches, tavernas and bars.

Each year a calendar was produced by his community, mainly featuring singularly unflattering views of the wonderful local churches, to which was attached a long list of forthcoming 'episodes' with their dates; there were religious episodes, musical episodes, folk dancing and traditional costume episodes. Andreas kept a supply of calendars in his van to distribute around the island and to thrust into the hands of all his clients and visiting yachtsmen on the marina. He seemed to know instinctively when we had arrived in Corfu and would scurry along to Sarava's berth, where we would suddenly find him standing on the pontoon, smiling patiently, waiting to give us the latest update on his village. Every time he saw us he would ask us to visit his home in the hills, but it was a long drive and usually we had friends or family staying on board; understandably they wanted to be at sea rather than trekking miles inland in the fierce heat of summer to see a remote village. His face would fall as we made our excuses which would always end with 'Perhaps on our next visit...' This time however Andreas had struck lucky, as Jeremy had been attending to a winch in the cockpit and I was on the foredeck hanging out washing. We had no guests on board and he had us well and truly cornered.

The day of the celebration was perfect, with clear sky as blue as a jay's wing, warm sun and a gentle early morning breeze. As we climbed away from the coast the hillsides were covered with patches of fragrant, butter yellow broom; outsize daisies, purple wild orchids and shiny celandines spangled the verges either side of the road. We drove our hired car to the outskirts of the village and I called Andreas on my mobile phone.

"Staying where you are please," he said, " I will be in five minutes."

From our vantage point we could see two churches and wondered which would host the service, there was no sign of life at either, in fact we had not seen a single person since entering the village. Enjoying the tranquility, gazing out over the verdant green valley filled with grapevines and fruit trees, to the hills and mountains beyond and listening to the birdsong, we were startled by the sudden roar of a loud, growling engine. Round the bend rattled a shiny, electric blue Land Rover, only slightly paler than the ultramarine stripes of the Greek flag, looking as if it had escaped from a child's toy box. Andreas' grin could only just be recognised as he peered over the steering wheel, set as it was at the level of his nose.

"Leaving your car there," he instructed, "We need the four wheels drive where we goes."

We clambered in and bumped off up the hill, the few crumbling houses flashing past, until we ran out of road. Ahead lay a very narrow, stony path, a goat track not quite wide enough for the Land Rover to pass without the prickly hedgerow scratching its smart paintwork on both sides.

"I just had it sprayed," said Andreas with pride. "You like the colour?"

"Very much, Andreas," I said, "I've never seen another like it before."

"Ah, yes," he nudged me conspiratorially; I was sitting in the middle of the bench seat, next to him, with the gear stick between my knees; luckily my safari-style skirt was long enough to keep my modesty intact.

"I gets it from my cousin in Thessaloniki, it is special paint for the national buses of Greece."

The path was getting steeper and narrower; tufts of grass and weeds appeared in the middle, always an unpromising sign according to my father when exploring the lanes of Devon and Cornwall. As the Land Rover rocked and jolted I was thrown from Andreas to Jeremy in turn like a pendulum. Clouds of white dust rose behind us, marking our progress from the village far below. Suddenly Andreas slammed on the brakes and we skidded to a halt at the top of a bluff.

"There! Our church. Beautifuls!" he exclaimed, pointing straight ahead.

Amongst the scrub and boulders on the edge of a precipice stood a tiny, whitewashed chapel, built on a rocky outcrop that literally hung over the sheer side of a wide and fertile valley. Green wooded hills rose from the far side of the plain to distant purple mountains, shimmering and undulating in the heat haze like a mirage; away to the south a glittering ribbon of sea sparkled on the horizon. Andreas parked at a respectful distance and walked ahead, beckoning us into the little building through its diminutive doorway, which had been decorated with fresh greenery and festooned with scarlet ribbons as if for Christmas. Within was a perfect church in miniature, where no more than ten people might stand. Dark, cool and windowless, the only light glimmered from ornate, silver oil lamps hanging on chains from low beams; faint ripples of golden radiance flickered over ancient, faded icons and peeling frescos on the walls and ceiling. The altar, no bigger than a child's dressing table, was covered with a crisply starched white lace cloth; upon it a vase of arum lilies stood between gold vessels and silver ewers brought out especially for the service. Baskets of bread were placed around the altar, the mouth-watering scent of *glykaniso*, sweet aniseed, from the freshly baked bread filling the air and arousing our appetites. I wondered where we would find lunch in such a remote place.

"This church is the very special; many miracles have happened here," he whispered in hushed reverence, relating stories of candles mysteriously lit, of untended oil lamps replenished behind locked doors, of freshly offered flowers, of unexplained scents and sounds, of pilgrims healed and visions seen.

More recently during a devastating forest fire in the area when everything around was completely destroyed, the church alone remained untouched; this much we could easily imagine from the charred tree stumps and stunted ilex nearby. The village, he explained, had been saved from German air raids during the second world war by the protection of the church alone; although, he admitted, that might have been due in part to the position of the village, hidden by the hills from enemy planes as they flew in low from the sea. Fortune had not always smiled on it, however. In the sixteenth century Corfu was besieged by the Ottomans and during one of their raids they had headed for the village. The alarm was raised and the entire population ran to hide in a secret cave in the hillside, save one old woman who was too infirm to join her neighbours; when the Turks discovered her they tortured her into revealing the hiding place of the villagers. A fire was lit in the entrance of the cave and all inside perished; the only villagers to escape the massacre were a handful of shepherds who were tending their flocks up in the high pastures – Andreas' ancestor amongst them.

Outside the villagers had suddenly materialised from nowhere and were assembling under a white awning, stretched from the church door to cast a welcome shade over several neat rows of wooden chairs. The mid-day heat was rising from the valley below, surrounding us like a shroud as we edged into the meagre shade and waited for the service to begin; far above us the faint cries of a pair of soaring eagles could be heard as they glided and wheeled on the thermals.

"Where are all the cars?" I whispered to Andreas.

"The peoples all has to walk. They arriving here from the path at the side of the valley", he answered, pointing to a sinuous track that wound steeply up the hillside and ended at a small gap in the thicket next to the little church.

"All the way from the village?" I asked, amazed that everyone in the congregation, dressed in their Sunday finery on this hot day, had trekked a kilometre or so up this stony path; I had noticed many pairs of dainty, high-heeled shoes amongst the ladies' footwear.

"Of course. This is what they must do to get blessed."

"But why didn't we walk too?" I almost knew the reply.

"Yous English and don't have to walk, that's why I bring the Land Rover!"

Goodness knows how we, the English, have been awarded such status – rarely having to queue, walk or, as anyone who has been out for a meal with a Corfiot will know, to pay the bill. Given the maccho presence of some of Great Britain's finest football hooligans, lager louts – invariably overweight and wearing the unattractive sleeveless vests which the young call 'wife beaters' – who happily eat at restaurants dispensing foul oaths and displaying hairy armpits and salacious tattoos to all and sundry, it is amazing the British are tolerated on the island at all – let alone treated with the deference, respect and affection hitherto afforded to our forbears in a more genteel age of foreign travel. Obviously the Corfiots are highly tolerant; a waiter in the town had once confided 'Yes, they look horrible, but we must remember they are on holiday'. But this, I had countered, was their normal behaviour at home; moreover there was no element amongst tourists from other countries that dressed or behaved so appallingly. Luckily these less desirable compatriots were generally collected from the airport in coaches and deposited at the enclave of Kavos, on the southernmost tip of the island, to drink and debauch to their hearts' content, largely unobserved by the rest of Corfu.

Two priests approached the altar, resplendent in elaborate robes of blood red, intricately embroidered with gold thread. Babes in arms, swathed in starched white frills and lace, were carried to the altar and blessed, followed by toddlers and young children accompanied by their parents; gold crosses glittered on chubby necks and even the youngest baby girls wore tiny gold studs in their pierced earlobes. During the service prayers were intoned by a small group of men wearing tight black suits as shiny as the perspiration on their solemn faces. The priests blessed the communion wine and the bread; the baskets were passed around the congregation and everyone took a chunk or two, the children eating theirs immediately. Outside, after the service, we were handed plastic beakers of neat ouzo, presented on tin trays from a little shed beside the church; the good ladies of the village, evidently some sort of Greek WI, were busy inside pouring ouzo and preparing paper plates of food. Andreas was at the head of the queue, having already placed us in a select spot away from the crowd. Within seconds he returned to us with three plates wobbling on his arms.

"A picnic!" he explained, sweat trickling onto the tight white collar beneath his beaming face.

How lovely!" I replied, as convincingly as I could manage.

"Gosh, Andreas, you're really spoiling us!" said Jeremy, who loathed picnics but was on his best behaviour.

On each plate was a piece of feta, some thick slices of peppery local sausage flavoured with a healthy dose of garlic, a lump of a hard *trikalino* cheese and a shiny, crimson hard boiled egg, its shell looking as if it was made of Japanese lacquerware. I perched on a convenient boulder, glad of my straw hat as the sun was directly overhead and there were no trees tall enough to provide shade. I studied my ouzo with trepidation, aware of its reputation for inflicting serious hango-vers; our beakers surely contained enough to anaesthetise an elephant.

"I don't think I can drink this!" I whispered to Jeremy, not wanting Andreas to hear me. But I was very thirsty and the dry bread, spicy sausage, salty cheese and crumbly egg were hard to swallow without liquid of some sort. Just then Andreas reappeared with a bottle of mineral water,

"You would like a little?" he enquired, the bottle poised over my cup. I would have liked the whole bottle but obviously it had to be shared amongst the brethren.

"It's just like the loaves and the fishes isn't it!" quipped Jeremy, as I gave him one of my withering looks.

"Up to the top, please," I urged, hoping my head would survive if the ouzo was diluted in this way.

It was surprisingly refreshing and went deliciously well with the food; in fact I hardly noticed finishing the second beaker. But our heads felt light as the milky white ouzo took instant effect and the ground under our feet started to undulate gently.

"Would it be all right if I took some photographs?" I asked Andreas. We were the only foreigners present and apart from Andreas I was the only one with a camera.

"Certainly of course, I will tell to the *papas*," he replied cheerfully, trotting off before I could protest towards the group of church dignitaries assembled in front of the church, where they prepared for the long journey home.

A wonderfully ornate gonfalon depicting a suitably pious saint was hoisted aloft, held upright by a sturdy devotee; others amongst the congregation held framed icons and one brave man grappled with a fifteen foot pole wrapped in a vast embroidered flag. To my horror and acute embarrassment Andreas bustled up to the assembly and started rearranging them, deftly wheeling the group until they faced me. Then, like a tetchy wedding photographer, he pushed one priest in front of the other at the centre, squeezing the group into a huddle and condensing the party to fit into my viewfinder. Commanding them to stay still he turned to face me and, with a flourish of his arms, presented his tableau for my camera. He stood grinning amongst them as if the whole event had been organised solely for my benefit; I did not have the heart to ask him to move out of the frame. All eyes were on me as I snapped the shutter, feeling most unworthy for having arrived by car like some dignitary. Andreas then released his prisoners and graciously allowed them to continue, whereupon they processed with slow dignity towards the footpath. As they approached us the chief *papas*, probably a priest or bishop of some seniority judging by his regalia, left the group and walked straight towards me.

"Oh Lord," said Jeremy, "Now you're for it. I knew you shouldn't have taken those photos; he's coming to tick you off!"

My knees turned to jelly as I frantically rehearsed an apology in Greek, desperately trying to remember any words vaguely close to *sacrilege* or *penance*. The priest stopped in front of me, took my hand and solemnly kissed it. I was speechless; perhaps he thought of me as a lost sheep. Then he started to rummage with both hands – there was no other word for it – to rummage under his cassock. Unsure what to expect I glanced at Jeremy for moral support; his eyes like saucers, he looked as if he expected the priest to pull out a gun and shoot me. I was frozen to the spot, but the priest's expression suddenly broke into a handsome smile as, with the air of a conjuror, he produced three red-stained eggs and pressed them into my hands.

"Χ*ronia sou polla*," he said in a soft, deep voice: may you have many years.

An effusive thank you was all I could manage. I wanted to say so much more, how overjoyed we were by such a wonderful day and how honoured we felt to be included, but my Greek was not up to it; even the familiar words had evaporated, particularly after the ouzo. Welcome distraction came from behind the church, where a commotion had erupted amongst the villagers; the throng was making its way slowly towards us, following the priests. We looked around for Andreas and he appeared out of nowhere, waving his arms wildly.

"Jesus is coming!" he shouted loudly, "Make a path! Jesus is coming!"

More than slightly alarmed Jeremy and I leapt backwards into the undergrowth as if we had walked into an electric fence. My sandalled feet and bare ankles were in the prickly bushes but I was unable to move; we stood like pillars of salt, hardly daring to breathe, our eyes fixed on the approaching group. I caught my breath as the crowd parted and there, crouching under an enormous wooden cross, was a tall, bearded, barefoot young man, dressed in loose white shirt and trousers, his long, curly hair falling over his face. He looked eerily Christ-like as he dragged the heavy cross laboriously up the hill, his Calgary.

Andreas explained that every year a young man from the village who was suitably good and pious was chosen for this honour. Followed by his entourage he would carry his burden all the way back to the village, re-enacting the Stations of the Cross.

"He is not the real Jesus, you understand," whispered Andreas, as if to dispel any lingering doubts that the second coming was upon us.

"Oh?"

"This one coming in at the last minute," he added somewhat derisively.

"Why?" I asked, by now thoroughly bemused.

"The other Jesus gets the chickenpox," he scoffed.

One bent old lady, dressed from head to toe in black, was picked up by two strong fellows as if she weighed no more than a flake of ash and placed on a sack of potatoes in the back of a decrepit truck.

"She can't walk, so she must ride," Andreas explained when we looked puzzled.

Jeremy and I felt feeble, pathetic and very embarrassed as we climbed into the Land Rover. Luckily the villagers took the narrower goat path back to their homes, so we did not have the added humiliation of overtaking them in our transport.

"You like to walk a little?" Andreas enquired after a few minutes of jolting along the track.

Actually we wanted only to curl up in the shade somewhere and fall asleep, our heads were starting to pound and the sun was scorching our bare arms. Andreas parked the Land Rover in a rough field and jumped out.

"There is the very beautiful views from this place, *mia poli orea thea*," he said, pointing towards the top of a bluff, his enthusiasm too touching to refuse. Jeremy gamely kept up with Andreas and strode off across the rocky ground. The land was baked to a crisp, its rough clods of earth and stones were interspersed with vicious thistles, which spitefully pricked my feet through my sandals. I was hot and sticky, longing for a cold shower and a few gallons of drinking water. I picked my way carefully, falling further and further behind the two men. Occasionally they stopped and turned round to see where I was.

"Are yous OK?" shouted Andreas over his shoulder. My head had started to throb.

"Oh yes, I'm fine," I lied. "I'm looking for butterflies; I'll catch you up."

I hoped this would explain my snail's pace, not wanting to admit to a hangover and silly shoes.

"Ah, yes," said Andreas, scrambling back over a low stone wall to join me in staring at the dry weeds that had ostensibly caught my attention.

"We have some very interesting plants here that grows nowhere else on the island, also rare birds," he continued. "And as you see, here in Corfu the *petaloudes*, the butterflies fly backwards."

Indeed, I reflected, nearly everything on this fascinating island defied appearance and expectation. I laughed at his description but knew exactly what he meant. The butterfly he was describing was the Scarce Swallowtail, quite common in Corfu; it has beautiful large wings of palest yellow with delicate, black filigree markings and a tail that mimics a head and antennae. A friend who knew I wanted to study and paint this butterfly had brought me a specimen he had found dead in his garden, leading Jeremy to remark that the butterfly was now the even scarcer swallowtail. In flight this butterfly resembles a scallop propelling itself through the water; it beats its wings curiously slowly and spasmodically, with its body held almost vertically, the markings heightening the illusion of flying backwards. Early on summer mornings I have often followed these butterflies along a pebble beach, watching fascinated as they land on tiny globules of sticky tar. I was amazed that their thread-like legs did not stick to surface and was baffled by this behaviour. Being very long sighted I had to take my reading glasses to the beach before I could discover what the butterflies were doing. Studying one closely I saw the butterfly land on the tar, extending its long proboscis onto a minute droplet of water, obviously drinking. Fresh water is in short supply during the summer months and these impervious blobs of oil retained the previous night's dew on the surface, which would later evaporate in the heat of the sun.

Jeremy and Andreas reached a ridge on the far side of the fields and were admiring the view, some four hundred metres above the sea, by the time I joined them. I wished I had worn wellies and brought a bottle of water, but the panorama was indeed glorious; a vast expanse of sapphire blue sea spread far below us, its even corrugations marching in orderly procession towards Sivota, Paxos and Levkas, refracting around the headlands and capes to the south. As we drove back to the village we started to make our farewells to Andreas, but he insisted the day was not yet over.

"Now we eat and drink," he said gleefully.

We had already eaten enough and certainly drunk more than we should in the midday sun; decidedly lightheaded we got out of the car and followed Andreas down a long, narrow path that was actually the main street of the village. It was paved with a jigsaw puzzle of large, dove grey, foot-worn flagstones, each one surrounded by wide cement grouting that was neatly and freshly painted brilliant white; above our heads the upper stories and rickety balconies of ancient houses leant at precarious angles, almost touching each other. Andreas led us down shallow, eroded steps that gave onto an open space, dominated by an enormous walnut tree; a wooden bench encircled its gnarled trunk, against which a pillar-box red motor bike was casually propped.

"Here is the village square of my family!" announced Andreas, pointing to the tiny courtyard enclosed between four dilapidated houses, which had long ago turned their backs on the wonderful open views of the surrounding countryside and distant mountains. The square overflowed with flowering plants, its perimeters studded with numerous pots and gaily painted tins, which had previously housed feta and olive oil and were now full of growing flowers; a profusion of freesias, jasmine, pelargoniums, roses, and tall carnations scented the still afternoon air. In the middle of the square stood a long table laden with food, around which Andreas' relatives and friends already occupied an assortment of wooden chairs. After a hearty welcome more chairs were quickly drawn up for us; as we sat down to freshly proffered glasses of ouzo I noticed a familiar face at the head of the table opposite me; with his long grey beard and short ponytail he was unmistakably the priest who had given me the eggs. Laughing and drinking with abandon he was the embodiment of Friar Tuck; however I was a little shocked to see that he was now a defrocked priest, dressed in what can only be described as a long petticoat, buttoned down the front, in a delicate shade of washed-out grey.

"Jolly practical in this heat," remarked Jeremy when I surreptitiously pointed this out to him. We drank lots of water as countless dishes of simple delicacies arrived in an endless stream from an unseen kitchen. As the sun began to sink we told Andreas we really had to leave.

"You must forgive us, but I have so much work to do on the boat before we fly home tomorrow," Jeremy said.

"But now we are going to make barbecues!" said Andreas disappointedly. A firm hand was called for.

"Thank you so much for everything," Jeremy insisted. "It has been a truly wonderful day, but we really have to go now."

With the cooler evening air I was just beginning to get a second wind and would have enjoyed something from the barbecue; I could eat shoe leather if it was cooked over charcoal. In fact I probably have, come to think of it.

"Well perhaps ..."

"We must go," Jeremy repeated, sensing my weakness and taking my arm.

We said our goodbyes and thanked Andreas and his family for their hospitality, shaking hands all round the table. I asked Andreas to tell the priest everything I had wanted to say earlier.

"*Po, po, po! Parakalo, paidia mou!* " said the priest and wished us *Xronia polla* again. All the way down the winding road through the hills we talked about our wonderful day and everything that had happened, chasing a crimson sunset that seemed to be racing us to sea level. We marvelled at the tiny church and its spectacular location, the local legends, the warmth and friendliness of the people, the way Andreas shepherded us and the unexpected feast; we regretted the ouzo however. By the time we got back to the boat the sun had disappeared behind the hills, throwing the marina and the bay of Gouvia into cool, blue shadow. We ate a couple of the blessed scarlet eggs with some holy bread we had saved and went to bed early, nursing headaches that kept us docile throughout our flight home the following morning. Despite the hangovers so lovingly inflicted upon us we were unusually sanguine about leaving Corfu, knowing that we would be returning in just a fortnight's time to show off our island to two different sets of friends in succession.

Chapter Five
Cruel Hearts and Coronets

What is there more kindly than the feeling between host and guest?

Aeschylus.

The first friends to arrive were titled folk. The week of their visit was most enjoyable, although it had got off to an inauspicious start. At Bristol Airport the four of us presented ourselves at the departure lounge for the late evening charter flight to Corfu. It was not as if our friends were in the habit of wearing their coronets, nor did their appearance give any clue to their ancient titles; in fact they preferred and sought anonymity wherever possible, but passport control was one of the few times when they would necessarily be unmasked. The Duke approached the control first, where a surly airport official glowered at his passport before asking him to stand still while his mugshot was taken by a camera behind the desk.

This seemed a rather unreasonable request in those gentler days before the attack on the twin towers, particularly as a dozen other security cameras were already trained on us. The Duke wanted to know the purpose of this extra level of scrutiny and, more importantly, who precisely would have access to these photographs, linked so recklessly as they were to passport numbers and itineraries.

"And if I don't want my photograph taken?" he asked with a genial smile.

"Then you won't be getting on the plane, mate" replied the official, his face turning puce as he summoned security on the airport's public address system; this announcement alerted the entire concourse, including the gently fuming queue behind us, to our perceived obstinacy.

Seeing he was getting nowhere the Duke eventually capitulated, telling the bemused official he would be raising this breach of data protection as a matter of urgency in the House. It was surely no coincidence that the the four of us were allotted the very worst, non-reclining seats in front of the aeroplane's loos. Our fellow passengers, all bound for Kavos where they could drink and party to their hearts' content, stared at us as if we were a different species.

'What extraordinary people we've been flying with!" remarked the Duchess without the slightest hint of disapproval, as we disembarked in Corfu, unaware it was the four of us, dressed in our remarkably inconspicuous travelling clothes, who had provided the freak show.

As we sped away from the airport in K9, I asked Christos to take us first into the town's market. I knew our friends would love to see this colourful and fragrant place where the Corfiot smallholders, farmers and fishermen brought their wares from all over the island. Christos pulled up by the fish stalls to choose some fresh swordfish from the glistening beds of melting ice. We would be cooking it on the barbecue installed over the davits, where any falling embers would drop safely into the sea. Unfortunately our barbecue implements often went the same way; in fact the sea bed of many secluded bays in the Ionian must be littered with such an assortment of our tongs that visiting divers must wonder if the local mermaids have been busily cooking up a storm.

I opened the door of the taxi but Christos signalled me to stay put.

"I go," he said, "I get better price for you." Greeks love to haggle, even for a discount of a few drachmas.

However the Duke did get out, unable to resist the sight of all the varieties of fish caught that morning off the coast of Corfu. If we hadn't known already, it was a delight to see how genuinely interested he was in anything and everything that was new to him. Christos bargained briefly but firmly with the fishmongers, returning with four large swordfish steaks and some sea bass wrapped in paper, which he put in the boot.

Sarava glowed in the early morning sun as we piled on board and showed them to their cabin. The Duchess said it looked like a five star hotel, having no idea a boat could be so comfortable. Most of the preparation had been done on our previous visit, using freshly laundered Egyptian cotton sheets and pillowcases on the double bed, covered with an embossed white cotton bedspread bought in Sardinia. But I had added some jasmine and a couple of pale pink roses, picked from the marina flower beds as the taxi was unloaded; once in a vase their scent filled our guests' cabin. Everyone was unpacking so I left them to settle in and headed straight back to the taxi with my largest shopping basket. We were going to sail south later in the morning, as soon as Jeremy had got the boat ready for action. This gave me time to shop for the first part of the trip, after which we would eat out every night and have easy access to the eclectic selection of shops in Gaios and anywhere else we fancied.

I was back within the hour, having bought ripe tomatoes the size of grapefruits, basil and mint growing in earthenware pots, salad vegetables, thick and creamy Greek yoghurt straight from the farm, proper *mozzarella di bufala*, a selection of olives in differing shades and sizes, some local garlic with papery brown skins and an enormous water melon. I did not need to buy fresh bread as Christos had brought some to the airport for us. 'This is with love from Yiannis', he had said, grinning from ear to ear. He also brought me the largest and freshest cucumbers I have ever seen, straight from his vegetable garden. I think I counted thirteen cucumbers and, as I thanked him, I secretly wondered how we were ever going to use them in a week. In fact they came in very handy; they made copious quantities of tsatsiki, dozens of delicate cucumber sandwiches for afternoon tea beneath the awnings and perfect Pimms served with a veritable eiderdown of cucumber slices.

Our friends were having a nap to recover from the late night flight as we cast off and glided slowly out of the marina. Turning to starboard into deeper water, Sarava's bows sliced through a calm sea as I put the food away in the galley and prepared a cold lunch. An hour later the land had disappeared into the heat haze and after a leisurely lunch under the shade of the awnings we were soon moored on the quay in Gaios. We went ashore to explore the village, do a little souvenir shopping and book a table for dinner; but to our great surprise the Duchess strode ahead purposefully and settled herself on a wooden chair outside one of the tavernas, where a large television hung from the rafters. An eager waiter was at her side in seconds, notepad in hand, asking what she would like to order.

"Oh no thank you, I don't want anything. Do you mind if I just watch your television?" I heard her ask.

This was not quite what we had expected. The Duchess was engrossed in a football match showing on satellite television. I walked over and asked her why she wanted to watch football.

"So sorry, Jani," she apologised. "But there are some qualifiers today and my youngest is passionate about football, especially Lazio, which he has followed since we lived in Rome. If I don't watch the games I can't talk to him about them when he 'phones me from school." I understood perfectly, as I had to do the same with Rory and cricket and with Miranda and show jumping.

From then on, in every port of call, a frantic television hunt would ensue. Sometimes a local fisherman with a tiny cottage would be surprised to see an English lady peering eagerly through his open window at a vintage television set if a match was on; no back street barbers' shop or one-room bar was off limits for a visit from this unlikeliest of English football fan.

The Duchess, an extremely elegant lady who always wore the most beautiful shoes at home, looked horrified at the selection of plastic beach shoes on offer in the little harbourside shops of Gaios. She knew they were essential, but turned her pretty, aristocratic nose up at all the childish jelly shoes with sensible ankle straps and buckles. Then she spotted a pair which resembled the dainty ballet pumps that were very fashionable at the time; they were made of soft, thin plastic which wouldn't deflect a prickly thistle, let alone a sea urchin or stone fish spine and had absolutely no chance of ever staying on the feet in water. I pointed this out to her, but before I could persuade her otherwise, she had put them in her shopping basket. Needless to say, as soon as she stepped into the crystal clear waters of Voutoumi next morning, both shoes instantly slid off her feet and floated defiantly to the surface.

I lent her a pair of mine for the rest of her holiday, which she obediently strapped on whenever she went swimming from the shore. With true generosity of spirit that was so typical of her nature, she admitted they were really practical, comfortable and, despite their ugliness, she should have listened to me in the first place.

Our next guests, some childhood friends of Jeremy's, arrived on the same morning as our Duke and Duchess were flying home. To their astonishment and evident distaste, they were greeted with bear hugs and whiskery kisses on both cheeks by Christos, who was again transporting us to and from the airport. He had been parked in front of the main entrance for at least an hour by the time we emerged, although it was entirely illegal to stop there; but this was Corfu and Christos was a proud citizen of Greece who, like his compatriots, never bothered about such trivialities. He had begun arguing with the airport security guards as soon as we dropped off the Duke and Duchess and was still in animated discussion with them as we drove away.

Oh beware, my lord, of jealousy! it is the green-eyed monster that doth mock the meat it feeds on.

William Shakespeare – *Othello*

It came as a surprise to find that such old friends could have been so singularly unimpressed with their free holiday, never commenting on anything unless it was to find fault. It was a further surprise to discover they had brought along a teenage nephew, who we had never even met. From the moment we drove away from the airport their observations were critical: the town was altogether too scruffy, the roads were excessively bumpy and the countryside was sadly lacking in palm trees. Their first lunch on board Sarava was even less acceptable: 'How do you know where this meat comes from?' one of them would say, or 'I'm certainly not risking *that*!'

The sea temperature, at seventy-eight degrees in late May, was considered far too cold for bathing, while every Corfiot was viewed with suspicion and treated like a convicted felon. Refusing all offers of advice on the use of sun creams – 'We don't need them; our skin is used to *really* strong sun in Barbados every Christmas' – they turned the colour of freshly cooked lobsters after the first hour on deck.

This happened so often, especially with teenagers who are desperate to get a tan as quickly as possible, regardless of skin damage or the inevitable peeling, that I had learnt to keep a large supply of soothing after-sun balm to ease the pain. Their sullen nephew's exposed skin was badly burnt, although most of his body was sealed within the same sweat-soaked black lycra cycling shorts and tee-shirt every day of his holiday. Needless to say I was asked to produce some after-sun cream before bedtime, by which time our old friends were trapped stiffly within carapaces of tightening skin. The following day had begun with a glorious morning at Antipaxos, snorkelling in the clear turquoise water, before lunching on fresh king prawns cooked over the barbecue, accompanied by a rocket and parmesan salad with crusty village bread, followed by thick, creamy natural yoghurt with sliced Italian white peaches, honey and walnuts. Having already served them breakfast and iced morning coffee, I had tidied our guests' cabins, removed wet towels discarded on the carpet and hung them to dry in the sun. I had then spent the rest of the morning in the heat of the galley preparing our lunch. Inevitably their question came.

"How do you know if these prawns are fresh?" asked the man, sniffing suspiciously at the crustacean on his fork.

"Well, they were wriggling in the basket when Jeremy carried them back from the fishmonger in Gaios this morning while you were still asleep!" I delighted in answering.

On the way back to Corfu up the west coast of Paxos we found a fair wind and enjoyed our first really good sail of the year. A steady westerly blew across the decks as Jeremy set the ghoster and mainsail, switching off the engines. Sarava glided effortlessly over the waves at twelve knots, the only sounds the soft swishing of the sea running under and the soughing of the wind in our sails.

"This is more like it! We thought you were never going to turn off the engines," commented our guests from their prostrate positions on the foredeck, unaware that we had been motor-sailing purely for their benefit, and at no little expense, to fit a personal and extensive guided tour of the islands within the six days of their stay.

Nevertheless we were slightly encouraged that the tide had seemingly turned, as this was their first vaguely favourable remark all week. Catamarans do not, thank heavens, roll from side to side like monohulls; rather they seem to surf the waves, very akin to the sensation of riding a horse bareback as it swims through breakers. Occasionally the twin bows would slice into a particularly large wave, such as the steep wash from a car ferry passing close, splashing any languorous sunbathers on the foredeck; the water would feel icy against hot bodies and invariably provoke shrieks from the victims. How Jeremy and I prayed for a ferry to pass by at that moment!

Suddenly a school of dolphins appeared from nowhere, like shiny grey torpedoes zooming through the water just fractions of an inch from our bows. They criss-crossed in front of the boat then leapt out of the sea in dripping, glittering arcs over the starboard bow wave, plunging into the water and out again to dive in front of the port bow before disappearing in turn under the boat. Sitting in a row on the net trampolines between Sarava's bows it was possible to touch their sleek backs with our toes as they frolicked beneath us on the crest of each wave, sparks of pleasure flashing through us at each contact. One small show-off practised his circus act alongside us, shooting up out of the sea like a Polaris missile, flipping in mid-air and diving straight down again with hardly a splash. Having entertained us for a full ten minutes this roving troupe of tumblers and acrobats left as quickly and silently as they had arrived, heading out to sea in the direction of Sicily and fresh audiences.

Falling under the lee of the southern cape of Corfu our speed suddenly fell away and Sarava reverted to power until we reached our destination for the night, usually a great favourite with our friends, the tiny bay of Agni. Exactly as our anchor chain snaked into the sea grass forty feet below, so the sun dipped below the high hills that surround the bay, casting a deep and welcome shadow over our decks. The land here rises steeply behind the beach and is thickly wooded with a variety of trees and shrubs; silvery green olives, short, round and bushy clustered around extremely tall, slim cypresses, now black silhouettes against the evening sky. Emerald green Mediterranean pines, their umbrella shaped branches contrasting with their taller cousins, scented the air drifting towards us from the sun-baked land. Tufts of Spanish broom dotted the hillsides and cliffs, the heady scent of coconut and honey wafting from bright yellow flowers, covering the sea around us with broad drifts of their golden pollen. Cedars with perfect, marble-round cones rose above a luxuriant undergrowth of bay trees, prickly pear and myrtle bushes. Close to shore were several elegant eucalyptus trees with shimmering, fish-like leaves; the papery, peeling silver bark revealed flashes of the glowing raw sienna beneath, making the ghostly white trunks look as if they were permanently catching the last rays of sunset.

Of the three excellent tavernas on the beach, Taverna Agni was our favourite; it has a romantic story of its own. A decade earlier a young Englishman had come on holiday to Corfu looking for a quiet, unspoilt beach. He soon discovered Agni, a perfect little bay with a white pebble beach and three small tavernas. Everyday he swam in the warm, crystal clear sea, basked in the sun and ate traditional, home cooked Greek dishes at his favourite table overlooking the water. The family taverna was owned and run by Aphrodite, Harilaos and their children Theodore and Eleni. Many years ago it had been opened by Eleni's great-grandparents as a basic taverna for hungry fishermen who brought the day's catch with them. Leaving their boats tied to the makeshift jetty they would have a jolly time drinking home made wine and eating local dishes; the vegetables, fruits and salad grown in the garden behind the taverna. Although the simple décor remained the same, wooden, rush-seated chairs and small rustic tables with cheerful gingham cloths, by the time the Englishman arrived Eleni was a pretty and vivacious young woman who served at table. Her beautiful sea-green eyes and engaging smile attracted more of his attention than the menu. With the heady mixture of sun, sea, wine, taramasalata and first love, Nathan decided Corfu was to become his future home. Not long after this holiday he returned to the island, courted and married Eleni and began a new life as a restaurateur.

Known thenceforward as the *Shirley Valentine Couple*, they soon joined Theo in managing the taverna, a conjunction which proved to be pure alchemy. Eleni's parents were now able to take their ease sitting on the shady terrace, nevertheless offering the occasional word of advice. Eleni took over the kitchen, cooking wonderful dishes from recipes handed down from generations of grandmothers, as well as inventing new ones of her own.

From Sarava's decks that evening it was obvious from our first glimpse of the taverna that some sort of party was in progress; the customers wore lightweight summer suits and evening dresses, looking distinctly less casual than the usual clientele. The jetty belonging to the restaurant was a simple wooden structure from which old car tyres, painted white, dangled to fend off approaching craft; enterprising sparrows built nests in these tyres, tucked neatly within, just above the waterline and safe from marauding cats. Now transformed with a strip of bright green carpet and two dainty arches constructed out of tufty pine branches festooned with pink ribbons, the jetty was unrecognisable.

Small boats began to arrive at intervals to deposit more guests; one charming group consisted of some angelic looking girls in pastel party frocks, white ankle socks and bar shoes, who skipped onto the beach to join some even smaller boys wearing pristine Bermuda shorts. It was a scene straight from the pages of Enid Blyton, the children far more entertaining to watch than the adults. Left to their own devices as the grown-ups socialised on the taverna's terrace, they sat merrily on the beach, legs outstretched with total disregard for the odd globule of tar as they began the time-honoured game of lobbing smooth, white pebbles into the sea. Quite suddenly, after about five minutes of peaceful stone throwing, one little girl in a sugar pink ensemble decided to liven up proceedings by lying on her back, bringing her legs up over her head to touch the beach behind her with her toes, displaying her matching pink knickers to all and sundry. We waited for cries of horror from a mother, along with the expected admonishment, but none came; perhaps this was the child's usual party trick and had all been seen before.

A salmon pink sunset faded and as the sky turned to deep indigo, the myriad stars appeared. The taverna lights were reflected in the calm water and the guests took their seats at long tables under the canopy. Enticing smells of delicious cooking wafted over the water; charcoal grilled fish, fried *kalamari*, oven-baked *stifhado* with baby onions snuggling up to melt-in-the-mouth pieces of beef in red wine sauce. The taverna's little ferryboat puttered out into the bay past Sarava and the one other yacht at anchor. Just as it neared our starboard side we heard a female voice tremulously but loudly warbling part of an aria from a well-known opera, followed by scales and vocal exercises. *Greta the goldfish has gout in her gills* stood out as one I remembered with embarrassment from school choir practice.

At first we thought it must be a portable music system aboard the tiny ferry; but looking through binoculars, Miranda spotted a lady in a soft peach trouser-suit, standing in the prow, arms waving to full dramatic effect and singing into the night air for all she was worth. Could this be one of the harpies, or the local siren troupe, we asked each other. Was she perhaps the temptress of sailors, luring them with her hypnotic songs to founder on the jagged rocks? After a couple of turns around the bay, the boat and singing cargo returned to the jetty, from where the diva began her repertoire that included, *O Mio Babbino Caro* and ended with *Ave Maria*. The rendition was met with rapturous applause and a standing ovation ashore, to which we added our own approval by sounding some short blasts on the foghorn, a gesture quickly imitated by the only other visiting boat. We were merely bystanders eavesdropping on their special day, nevertheless we charged our glasses and toasted the happy couple, wishing them health and happiness in their future life together. A golden moon rose over Albania as the party continued until the early hours; operetta was replaced by Abba and the throng danced under the stars. As we fell into our bed, lulled by warm airs coming into our cabin through the open windows, we were rocked gently to sleep by the rise and fall of the water, the breathing of the sea. The distant hubbub gradually subsided until the night belonged once more to the Scops owls. Our guests were at last enjoying themselves.

Next morning Jeremy and I rose with the sun, donned swimwear and sunglasses and sped across a millpond of water in Sarava's tender to the next bay, leaving our friends comatose and snoring in their cabins. In the bay of Kalami, made famous by the White House once occupied by Lawrence Durrell and his wife Nancy, there is a tiny mini-market, just a stone's throw from the beach. This shop is one of many contributing to the failure of all good intentions to lose weight during the summer; tucked in a corner towards the back of the shop are shelves full of freshly baked Corfiot pastries and butter croissants still warm, fragrant and totally irresistible. The childrens' favourites are the pains au chocolat, while Jeremy and I favour the *milopitakia*, the bite-sized crispy filo pastries liberally dusted with icing sugar and filled with fresh apple compote flavoured with cinnamon; should one ever need an easy lunch there are mouthwatering filo pies filled with ham and cheese, spinach or the local yellow cheese. Wading up to our knees in the warm shallows we stowed our breakfast in the tender and sped back to Sarava before the pastries could get cold. I made fresh coffee and squeezed some oranges, while Jeremy zipped one of the blue canvas side awnings onto the bimini; for although the rays of the morning sun were still low their heat was intense and it was impossible to sit at the cockpit table without shade.

As I laid the table I saw some boys waving at me from the beach; it was Eleni's brother Theo and the Taverna Agni waiters, George and Alex. They were unloading freshly caught fish and mussels into a wheelbarrow from a fishing smack, George, being the youngest, was then given the difficult task of pushing it uphill over the pebbles to the taverna. I giggled as I watched George's laborious and wobbly progress up the beach, the barrow in danger of capsizing with each shove as pebbles crunched beneath the perished tyre. Our guests appeared bleary-eyed from their cabin to find breakfast awaiting them, a five star service which they had taken for granted all week.

"Oh dear, don't you have home made marmalade?" chirped our lady guest, adding the last straw to the camel's back.

Later that morning we bundled them into a taxi for the airport with relief, but also with heavy hearts, wondering if lifelong friendships had already come to an end. The week had left us feeling hurt and rather cross, having done everything possible to make our friends' stay enjoyable and memorable. We had pulled out all the stops, put extra effort into taking them to all our favourite haunts and simply couldn't understand their lack of enthusiasm for the island and its people we loved so dearly. Jeremy put their attitude down to being too rigidly set in their ways, much as we might have reacted to an enforced holiday at a nudist colony in Antarctica.

* * *

If a man insisted on always being serious, and never allowed himself a bit of fun and relaxation, he would go mad or become unstable without knowing it.

Herodotus

Corfu usually managed to conjure up some unexpected consolation for any setback and that afternoon did not disappoint. My phone sprang into life: an invitation to drinks the same evening. Handily the newly completed buttercup yellow villa, perched on the edge of the bluff which dominated the water between Agni and Yialiskari, was right above us. It had recently been bought by a charming English couple, who we had met through Rory and Miranda when they had befriended their eldest son, a loyal supporter of the Harbour Bar. Leaving Sarava at anchor just below the villa, we took the tender to the beach at Agni and walked up the narrow goat path that connects the two bays and led into the garden of the villa. Very sensibly I was wearing my wellies with my cocktail dress, carrying a pair of dainty heeled mules to change into once we reached the terrace. I knew this particular goat track well as it was one of Burberry's favourite walks ashore, shaded as it was during the day by tall, ancient Cypress trees. Underfoot the steep incline was riddled with fir cones, loose pebbles and stones as large as boulders, which could trip the most careful walker – let alone anyone foolish enough to be unsuitably shod. A fall on this path could easily send one tumbling down the sheer drop into the sea below.

Discarding my boots by the front door we made our way across the terrace to be greeted by our host, Andrew. His wife, Vicky, was in the kitchen preparing the canapés, so I took her my contribution of 'Drunken Tomatoes', a sort of edible Bloody Mary. A great favourite with my family, they are tiny cherry tomatoes marinated for a day in a concoction of vodka, Worcestershire sauce and Tabasco, then drained and served on cocktail sticks with an accompanying dip of celery salt; luckily I had bought the salt in Sardinia on our passage to Corfu, for it would have been tricky finding it on this part of the island. The party was in full swing and in this stunning setting, watching the distant shadows lengthening on the foothills of Albania as we sipped chilled Bellinis from frosty glasses, we enjoyed ourselves immensely. Jeremy was able to keep a watchful eye on Sarava while chatting with guests we knew and others we were meeting for the first time. Gradually the party began to thin and we were just saying our own goodbyes to

Andrew and Vicky when they asked us to join their family and house guests for dinner at Agios Stefanos.

"You can leave your tender on the beach and come on our RIB," he said. "There's plenty of room."

"Thank you so much, we'd love to – I'll just collect my boots." Andrew looked puzzled, but laughed when he saw them.

"Only you could have pink Hunter wellies in Corfu!"

I was looking forward to this ride up the coast and back on such a lovely evening; Andrew's powerful RIB was a thirty-foot long affair with ample seating for the twelve of us, but I dispatched Jeremy back to Sarava to pick up a pashmina from my cabin, thinking I might be cold and wind-blown. I needn't have worried as the air was as gentle and balmy as a South Sea Island breeze and the sea was like a mill pond. Perhaps it was the cocktails I had enjoyed over the last two hours, but the boat seemed to glide smoothly over the water like a hovercraft; it was probably me that was floating on air. Dinner was a jolly affair and the trip back after midnight was enchanting; we lost count of the shooting stars as the sliver of descending rose gold moon fell behind the hills, leaving the Milky Way, *Galaxías* in Greek, suddenly visible, as if an angel had sprayed cosmic platinum glitter across the heavens. As I stepped out of the RIB onto the shingle of Agni beach, I stooped to pick up a perfect heart-shaped pebble which I gave to Andrew as a souvenir of such a wonderful evening.

"Oh how lovely, you're such fun Jani!" he laughed.

Back on board Sarava we fell into our deliciously comfortable bed with its cool white, lavender scented sheets and were asleep in seconds, lulled by the hypnotic song of Agni's resident Scops Owls calling to each other from the tree tops. Seamlessly the star filled night slipped into sunlit day with barely a whisper of sleep in between; I had closed my eyes by the light of the moon and opened them, seemingly a mere moment later, to the view across the water of a crimson sun rising over the distant Pindus mountains, flooding our cabin with its warm glow. A new Corfu day was beginning.

To cheer ourselves up even further we decided to have lunch at Agni to make up for the meal we had missed two nights before. I swam ashore to book a table; rather than walk into the taverna in a wet costume I lolled in the shallows and beckoned to George.

"*Kalimera* George, can we reserve a table for lunch?"

"Sorry, no room! We are full until October!" he replied cheekily. Amongst other well-rehearsed lines of repartee was a quip he used whenever he read out the dessert menu to diners: 'Baklava, home made by Eleni's mother, very nutty – the baklava not the mother!'

At two o'clock we piled into the tender and George came running to the jetty to take our line, gallantly offering his hand to help Miranda and I out of the boat. We looked for our table as George made fast, aware that Nathan enjoyed designing his very own range of bespoke *reserved* signs. If a customer who has previously given him or his staff any trouble, or failed to leave a proper tip, the sign might read *Reserved for a discerning and highly esteemed customer.* Our sign often read *Sarava AGAIN,* but this time *O Petherós,* was written on it.

"What does that mean?" asked Miranda.

"It means father-in-law!" Jeremy laughed.

This was Nathan's joke at George's expense, alluding to his growing infatuation with Miranda. Alex came forward to welcome us and to take our order for drinks but was soon elbowed out of the way by George. Alex and George were best friends and spent most of their free time together; they made an incongruous pair. Alex was the gentle giant, very tall and robust with thick fair hair making him look more like a Scandinavian wrestler than a Corfiot waiter; George on the other hand was lithe and wiry, with dark curly hair and a mischievous grin. Seeing the two of them side by side it was impossible not to think of Don Quixote and Sancho Panza – more so when one watched them haring around North Corfu on a small motorbike, George crouched intently over the handlebars with the huge frame of Alex riding pillion, towering over his friend with ham-like hands clinging on for grim death to George's shoulders.

* * *

The course of true love never did run smooth.

William Shakespeare

What George lacked in stature was more than compensated by personality, which he had by the bucketful. More Puck than Romeo he nevertheless had an endless stream of young, and not so young, female admirers. George's fan club was worldwide and at the end of each summer season letters and cards would arrive by the sack load at the local bakery, the delivery point for all mail in his tiny village above Nissaki. Small but perfectly formed, with the most disarming and engaging smile on the island, beautiful white teeth grinning in his suntanned face, George would beguile all the customers at Taverna Agni where he worked in the school holidays. His brown velvet eyes sparkled with glee as if he were constantly plotting his next mischief.

George's most distinctive characteristic was his gait. He was fanatical about football and a proud member of the Kassiopi Football Team. Playing as he lived life, George hurled himself enthusiastically into every game, tackling all comers, most of whom were twice his size. Unfortunately this behaviour led to many accidents and George was a frequent visitor to Corfu Hospital. His knees in particular seemed to bear the brunt of his injuries, which resulted in his distinctive walk. My son, always quick to recognise idiosyncrasies in others, likened him with affectionate jollity to 'Woody', the wooden toy cowboy with rather jerky movements, voiced by Tom Hanks, from the computer-animated film *Toy Story*; even at a few hundred yards we could spot George from our position on Sarava as she lay at anchor. More part-time student than part-time waiter, George was ostensibly a reluctant pupil of a school in Corfu Town; although the day officially ended at one-thirty, George rarely stayed the course and frequently escaped before eleven o'clock. Despite his charm, good humour and generous nature George had a streak of impulsiveness and bravado that could occasionally land him in hot water.

One memorable morning during an October half-term holiday, as

Miranda and I stopped for coffee during a shopping trip in town, her mobile phone had beeped urgently to signal that a text message had arrived. More an implant within her right hand than an accessory, Miranda was already replying by the time I enquired innocently after her caller. She had blossomed that year with alarming rapidity, phone calls and messages arriving in a continuous stream these days; my own phone hardly ever rang.

"Who is it from, darling?" stirring my cappuccino and feeling very content on this sunny autumn morning, sitting at a café overlooking the lush greenery of Vido Island. I really felt this week had brought us very close, sharing so much time together without the distraction of the hoard of visiting friends we always accumulated during the summer holidays. We were more like best friends than mother and daughter I mused.

"You don't need to know," she replied curtly, fingers tapping on the keys with lightening speed. My illusions shattered I bravely persevered.

"Oh go on, don't be so mean, I'm just interested and I haven't had a message for days."

Before she had time to answer I saw her glance up as a shy smile illuminated her face. Following her gaze I spotted a familiar figure hurrying towards us along the smooth paving stones, grinning from ear to ear, eyes firmly fixed on my daughter.

"Hi George! What a surprise to see you, I thought you had college today," I exclaimed in an attempt to cover Miranda's feigned indifference.

"I know you are here so I came out."

"But George, don't your teachers say anything? Won't you get into trouble?" I asked, trying to compare the rules of a Greek college with my own experience of English public schools.

"They don't know. I climbed out of the toilet window!" he said, his grin getting bigger by the minute. Astonished, I asked him if he would get punished the following day.

"Not for that," he said, then stretching himself to his full height, hoping to impress Miranda with his derring-do. "Last week I threw a desk out of the window. For *that* they telephone to my mother!"

From our earliest visits to the island we had always seen George at Agni, running to catch the lines of visiting boats at the taverna's jetty. He could have been no more than twelve when we first brought our catamaran into the bay; he a little Greek boy in tee shirt and shorts, and Miranda a mere slip of an eleven year-old girl. Although too shy to talk to us, George was given more responsible tasks each year, eventually being elevated to official table clearer and occasional drinks waiter at the taverna. His confidence grew with his command of English and by the summer of 2000 he was bold enough to start a conversation with us; by 2001 we were practically his new family and he asked if he might be allowed to see our boat.

"Of course you may," said Jeremy, "Come over when you've finished work."

It was a particularly hot afternoon in mid-July and the taverna was full of customers until five-o'clock, George would only have an hour off, having started work at eight in the morning; soon he would need to start laying tables for the evening. George was evidently in a hurry as we watched him run down the jetty, throwing off his tee shirt before diving like an Olympian into the clear water; minutes later he was dripping and grinning on the aft deck, touchingly pleased to have been invited aboard. From that day on he became a regular visitor, finding us wherever we were at any time of day or night, whether in another harbour or anchored in some remote bay; we would hear the asthmatic coughs of his motorbike and everyone would chorus 'Here comes George!'

Half term fell late in October that year and Corfu had slipped quietly into autumn mode. The seasonal tavernas were closed and shuttered, the deserted beaches piled with neat stacks of sunbeds, below which tide lines had appeared with all the flotsam and jetsum washed up on the white pebbles by the first storms. In town the street vendors had replaced the flowers they sold in the summer months with hot roasted chestnuts and charcoal grilled corn-on-the-cob. The sun was still very hot and having spent a couple of wet, cold and windy months in England we were shedding our winter clothes like butterflies emerging from chrysalids. We pulled out cotton trousers and shirts from drawers and cupboards on Sarava, having put them away at the end of the summer thinking they would not be needed until next spring.

The Greeks, of course, thought us completely mad, for as soon as August has drawn to its close – despite September being hotter than an English heatwave – they cover themselves from head to foot in autumnal fashions. Out come boots, tights, trousers, polo-neck jerseys, jackets, scarves and gloves; even babies and toddlers are swaddled in woolly cardigans and hats against the ravages of the Mediterranean winter, when temperatures begin to fall below seventy-five degrees and the danger to life and limb becomes acute. A Cypriot friend had once confided to me, when challenged about this frenzy to discard summer clothes for winter ones, that the reason was very simple: the climate was summer for nine months of the year and people became so bored with wearing the same clothes that they could not wait to change into something different. As Sassa was the sole agent for Louis Féraud in Cyprus and the Middle East and also ran a very successful boutique, I could see she had little reason to discourage this national custom.

George had invited Miranda and me to Corfu Town to watch the annual parade which was part of the celebrations for *Oxi* Day; 'No' Day proudly commemorates the Greeks' rejection of Mussolini's ultimatum to annex their country to Italy on 28th October 1940. We, of course, felt obliged to accept and were flattered and honoured he wanted us there, although it was so hot by ten that morning we would really have preferred to go swimming. The town, bedecked throughout in the cheerful blue and white of the Greek flag, was already ringing with the laughter and chatter of all the Corfiot families and friends gathered for the occasion; many of them would not have seen each other for the six full months of unremitting work during the tourist season. We were the only foreigners to be seen amongst the crowds of proud parents, grandparents, aunts, uncles, teachers, pupils and their younger siblings; they lined every street ten deep where the procession of countless schools and representative troupes would pass. Scuttling to the nearest tree to find shade from the fierce sun, I held my handbag over my head having stupidly forgotten my hat. The noise was intense, everyone talking loudly and calling enthusiastically across streets to one another, obediently avoiding walking on the chosen route for the parade. The first group appeared, smart and dapper in navy and white uniforms, marching almost in unison behind a sweating, dark-suited teacher who tirelessly exalted them, '*Ena, dio, ena, dio*'. Much applause and clicking of cameras welcomed them, fathers craning video recorders over our heads trying to capture the moment. The next school party followed immediately behind the first, different uniforms but the same march, the children looking hot and uncomfortable in stiff, new black shoes.

By the time we had counted the tenth group I was beginning to wilt and wonder if we would ever catch a glimpse of George with his band of fellow students. Miranda was determined however; being taller by a head she was able to spot George's imminent approach and warn me to ready the camera. Through my viewfinder I suddenly saw George looking as smart as paint in his new black trousers, crisp white shirt and black tie, all borrowed from a friend who had recently attended a funeral. I pressed the button decisively and my stupid camera, making full use of its sluggish auto-focus, captured a wonderful view of George's back disappearing into the distance. There must have been at least fifty groups in the parade and, as they dispersed into a seething mass under the trees by the cricket pitch, I wondered how there could be so many schools on such a small island and how we would ever find George again. My anxieties were groundless, for within minutes, with the tracking instincts of a bloodhound, he was standing beside us, sweating profusely, red in the face but as happy as a dog with two tails that the Fair Miranda had witnessed his triumphal march. Alexander the Great could not have been prouder at the gates of Tyre.

We had the immense pleasure of George's cheerful company every day during our week's holiday. Sometimes he would come to the boat in the evenings politely enduring my indifferent cooking, sitting contentedly for hours playing cards with Miranda and teasing her affectionately, she treating him like an annoying elder brother but secretly revelling in the attention. One evening we took them to the smartest restaurant in town for dinner, George, looking very dapper with a stylish new shirt bought for the occasion, surprised us by chatting knowledgeably with the waiter about wines, ordering for us with the panache of a seasoned sommelier. Another night he surprised us by arriving at the boat with bags full of hot *souvlaki* kebabs for us all, *For me*, as the Greeks say, meaning 'On me', my treat. These local delicacies consist of delicious, tender cubes of pork or chicken which have been grilled over charcoal, enveloped in crisply toasted pitta bread stuffed to overflowing with salad and *tsatsiki*, a concoction of grated cucumber, garlic and mint mixed into thick and creamy natural yoghurt. The filling was topped with a few thin French fries, a dollop of savoury gravy and the complete pitta envelope came wrapped in a greaseproof paper bag, the Greek equivalent of fish and chips. We learned so much from George, not only local customs and traditions but the delicate intrigues of Corfiot family life and the stark contrasts between his teenage years and those of our own children.

On the evening of our departure at the end of that week George insisted on accompanying us to the airport. Waving and swerving merrily on his noisy bike, hair flattened by the wind, he followed our taxi. George had a very large, shiny crash helmet that he used to carry under his arm whenever he arrived on the boat to see us, always placing it tenderly on the cockpit table, although we had never seen him actually wearing it whilst riding his bike. Jeremy challenged him about this one day and somewhat predictably George replied that he could not possibly risk damaging the expensive helmet in the event of an accident. Despite our protestations, George carried all our luggage to the check-in himself. Our plane was delayed by about four hours; our luggage had already disappeared on the conveyor belt. Unable to stand waiting in the crowded airport, which was always thick with cigarette smoke in those far off days, we summoned a taxi, piled in and headed off to Corfu Town. In need of sustenance, and in fear and dread at the prospect of plastic airline food on the journey back to England, we followed George to his favourite café and ate our toasted sandwiches, all the while noticing George becoming quieter by the minute – a very rare phenomenon.

The evening was growing cool as we walked through the park, past the English bandstand under the horse chestnut trees, heavily laden with conkers, until we reached the walls of the Old Fort. George was now long-faced and not speaking at all. As we watched the sun going down over the sea he and Miranda sat on a low wall hand in hand, both realising we would soon be driving to the airport, she going back to boarding school and unable to return to Corfu until the following April, while George would have no more excuses for playing truant and would have to knuckle down to work at last. Jeremy and I felt the weight of a black cloud hanging over us, leaving our beloved Corfu to resume our other life in England. At the airport once more we were a sorry little group. George stuck close, reluctant to take his sad puppy-dog brown eyes off Miranda or to let go of her hand. I had such a lump in my throat that I couldn't speak at all for fear of bursting into tears. As we reached passport control George made no effort to stand back and Jeremy had to take charge.

"We will have to say goodbye now George", he ventured. "You can't come any further; sorry old chap".

George looked most hurt and crestfallen. Suddenly he lunged at Jeremy and threw both arms around him in a bear-hug. Unfamiliar with this sort of treatment, being a typically reserved Englishman, Jeremy looked rather embarrassed as he patted George on the back and muttered 'there's a good fellow', before gently disentangling himself to present our passports. I was totally unabashed and gave George a huge hug and a kiss on both cheeks, I knew I would miss him dreadfully in the long months before we were back on the island again. He and Miranda hugged too and he unwillingly let her follow us into the departure lounge, watching her intently until she disappeared from his sight. As soon as we took our seats on the plane a message came through on Miranda's phone.

"Just George saying goodbye and *kalo taxhidi,*" she said.

"How sweet," I replied.

"Hmph," came from Jeremy, "I'm half expecting to see George pop up in the seat behind us."

"Or running along the tarmac!" I quipped.

"Even he couldn't manage that," he said. But as the plane accelerated down the runway all three of us were peering anxiously out of the window.

Back at home a few days later my phone rang as I was driving; it was George.

"How lovely to hear you, George dear, how are you?"

The sound of his voice was so welcome, his Greek accent bringing memories of sunny Corfu and our floating home flooding into this cold, grey, rainy day.

"I very bad," he said huskily.

"Why, what on earth's the matter?" I said, trying to negotiate the bends in the narrow country lane with one hand on the wheel, the other holding the phone to my ear.

"I broken my arm," he continued with a catch in his voice, followed by what could only be described as a deep sob.

"My mother had to take me to hospital and now my arm in plaster."

"Oh no, you haven't fallen off your bike again?" I asked.

"No."

"Then how did you do it?"

"I hit a wall," (sniff).

"On your bike?"

"No, with my arm," (deep sigh). "I was on the phone with Miranda and she say she have to go because she is with her boyfriend," (more sniffing). "I haven't look at any girl since she left!" (less than a week). "I so angry I hit the wall with my arm. I feeling very, very bad."

I tried to console him and assured him that although Miranda had friends at Millfield she did not have a boyfriend in the way he meant.

"Her friendships are just platonic, George."

"Ah yes, I see," he replied, sounding a little chirpier. "From the Greek, is named after *o Pláton*!"

I didn't have the heart to remind him that Plato never used the term himself, perhaps because his friendships were simply not of the platonic variety.

"I will talk to her," I reassured. "Don't worry, George, she is very fond of you."

"*Daxi*, okay," replied George, letting out a lengthy sigh worthy of the most tragic of Greek tragedies. "I leave it to you."

Later that evening I telephoned Miranda at school, she confessed rather guiltily that she had been receiving constant flow of text messages and calls from George and she had got fed up with his attentions. Gentler persuasion having failed, it had been the only way she could put him off, she explained. Poor George. Nevertheless I was still worried about him and telephoned Nathan to ask him to have a 'Dutch Uncle' chat with George; he looked up to Nathan and I knew he would take his advice. Nathan handled the situation with tact, kindness and diplomacy, mindful of George's youth and delicate sensibilities; unfortunately Eleni had no such scruples and gave George her opinion in no uncertain terms.

"A girl like Miranda would *never* look at you!" scolded Eleni. "You who play truant are nobody and will not make anything of yourself. You are not good enough for her!"

It was completely unfair and untrue of course, as Eleni must have known full well, but it seemed to do the trick. Things gradually calmed down after that, communications tailing off to about one message a week and a Sunday phone call. Devoted George had learnt a hard lesson: teenage girls love attention, but too much of a good thing will send them flying in the opposite direction.

In the intervening years George has made a very great deal of himself, as we always knew he would.

Chapter Six

Caveat Emptor

Twenty years from now you will be more disappointed by the things you didn't do than those you did. So throw off the bowlines. Sail away from safe harbour. Catch the wind in your sails. Explore. Dream. Discover.

Mark Twain

In June 2002 we chose to drive from England to Corfu, partly for the convenience of having our own car on the island, but also to allow our one remaining King Charles Cavalier, Burberry, to spend the summer with us. We had obtained a Pet Passport after many visits to our vet for inoculations and endless form filling started months before our departure; the rabies vaccine had to be administered at least six months prior to a dog re-entering Britain. Interestingly none of the resulting dossier of documents and permits, granting Burberry diplomatic immunity in any country into which he might accidentally stray, were ever requested until we returned to Dover three months later. This confirmed our suspicion that the whole caper was a job creation scheme for vets, dreamt up by the bureaucrats of Brussels and London.

Our chosen route took us via Epernay and Alsace to friends in Munich, thence through Austria to Italy, where we would take the ferry from Venice to Corfu. Fully expecting this ferry to be as unsavoury as our own grimy cross-channel service, we had booked the most luxurious cabin in the hope that it might be passable. Strictly speaking pets were not allowed in the cabins, so we had given Burberry several practice sessions at home to prepare him for his stowaway performance to come; having read about the ferry company's idea of doggie accommodation, we had no doubt about its unsuitability for Mr. B. At home he used to sleep on our bed or beside it; he was obedient, quiet, better behaved than most children and a great deal cleaner and more fragrant than many adults. Canine passengers were expected to remain caged in small metal kennels on the top deck for the duration of the twenty-four hour passage. In these prisons the air was full of toxic fumes from the ship's funnels directly overhead, moreover the location was in full sun during the day, with scant shelter from wind, rain or sea-spray in the daytime or at night.

Placing a soft canvas holdall on the floor, zip fully open, we would drop a bit of biscuit inside and ask Burberry to hop in; then as he put his head down to search for it, the case was smartly zipped up and carried to the car; once on the back seat we would open the bag and he would cheerfully climb out to be driven off for a walk on Dartmoor. After a few of these bagged excursions he was so enthusiastic about them that he would often climb into any open bag by himself and fall asleep, head over the side, optimistically anticipating his next outing. Arriving in Venice from our final overnight stay on the shores of Lake Garda in good time for our ferry's departure, we parked the Jeep cheek-by-jowl with the other vehicles on the car deck, said the magic word, 'Biscuit', to Burberry, zipped-up the bag and climbed the stairs towards our cabin. We quickly realised we had seriously under-estimated the ferry, which had the air of quite a smart cruise ship; our expensive cabin turned out to be an unnecessary extravagance, but Burberry was delighted when he was shown his own personal sofa, covered with the new rug we had bought for the purpose. Having unpacked our luggage, we smuggled him out onto the designated 'poop' deck for our departure, from where we could admire the view of Venice as we left the dock.

In those days the ferry was piloted from its berth at the western end of Venice along the Giudecca and San Marco channels, finally entering the Adriatic through the lagoon entrance north of the Lido. Making sedate progress through the narrow channel bustling with va-poretti, the top decks afforded majestic views of Venice's familiar land-marks as they passed tantalisingly close beneath us, those wonderful monuments and buildings, galleries, restaurants and shops just out of reach; interestingly it is only from the top deck of a ship, or possibly from the height of a campanile that one can see the dozens of secret roof gardens concealed above the city.

Out on deck it was extremely hot, especially after the air-conditioned comfort of our cabin; it was mid-afternoon and the sun was still high. We found a slice of shade on the San Marco side of the ship and I told Burberry to sit, but he got up very quickly. I couldn't understand this behaviour or why he was so reluctant to settle. As my feet were hurting I slipped off my sandals and realised to my horror that the shaded steel deck was scorching – hot enough to fry an egg. He had obediently sat on the scalding metal, griddling his nether regions in seconds. Forsaking the views of Venice I whisked Burberry into my arms and rushed him back to our cabin, where I put him in the shower and doused him with cool water. He looked very relieved. Afterwards I examined him, wrapped in a towel like a baby. We could clearly see the skin on his private parts was blush pink, having little hair for protection in such a vulnerable area. Feeling terribly guilty I smothered him with Aloe Vera gel from my sponge bag, while Jeremy explained that our patch of shade had in fact been in the blazing sun for several hours before the ferry had turned around for its departure. For the remainder of the journey we amused ourselves composing schoolboy versions of the poem *Casabianca,* which started predictably with *The dog sat on the burning deck ...* and ended with ... *rowlocks.*

* * *

Having a car permanently available brought a new dimension to our summer in Corfu; it also found us the piece of land we had been looking for so fruitlessly. We had looked at several plots in the north-east of the island over the last few years, but none had been perfect; either they faced the wrong way, lacked clear views, were too steep or too rocky, had too many close neighbours or lacked access. Then, one very hot morning in August just as we were about to set sail once more for

Kefalonia, I suddenly remembered an errand I had agreed to run for Simon, a charismatic English friend of Miranda's who was finishing his gap year in Fiskardo. Working in a busy harbourside taverna he was finding it difficult to buy smart shirts suitable for the hot weather, so I had promised to bring him some pure linen short-sleeved shirts from Corfu. Accordingly Jeremy took Sarava to refuel at Gouvia, where I would leave the Jeep for safekeeping during our absence. Approaching the small turning to Agios Stefanos I swung off the road down the narrow lane in the direction of the village; I always enjoyed winding down this tortuous little road, which culminated in a series of steep hairpin bends from where the most wonderful, but treacherously distracting, views opened onto the hamlet far below, looking like a lovingly laid out model village complete with toy boats bobbing in its own miniature horseshoe bay.

I was also happy to be visiting one of my favourite gift shops on the island, a little wooden cabin by the beach. Not much more than a hut with a polythene roof, this was an Aladdin's cave of lovely things: pure cotton mats woven with Greek designs of dolphins, turtles, key-patterns, Venetian galleys and, oddly, with footprints – wonderful presents no doubt for reflexologists. Sarongs hung outside swaying in the breeze in a profusion of colour next to sun-hats and flip-flops that jostled for position on wobbly shelves with beach balls and children's fishing nets. Inside you could find piles of crisp white cotton sheets and pillowcases, some with delicate embroidery, locally hand-made crochet tablecloths, throws and bedspreads; revolving display cases held paperbacks on olive oil, herbs, wild flowers, Greek mythology and cookery. The ceiling had been lovingly disguised with dozens of coloured plastic coat hangers from which bikinis in every shape and size dangled overhead.

The air-conditioning was on full blast and the car was blissfully cool; much to Miranda's disgust the CD player was blaring out Simon and Garfunkel's *Cecilia* as we threaded our way along the lane.

"Oh Mummy, where are you going now?" moaned Miranda,

already settled down with Burberry on her lap for a nice long nap in the soft, leather seated comfort of the Jeep.

"I've just remembered Ass's shirts, darling," I replied.

This nickname had been given to Simon the previous summer when, after demonstrating his proficiency at deck swabbing, I had promoted him 'Able Seaman Simon'. Jeremy promptly shortened his rank to the less flattering acronym, which stuck. From then on Simon became ASS, a nickname he accepted in his usual genial way.

"Oh no!" groaned Miranda, knowing as she did how a quick visit to the shop could turn into an eternity.

We drove through the cool green shade of the olive groves, diffused hazy shafts of sunlight filtering through the silvery canopy of leaves. In the dim pools of light beneath the trees a carpet of ferns grew in profusion, strewn here and there with long rolls of black netting, resembling the discarded skins of giant snakes, ready to be unfurled to catch the falling olives later in the year. Rounding a bend we came suddenly upon a stunningly open view, where the olives by the road had recently been pruned bare to their trunks, revealing a wide, perfectly shaped valley on the right hand side of the road. The land was thick with every type of tree and shrub; a green patchwork of ancient, gangly olives leaning haphazardly in all directions, tall dark cypress, mature oaks, laurel, Spanish chestnut, juniper, arbutus, myrtle bushes and figs spread out in a profusion below. The flanks of the valley framed the cerulean sea in the Straits and the paler waters of the inlet leading to Lake Butrint; beyond a backdrop of dusty pink hills the distant mountains of Albania hung in a shimmering heat haze. It quite took our breath away, a completely unspoilt piece of this magical island, hitherto untouched by human hand for hundreds of years, save for the working of the olive groves; there was not a single villa or building to be seen in the panorama. Birds flitted from tree to tree, blue-tits, collared doves, unidentifiable species with black, white and yellow plumage and dainty flycatchers. We opened the windows and the urgent rasping of the cicadas leapt into the car. There was no other sound; the peace was deafening.

"I don't think we've driven along this road since last winter," I said to Miranda. "Only sailed past in Sarava."

"Look Mummy!" she exclaimed. "There's a For Sale notice!" Unable to believe my own eyes I saw the tiny white board nailed crookedly on the gnarled trunk of an olive tree by the verge. I could hardly believe my eyes. Carefully painted in pillarbox red letters it read:

FOR SALE NICE LAND Tel 6135180

"Quick! Put it on my phone," I said. Even Miranda was catching my infectious enthusiasm now, punching on the keys with the speed and dexterity of a touch typist.

"Bet it's expensive."

"Bound to be, but I know someone who will know the price," she turned to me with a grin.

"BYE BYE SNAKE!" we both shouted simultaneously, as I sped off down the hill.

This affectionate nickname had been awarded to our friend Sotiris after he had shown us a piece of land two years previously. As I was strolling through an olive grove, wearing only a swimsuit, sarong and flip-flops, he had called out 'Beware of the snakes Jani!' I had frozen momentarily before taking great leaping, unladylike strides over the crackling dry undergrowth until I reached the safety of the path.

"Well you might have warned me earlier!" I panted. "I don't want a house with snakes in the garden," I protested. Sotiris just laughed at my fear.

"No Jani, you must not to worry, it is easy to get rid of the snakes,"

"How?" I enquired, still trembling slightly.

Sotiris was very tall, well built and good looking, but he had a sensitive and delicate disposition; his sing-song, lilting voice was almost hypnotic, yet far higher up the register than one might have expected for a man of his stature. He explained slowly and carefully, as if talking to a small child.

"You take a bottle with a wide neck, not too big so a cat could put his finger in, and put some milk in the bottom. In this milk you put some poison. You bury the bottle in the ground, leaving just the neck outside. The snake loves milk, so he comes along, goes inside the bottle, drinks the milk and BYE BYE SNAKE!" he exclaimed, waving delicately in the Greek manner – locked fingers flapping over the palm as if he was clicking a castanet – as we all fell about laughing.

Miranda and I locked little fingers and made a wish, a habit of hers since she was at nursery school whenever two people said anything simultaneously. I had a feeling we both wished for the same thing: we had just driven past it. The car seemed to drive itself the rest of the way down the hillside at breakneck speed; I was urged on by an insistent niggle in the back of my mind that a potential purchaser, with ready cash in hand, was at that very moment closing a deal on the land that I had now, since five minutes ago, fallen for hook, line and sinker. I didn't even consider what I was doing, every instinct and fibre of my being urging me to act. I felt as if benign hands were leading me down, down to the village below where the answers to all my dreams would lie. It was as if I was surrounded by a host of well-wishers who wanted to help me and my little family. I was convinced I could hear voices in my head saying 'Go on Jani! Try to get it, it's the right place, the one you've been searching for'.

Abandoning the car crookedly on the shingle beach, Greek style with the engine still running, I left Miranda in the comfort of the air-conditioning and jumped out. I charged into the shop in a very undignified manner.

"Where's Sotiris?" I asked the owner breathlessly.

"In his house," he said staring hard at my flushed face and gauging immediately that something was up.

"I've found my land," I gasped, describing its whereabouts to him.

"I call him," replied Sotiris' elderly uncle Petros, who was succinct with his words, not having a great command of English.

He had known me for several years and could read me like a book; we were on the same wavelength and needed few words to communicate. If I was tired he knew; if I was fed up with difficult guests he knew; when I was energised and ready for a chat he obliged. Picking up the telephone he spoke to his nephew, who said he would find out the price of the land and ring back. I busied myself choosing Simon's shirts, one in each pastel colour, not really concentrating. It seemed an age before the phone rang.

"*Nai, nai, daxi,*" said Petros. Putting down the receiver he beckoned me nearer. Glancing around him with the furtive air of a traitor about to impart state secrets, fearful there were spies amongst his customers, he whispered the price in my ear, adding that the 'for sale' board had only been put up two days earlier. I thought I had misheard him, as the price was far below my own estimation.

"*Ti?.... Poso?*" I asked. Numerically my Greek was pretty good, due mainly to my perfectly honed shopping skills, but my bills rarely rose above the two hundred euro mark; maybe I had mistaken thousands for millions. This time he wrote it on a piece of paper and thrust it into my hand, closing his over mine like a schoolboy passing secret notes in class. I nervously unfurled the crumpled scrap. The figure ended in many zeros as it was in drachmas, the preferred currency of Corfiots and old school British, especially when discussing larger amounts; the euro was still despised and ridiculed by most older Greeks. The amount was not only well within our price-range but also much less than any comparable piece of land we had seen before. My friend looked as excited as I felt as I kissed him hurriedly on both cheeks, before dashing back into the car.

"Well?" asked Miranda.

"It's a good price!" I said, "We can easily afford it!"

"Bet Daddy won't think so," was her parting shot before she closed her eyes and settled down again for a nap, earphones firmly in.

I drove back to the marina faster than I should, given the busy winding road that follows the indentations of the east coast towards Corfu Town. Village houses, barking dogs and sleepy *kafenions* flashed past; startled coach drivers swerved and uncharacteristically gave way to avoid me. I was rehearsing the best way to break the thrilling news to Jeremy, knowing I would have to treat him with kid gloves. Usually the more I enthuse about something the more likely he is to play devil's advocate, often throwing endless obstacles and negativity in my direction. This infuriating habit stemmed from the deep-seated pessimism drummed into him by a Victorian father; he preferred to call it healthy scepticism, his theory holding that if you generally expect the worst you will often be pleasantly surprised. Conversely I am the exact opposite; a cock-eyed optimist always thinking the best of everything and everyone, sometimes but seldom disillusioned. By the time I reached the boat I was struggling to contain my enthusiasm, nevertheless I waited a full ten minutes to give Jeremy a chance to finish the nautical task he was busy with.

"Darling," I ventured, slowly and calmly,

"Hmm?" not looking at me as he coiled yards of new rope on the aft deck.

"Miranda and I have seen a beautiful piece of land!"

"Mmm," he murmured with his back to me, now bending over the stern with a spanner in one hand.

"It's for sale and amazingly reasonable!"

"Ah yes," was his only response.

"It's near Agios Stefanos. Can we go and look at it?"

"What, now? Of course not! We're expected in Kefalonia the day after tomorrow and we should leave while the wind's favourable," he answered, jumping into the tender to attach the davits falls.

I panicked. Kefalonia meant at least five days away from Corfu: four hours to Lakka, overnight there, then on to Kefalonia, another five or six hours; two nights in Fiskardo then, and only if the weather and winds were promising, back to Antipaxos or Parga for the night, before returning to Corfu. Should the weather turn, however, we could be further delayed; the benign pattern of prevailing winds in the Ionian can be interrupted by a Maestro, bringing north westerly gales and violent thunderstorms for two days at a time, particularly after an exceptionally hot spell of weather such as we were just experiencing. Bearing all this in mind I was suddenly less than enthusiastic about the forthcoming trip. All I could do was wait … Or was it? I rushed down to my cabin to call Bye Bye Snake in secret.

"Sotiri, I really want that land," I told him. "Can you contact the owner and see if he'll wait until we get back?"

"I do my best," he replied, "but already six people come to me and say they are interesting this land."

"Stall them 'til next week, please," I begged.

"Ok Jani, I will try. For you I will try." Click. That was it, I could do no more.

As Sarava moved slowly from her berth bound for Kefalonia, I watched the boats and marina buildings disappear from view out of my cabin window with a feeling of helplessness. I loved visiting other islands, but this time I knew I would be too preoccupied with the image, still swimming before my eyes, of that perfect valley and its wide, shimmering triangle of sea beyond. In Gaios that night we took our usual, eagerly anticipated fare of sea bream and lobster spaghetti at *Pan and Theo's*, from where we could keep a glancing vigil on Sarava's anchor light, twinkling away in the darkness at anchor beyond the bustling harbour. I had already visited my favourite delicatessen, stocking up with large quantities of wonderful prosciutto, ripe melons and mozzarella – always readily available to meet the exacting taste of the many Italians who swarm to Paxos. But the tiny, wonderfully tasty Paxiot olives were not to be found anywhere; the island's entire stock, I was told, had been delivered aboard one or other of an Arab Prince's matching megayachts the day before.

We arose before dawn and after a gentle sail through early morning mists, we soon found ourselves scurrying down the sheer western shores of Levkas, eventually mooring in time for lunch in the exquisite harbour of Fiskardo. The Ass's linen shirts – serendipitously instrumental in finding the land I was now so eagerly chasing – were ceremoniously handed over with detailed explanations of the part they had played in the continuing saga. Here we lingered for a further two days, relaxing as far as I could in the easy charm of the place and renewing casual friendships with some of the locals we have come to know. On the third day, still extremely edgy, I felt compelled to phone again for an update.

"So many people keep coming in to ask me about this land," Sotiris said. "Lucky for you the owner has gone away for a few days so they cannot contact him."

"Oh thank you so much," I breathed with some relief.

"I went there last night to see the *fengari*, a full moon actually. It was so beautiful and there were many wows," he continued.

"Wows, Sotiri?" I asked, bemused.

He sighed and tried to explain with great patience; once again this English woman was proving to be a bit thick.

"You know, birds who flying at night ... big eyes ... and say woo-woo."

"OWLS, Sotiri!" I said, trying to stifle a laugh.

"Yes, that's it, lots of wowls there, *poli orea*. Also, Jani, I have a copy of the topographical plan for you when you come back ... *yiassou*, bye bye."

Not a moment too soon for me, the anchor chain was clanking over the bow-roller and Sarava was edging out of the crowded harbour entrance, where a handful of leviathon yachts had shouldered mere superyachts into huddled, sulking groups, their crews in heated argument over crossed anchor chains and tangled stern lines. Miranda would never allow me to hang washing, or even beach towels to dry on Sarava's railings when in any harbour, saying 'You make her look like a Chinese laundry Mummy, it's *so* degrading!' But the washing machine had just finished and a pile of laundry was waiting to be hung out as soon as we left Fiskardo; I had just started this chore when I heard Jeremy calling to me.

"Take a really good look at that tender." From his position at the helm he was pointing to a very smart tender approaching us through the milling boats. I stared hard from our foredeck as it glided slowly past and there, not ten feet away seated amongst a casually dressed group of yachties, was the unmistakable smiling, suntanned and bearded face of Tom Hanks.

"Have a good trip!" came the instantly recognisable lilting voice, a riveting mixture of a dozen familiar films and animation voice-overs.

"Oh thank you! You too!" was all I could manage in response, completely dumbfounded.

Only then did I realise that Tom Hanks, my very favourite actor, had greeted me surely for the first and last time in my life, as I was pegging my freshly washed knickers to the guardrails. I was utterly mortified.

* * *

Our return northwards to Corfu always followed a familiar pattern: lunch on board was a delicious recipe I heard on BBC Radio 4 one day, quickly scribbled on a scrap of paper in the galley and used time and time again. '*Kleferti*', as I heard it, is a simple pancake batter poured over slow baked fresh plum tomato halves, sprinkled with chopped fresh oregano, crumbled feta cheese, salt and pepper. The instructions called for the tomatoes to be baked for two hours on a very low heat, but I could not do this on Sarava as the oven would heat the whole boat. I had a better idea which I thought was ingenious: I cut the tomatoes in half, poured on some olive oil, sprinkled fresh oregano and black pepper on top and put them on a tin plate, which I laid on the coachroof in the full midday sun. It worked perfectly and gave a whole new meaning to sun dried tomatoes. I put the 'baked' tomatoes in a shallow ovenproof dish then poured the batter over them, adding cubes of crumbled feta cheese and finishing the dish in a medium oven for 20 minutes. The only drawback occurred if ever I forgot about my tomatoes when a particularly heavy wash from a passing ship would send the plate sliding off the roof like a frisbee. I haven't found this recipe anywhere, so I have probably got the name wrong; if any reader can enlighten me I would be delighted.

After lunch we often swam in the warm shallows off Skorpios, the small private island once owned by Aristotle Onassis. It was usually deserted but I was always intrigued, having read a fascinating book, *The Onassis Women*, by Phyllis Karas and Kiki Feroudi, a former PA to Onassis. The place had a strange atmosphere and lingering sadness about it; unsurprising given the tragedies that seem to follow the Kennedy and Onassis dynasties. Although still owned by the family, Skorpios seemed abandoned and unloved. It is not permitted to step onto the shore, but under Greek law visitors by boat could not be prevented from standing in the shallows, just a few yards away. Far from being a haven of solitude, the island was actually a goldfish bowl.

Then, threading our way through the ancient canal that gives Lefkas its notional island status, Sarava would head out into the midnight calm towards Antipaxos. The handful of people who live on this diminutive island are supplied and victualled through one miniscule dilapidated harbour, suitable only for the smallest launch, from where a tractor hauls provisions up a winding track to the ridge along which most of the dwellings are dotted. The steep land, interspersed here and there with neat patches of cultivated terracing, is covered with dense maquis that rolls down to the sheer edge of elaborately whorled and stratified ivory cliffs. We always enjoyed nosing through the fading evening light into one of its deserted anchorages, letting go the anchor in ten feet of phosphorescent water. The youngsters would dive from Sarava's decks, illuminating the dark water with blazing trails of shimmering light; for a second or two as they climbed the boarding ladder, their bodies would glow as if they had been covered with luminous paint. Rising early with the sun next morning Jeremy and I would swim in water as clear and smooth as aquamarine jelly; here the colour of the sea can be so intense that it seers the retina, forcing you to look away and rub your eyes until disbelief makes you return the gaze once more. Dabs, hermit crabs, starfish and sea-cucumbers move over the pure white, sandy bottom, while small fish hang just below the surface and swim lazily around you.

As the early morning shadows shortened we would climb the ninety or so donkey steps, hewn out of the rock to twist their way precariously through a dwarf forest of holm oak and myrtle up to a solitary taverna. The Bella Vista lived up to its grand name; from its rustic vine covered terrace the panorama was utterly breathtaking. Promontories stretched into the distance like dark green fingers from turquoise shallows to the deeper indigo waters, leading the eye beyond Paxos to the southernmost tip of Corfu in the far distance.

But we could never linger after our morning coffee and croissants. By ten o'clock the first of the tourist boats would appear over the horizon from Parga or Preveza on the mainland, unsuitable pop music blaring. Overladen with a hundred or so rowdy passengers intent upon jumping into the sea from the same side of the ship, the whole vessel would list so alarmingly that you feared a capsize. Suddenly the water would become a boiling cauldron of hot, Germolene-pink bodies, splashing, swearing and shouting; those left on board would lie in the blazing sun guzzling as much lager as they could before the return trip, entirely oblivious to their exquisite surroundings. Beating a hasty retreat from a paradise we knew would still be there for us next time, we would weave our way between loutish, foul-mouthed bathers and bobbing beer cans before heading out to the peace and tranquillity of the open sea. Timing is everything, even in the Ionian.

* * *

Never give up because you never know what the tide will bring in the next day.

Tom Hanks

Miranda and I were in the Jeep as soon as we arrived back at the marina in Corfu, heading straight up the coast road to visit the land; there to our utmost relief we were not greeted by a 'Sold' sign. Leaving Miranda on watch for passing cars, I took the small pot of white nail varnish I normally used for a French manicure and approached the 'For Sale' sign on the gnarled olive trunk. Carefully I painted out segments of the red number eight of the phone number, neatly changing it into a three. Miranda beeped the horn whenever a car came along the narrow road and I would instantly cease my sabotage, adopting the extravagant gesture of a pantomime actor raising a hand to scan the horizon for imaginary passing ships. My heart thumping and feeling like an arch criminal I jumped back into the car, varnish in pocket, and drove to the village to collect the *topografico* from Sotiris, thanking him profusely for his efforts on our behalf.

Two days later I eventually persuaded Jeremy to visit the land, which I had since learnt from one of the villagers was in a little area called, '*Liondari*', Greek for lion. Legend held that in ancient times a mansion owned by a prosperous Venetian merchant had stood there; in its grounds was the stone statue of a lion, no doubt winged, from which the area took its name. The house was ransacked and the statue stolen by marauding pirates; henceforth the house was abandoned and fell to ruin, never to be re-built and most of the inhabitants left the settlement. From that moment, should we ever own the land, I knew not only the name of the house we would build there – The Lion House – but also the first thing I would need to buy for it.

Dusk had slipped into starlit darkness before we left the land that evening. Obligingly a cruise ship glided silently over the stretch of water below us, illuminated like a floating basket of light, just as a cluster of fireflies sprang into life beneath the sprawling umbrella of olive trees. These tiny creatures produce rhythmic flashes of green-white light from their abdomens, the sight entirely magical. At night the insect itself is invisible and all you see are a thousand slowly drifting pinpricks of light winking in the darkness. I gently caught one in my hand and for the few seconds I held it I could feel its radiated warmth. A Scops Owl called to its mate from one side of our valley, almost instantly the call was returned, as if in stereo, from a large oak tree on the opposite side. I had thought this piece of land was stunningly beautiful during the day time, but at night it had turned into fairyland.

Teenage George had been the first to tell us the fireflies' Greek name, during a May evening spent with us on the boat. After supper I asked him to come with us to see the fireflies; they always assembled above the stream which ran beneath the avenue of tall eucalyptus trees lining the narrow lane leading to the marina. As we watched their courtship dance I asked George what they were called in Greek. He blushed profusely and giggled, pretending not to know.

"Oh come on George, you must know," I persisted.

He glanced at Miranda and shrugged.

"*Kolofoties,*" he muttered under his breath.

Jeremy laughed as he translated the word in his head. I had to ask George again and he looked even more embarrassed as he mumbled 'light-up bottoms'.

Jeremy was grudgingly impressed with the site but could not believe the price, insisting there must have been a misunderstanding. I took him to see 'Bye Bye Snake' who confirmed the land's asking price, adding that many people were asking him every day if he knew the owner; more ominously he knew of a wealthy Englishman who had offered three times the usual deposit if the owner would wait until the end of September, when he could return with the balance in cash from England. It was now the third week in August.

"Oh no, I knew this would happen! What can we do?" I implored.

"Well, I give you name of lawyer and ask him to make enquiries for you; but don't worry about the other peoples," continued Sotiris. "It's something strange that happening, because every time somebody tries to call to the owner they getting a wrong number ..."

I smiled to myself, feeling only the merest twinge of guilt.

First thing next morning, before the shops had opened, we were in Corfu Town having breakfast beneath the leafy shade of the acacia trees on the Espianada. The town was quiet; only the café staff and a few shopkeepers strolled along the smooth paving stones of the promenade on their way to work. Scents of jasmine and freshly cut grass mingled with the ever present salt tang of the sea which surrounds Corfu Town on three sides; rare whiffs of a slightly unsavoury drain only served to reassure you that you are in a foreign land. The freshly watered cricket pitch sparkled in the early morning sun, as Mediterranean swifts, like navy blue paper darts, wheeled over our heads, filling the air with their shrill, piping cries. At our feet tiny house martins and swallows flitted about gathering wet mud for their nests from patches of bare earth at the side of the pitch.

Friends from Devon had arrived for a week's holiday with us the night before; nevertheless they were unceremoniously dragged out of bed to accompany us into town early that morning, gamely joining us as the hastily arranged appointment with our solicitor became necessary. After breakfast they amused themselves with a little sightseeing while we spent a couple of hours with our new 'best friend', a lawyer we were sure would help us buy the land and guide us through a labyrinth of Greek legalities with the skills of an ancient mariner. The lawyer was, to our surprise, a forty-something Greek dish with the smooth good looks of a matinée idol and dressed with the casual elegance that comes so easily to continental men; not a pin-stripe or tie in sight, he wore instead a black, designer polo shirt and beige chinos with a tan leather belt. He exuded chic and savoir-faire from the top of his perfectly coiffed head to the toes of his tasselled Italian loafers. Hugely impressed by this Adonis I had every confidence that he was obviously the best lawyer in Corfu, if not in Greece. 'Handsome is as handsome does' as the saying goes, or as Jeremy would prefer 'Appearances can be deceptive' ... Naturally the more I waxed lyrical about him the more Jeremy came to mistrust him and by lunchtime he had him down firmly as a 'bottom pincher', Jeremy's term for any type of womaniser.

'Angel Gabriel', as I had nicknamed our lawyer Gabrilis, explained all the Greek formalities to us while we sat in his stylish but stifling top floor office and drank coffee. Air conditioning was not allowed in these traditional old buildings in what used to be the Jewish quarter; the local authorities, to their credit, will not tolerate the unsightly

compressors on the exterior walls. It must have been ninety-five degrees indoors and I was beginning to feel faint. Within half an hour
we had learnt about the various searches that must be done on our
behalf. The *topografico*, a detailed survey which marks every tree, rock
and contour, would need to be submitted to the land registry to confirm that the plot is *a.* not a forest, *b.* not an archaeological site, *c.* not
owned by someone who is unwilling to sell, (in Greece it is common
for land to be registered in the names of eight or more relations who
will hardly ever agree to sell at the same time, let alone concur on a
price), *d.* is not considered too steep to build on, *e.* is not too near the
shoreline, *f.* has access from and sufficient frontage onto the nearest
lane or track and *g.* is truly the size stated on the topographical plan.
In practice most of these hurdles could be quietly ignored or overcome with some suitably irregular voluntary donations – as bribes are
known hereabouts – but Jeremy is a stickler for doing things by the
book and was still rather too English to contemplate such corruption.
The commonest problem concerned the exaggerated size of a piece of
land, often handily measured for a vendor's benefit to occupy just a
few square metres more than the critical minimum level for building
approval; it is said that if all the island's registered plots of land were
joined together, as delineated on the individual surveys, Corfu would
actually be the size of France.

Then our solicitor dropped a bombshell: he knew this acre of land
by name. During our absence in Kefalonia the mysterious Englishman
had also paid him a visit, instructing him to make all the same enquiries about *Leondari* and, all being in order, to start proceedings
towards an October completion. The race was on. I left the office,
teeth clenched, determined to outwit our competitor, while Jeremy
was becoming ever more hesitant and uncertain.

"I don't like being rushed into things," he said.

"If we *don't* rush we will lose the land!" I replied, exasperated and already very, very hot as we wound our way through the narrow streets,
two determined Arian rams at loggerheads.

"If we do, we do," he said, with resigned and infuriating nonchalance.

"But if we can pay a deposit quickly we will secure it," I retaliated.

"I won't be pushed into this. I need to think about it," he insisted, striding ahead and talking back over his shoulder. I struggled to keep up, trying to stay in control and keep my temper, open parasol and handbag in one hand and lead in the other, tugging Burberry away from street corners, walls, trees and every tantalising lamp-post in town which he felt was in need of his attention.

"Let's meet Angela and Geoffrey for a nice cold drink," I suggested, hoping to keep things on an even keel and drum some sense of urgency into him at the same time. I knew Angela would be in my corner but suspected that Geoffrey might take Jeremy's more cautious approach. We arrived at a café in the little square nestling under the monumental bulk of the New Fort, built by the Venetians in 1577 to ward off invaders, where Angela and Geoffrey were waiting for us with bags of shopping at their feet. Somehow the towering walls above us seemed as unyielding as Jeremy's intransigence.

As we were driving back to the marina my phone rang.

"Hello Mrs. Jani, this is Maria, your lawyer's secretary." I swallowed hard, certain something was amiss. "Just to tell you your land is not a forest."

"Oh good," I replied feebly, a bit weak at the knees. This meant we could either cut down or move the trees on the land to enable us to build.

Sadly for Corfu the law states that olive trees, often many hundreds or even thousands of years old, may be cut down and uprooted with impunity; indeed their very presence on any land is an indication that building permission will most likely be forthcoming. I was determined that none of 'our' olives would be sacrificed, instead we would carefully dig them up, wrap the root ball tenderly in wet sackcloth and place them under the shade of other trees until we could re-locate them. One morning I had counted every one of the seventy-two venerable trees and from that moment I felt they were my friends, guardians of the land; their fate would not be, as it was for so many others from Corfu, to fuel the pizza ovens of Italy. By the time we had turned into the narrow lane leading to the marina I had not only become a proficient olive farmer but had found an organic alternative to chemical pesticide for my trees, harvested the first crop, cold-pressed the fruit, received an award for oil of exceptional quality and purity, stored it in elegant Italian bottles, designed artistic labels and received my first order from Fortnum & Mason.

Angela and Geoffrey still had another five days with us on board, so we took Sarava up the coast and headed for Agios Stefanos. We could see 'our' land clearly as we approached from the straits, standing at the head of its unspoilt valley of olive and cypress trees. Most of the hillsides directly above the bay had become dotted with villas over the past ten years or so; every time we sailed in for the first time each spring several more scars would have appeared among the olive trees, signifying more building work in progress. Now we were hoping to add our own blemish, although we would try our best to blend the building into its surroundings. Such development was perhaps inevitable in this attractive area of the island where no hotels or apartment blocks have been built; however the effect of these individual villas upon the landscape has been further mitigated by the minimum requirement for plot sizes, often two acres per building. The area had attracted a growing following over the past thirty years, most families returning to the same favourite houses each summer; when the pressure of bookings led inevitably to disappointment, many of the regulars decided to build their own more luxurious holiday villas instead.

* * *

The attraction of the place was not difficult to see. Kassiopi was only a five-minute drive away for the young who wanted to go out at night; they could easily return to their parents' villas in the early hours, although the one taxi in the town used to be permanently booked and would never have an empty seat between midnight and seven o'clock in the morning. By day the holidaymakers could explore the peace and tranquillity of the numerous unspoilt coves and beaches in small rented launches. Everything needed for a relaxing holiday was close at hand; as well as four small shops Agios Stefanos boasts four extremely good tavernas and two cocktail bars, all overlooking the sea. Half a dozen jetties in varying states of repair extended just far enough to accommodate small motorboats and dinghies, larger yachts usually riding at anchor within the sheltered bay. In the height of the season one jetty was occasionally used for diners, the chairs and tables balanced precariously above the water on its narrow platform. On several occasions chairs vacated too vigorously have ended up falling into the sea, although we have not yet witnessed a customer toppling in; nevertheless my children live in hope. Each establishment seems to be competing in designer chic for a Best Dressed Restaurant award, colour schemes, chairs, cushions and awnings upgraded each season in a constant game of oneupmanship.

When we first came to Corfu these tavernas were cheerfully furnished with basic white plastic chairs and tables set with gingham cloths covered in thick overcoats of clear polythene sheeting, anchored against the summer breeze with metal clips at each corner. Napkins were of the thin, totally unabsorbent variety, wedged into wooden or plastic holders or simply stuffed in a water glass. Signs were functional and unattractive, usually adorned with the insignia of the credit cards they were pleased to accept. Dribbling oil and vinegar bottles were presented in sticky red plastic stands, the salt rarely ran despite being mixed with maggot-like grains of raw rice; the décor, however unsophisticated, was nevertheless charming and the food and service exceptional. The produce was fresh, cooked to order over charcoal or gently oven-baked for many hours; the aromas of cinnamon rich *stifhado*, oregano and rosemary infused *kleftiko*, pork chops, freshly caught sea bream, sea bass, and swordfish wafting across the water often proving too strong a temptation for many passing boats. One side of the bay was wooded, the other protected by a long, untouched headland beneath which a narrow beach with a dozen sunbeds and umbrellas stretched from the shade of two enormous eucalyptus trees towards the rocky promontory.

Out in the channel boats were always passing by, sometimes filling the frame as they headed north to the Adriatic or south to the islands; stately ferries, cruise liners and superyachts of the rich and famous swept past at intervals providing a constantly changing scene. Basking in the heat haze across the straits lay the barren, dusty-pink hills and mountains of Albania, their contours resembling folds of elephant skin bristling with a three-day growth of dark stubble. Up in the thyme-scented hills and high on the promontories of North East Corfu, half hidden amongst the houses of more ordinary folk, nestled the holiday villas of millionaires and aristocrats; as befitted their royal and stellar guests, their privacy was protected by high walls, dense hedges and heavy iron gates. During the summer months the owners of these houses or their staff popped down to the little supermarket every morning as soon as the English broadsheets had arrived from Corfu Town; blowing in the breeze on the wall behind the till, the scrappy newspaper order forms read like entries from Burke's. Even earlier each morning the race for fresh chocolate croissants from the tiny shop by devoted parents rivalled the stereotype of fanatical Germans bagging the sunbeds by hotel pools the world over. Every year the little village featured in the travel sections of at least one of the glossy fashion magazines or weekend supplements, some of whose journalists could actually have been there, although others obviously had not; it had perhaps been one of the first to acquire the dubious nickname of Kensington-on-Sea, which has unfortunately stuck like glue with many Brits who still use the Italian variation of its name, because they find the pronunciation easier than the Greek: 'It's San Stefarno, Darling', although 'San Stef' is even simpler for those suffering from the muscle paralysing effects of Botox.

The residents of this hamlet were friendly, generous, cheerful, and tolerant of all visitors; the same charm was dispensed equally to great and the good, to the quiet majority and even to the very occasional undesirables who dropped in. Luckily for everyone else the less respectful tourists rarely made a return trip; it was all too quiet and peaceful for them and their loutish manners did not go down well. However the locals still managed to treat them with a cool patience; it was the onlookers who got angry, particularly if the offending party were fellow countrymen. On one occasion I was enjoying a morning coffee on the waterfront, the few other customers enjoying the tranquillity from comfortable cane armchairs, reading papers, writing postcards or simply gazing out to sea. A group of young lads arrived, carrying rucksacks, filling the place with their loud banter and the clatter of chairs carelessly dragged to accommodate them around two tables. The waiter came to take their order.

"*Kalimera*," he smiled. No reply. He tried again in English, "Good morning, can I help you?"

Still no reply as they stared at their menus without looking up while the waiter stood quietly, pencil poised over his notebook.

"Ten beers," one of them eventually managed.

Incandescent, I waited until their drinks arrived; naturally there was no acknowledgement from the party.

"Excuse me," I began, " Do you speak English?"

The one nearest me looked up as the others stopped talking and glowered at me.

"Ya," he replied, in a distinctly foreign accent.

"Try saying please and thank you next time. Good manners cost nothing, after all."

A hush had fallen over the café and I was gratified that the boys were now rather subdued and looking, to my absolute amazement, rather sheepish. I had been expecting a torrent of abuse, if not a punch on the nose. I returned to my post-cards, a study of composure, but my hand was shaking too much to write and my knees were knocking under the table. I was very relieved when they left, having hastily downed their beers in silence. Just as I was gathering my things to return to the boat, another coffee and a glass of local brandy appeared unexpectedly on the table in front of me. I looked up enquiringly at the handsome young waiter.

"On the house," he grinned.

* * *

It is harder to subdue a woman than to tame any wild beast.

Aristophanes

Rounding the point Sarava edged gently into Agios Stefanos, weaving her considerable width between a dozen smaller craft at anchor. Suddenly Geoffrey let out a gasp, raising the binoculars once more to his eyes. On the smooth, flat rocks at the mouth of the bay were some scantily clad girls, semi-naturists actually, as their bottom halves were covered. They were being discreet, well away from the families with children on the beach and were only visible to passing boats. Although a little older than Jeremy and with three grown-up children, Geoffrey had led a more conventional and sheltered life. He was a true gentleman, charmingly old fashioned, kind and – given his illustrious forebears – infuriatingly modest.

"What ever's the matter, Geoffrey? What have you seen?" I asked, certain it was not the sun worshippers, so commonplace all over the world.

"Those girls!" he spluttered, raising the binoculars once more as he struggled for words that would give no offence. "They're wearing *topless bathing trunks!*"

Jeremy, Angela and I collapsed into helpless laughter at such a quaint turn of phrase, instantly conjuring up images of hundreds of empty clothes hangers dangling from display stands amongst the aisles of John Lewis, each rack promoting the latest range of naturist attire – *Invisible Brazilian Styling, Cool and Unrestricting to Wear*, or perhaps *Lighter than a Second Skin*. All would of course be prominently arranged in the exclusive *Emperor's New Clothes* department.

"Oh Geoffrey!" exclaimed Angela. "You are hopeless!"

In her younger days a Fleet Street photographer and journalist, Angela by contrast was extremely up to date with everything. Despite years living at their rambling family seat buried in the heart of the Devonshire countryside, where she kept ponies for her children, bred Jacob sheep and Cavalier King Charles Spaniels – Burberry being an example – she had not let the current trends pass her by. Nevertheless their first visit to Sarava some years earlier had also caused mutual amusement at the expense of their holiday packing list. Both seasoned English Channel sailors they had once chartered a small flotilla boat from Levkas at the tail end of a long distant summer; the weather had been unkind and the little boat leaked like a sieve for the duration of their week's holiday, after which they returned home with the first twinges of rheumatism and suitcases full of clothes covered with exotically hairy mould. Thus forewarned they had stepped from the plane at Corfu airport into the torpor of an August heatwave for their holiday on Sarava. It was not long before we discovered that Geoffrey – whose forbears had roamed uncharted oceans and claimed entire countries for Queen and country – had packed oilskins, sou'westers, woolly jumpers and socks, Oxford shirts, thermal vests, twill trousers and a hot-water-bottle, all wrapped in quantities of black bin liners to keep the salt water from soaking everything. We gently explained that Sarava did not leak, unlike Sir Edward Heath's yacht, *Morning Cloud*, which had moored alongside us in Bayona in 1980; her crew had delighted in telling us her nickname was *Morning Sponge*.

Andreas, the youngest waiter from Kaparelli taverna, came running along the rickety pontoon, beckoning Sarava in a frenzy of obscure semaphore to her usual mooring space. Geoffrey, still vaguely distracted by his close encounter with the semi-nudists, threw a line which Andreas deftly caught, looped through the mooring strop and threw back again. Jeremy manoeuvred Sarava into position while Angela and I hung fenders over the sides. Wearing only swimsuits and sarongs, the chaps in short-sleeved shirts and shorts, we disembarked and settled at a shaded table set right at the water's edge, where Andreas, Theodore or Marianna had already anticipated our order for supercooled bottles of dry Boutari rosé and fizzy water. Burberry waded delicately into the shallow water, his lead fully extended, and stood up to his chin in the lukewarm sea with all his silky hair and long, curly King Charles Cavalier ears floating around him like a cloud of sea-fern. Kostas, the mercurial owner of the taverna, bustled up to us, eyes sparkling almost as much as the heavy gold chain around his neck. His accent was a delicious Greek concoction reflecting the years he had spent in Italy and Melbourne.

"How's it-a goings? You has-a the land?" he asked, full of interest and concern that everything was proceeding correctly. The island's jungle drums never missed a beat, so it came as no surprise that he knew of our impending purchase.

"It goes well so far, but we have our fingers crossed, Kosta," Jeremy replied, now slightly more enthusiastic about the whole idea.

The little inlet of Agios Stefanos can get too crowded for Sarava to anchor safely in high summer, when charter yachts mill around like dodgem cars. During our first full summer in the Ionian Kostas had noticed Sarava's fruitless search for enough space to swing at anchor and had beckoned us towards the little jetty in front of his taverna, where the shallow water could accommodate our large catamaran's deceptively meagre draft without grounding. A sign on his jetty offered free water for yachts, a great rarity, as well as delicious traditional recipes; naturally we had felt obliged to eat at one of Kostas' tables on that first visit and since then, after countless breakfasts, lunches and dinners, the place felt like a second home. The other excellent tavernas all have a loyal and well-deserved following, but Kostas and his staff have earned the lion's share of our patronage since that day.

Next morning my phone rang, disturbing the peace with its urgent tone. It was Sotiris.

"Jani, I sorry to tells you bad news," he began in a sombre voice. "But I think you losing the land."

He went on to explain that our English competitor had secured the land by paying a very large deposit. My heart sank, thinking we had lost our chance to buy the land by just a week. Not knowing what to do with myself, I left the boat and went for a coffee at Kostas' taverna to ponder what, if anything, could be done. I felt there had to be a way to prevent it all grinding to a halt after we had been so close to success. Soon Kostas came over to wish me *kalimera* and enquire after my health.

"I feel awful," I confided. "I've just been told we have lost the land we wanted."

"No, impossibles! Come with-a me," he commanded, having listened briefly to my news. I followed him to his office, a small desk with a till and a telephone next to the kitchens.

"*Kathiste* Mrs. Jani."

Obediently I sat opposite him and read out the correct contact number for the owner of the land, which he promptly dialled. When it was answered he shot out a stream of Greek as loud and rapid as machine-gun fire. I could only understand one word in five, so fast and furious was the conversation. After less than a minute he barked a curt goodbye and slammed down the receiver and smiled at me.

"No, he has not-a the deposit. The land is-a still for sell"

"Oh, thank goodness!" I said.

"But you has-a to be quick, it is a true another men want-a to buy it and many mores are interesting."

I asked him if he knew the land owner.

"Sure, we are friends since many years, since-a the school. I tells him not-a to sell this-a land to anybodies else because you wants-a to buy it it and-a you are my friends. I tells him the other mans is-a too greedy and anyways I don't like his-a face. Also I tells him to take ten thousand-a euro less from you. He will do as I ask."

"I can't believe it! Thank you so much, Kosta, *efharisto para poli*. What is this man's name?"

"Kostas," replied Kostas.

I dashed back to the boat and asked Jeremy to call the owner to confirm our intention to pay the deposit, forgetting that we would need to transfer the funds from England.

"With the best will in the world the money wouldn't arrive here until the end of next week," he surmised. "In the meantime we would have to open a Greek bank account, which could take another week, so there's little point in calling."

"It's just a phone call; it'll buy us more time and look as if we intend to proceed," I retorted, reading out the telephone number.

A moment later, suddenly galvanised, Jeremy went below to the chart table; picking up Sarava's sailing log and flicking through it until he found the page where some useful phone numbers were scrawled.

"What did you say is this chap's telephone number?" he asked suspiciously.

I looked at my mobile phone and read it out to him again.

"Aha! I thought so!" he said triumphantly.

"What?"

"It's the fellow who owns the garage just outside Kassiopi, a most helpful sort. He's the one who brings his little tanker down to the harbour to re-fuel us sometimes ... I thought I recognised that number. I'll give him a call".

"Well there you are then, you already know him," I said delightedly in utter amazement.

Somehow this link between them had changed everything. No longer was this man some anonymous slippery customer, he was Kostas the Garage, purveyor of diesel to Sarava. Unaccountably this seemed to give Jeremy confidence; the hitherto faceless olive farmer selling a piece of land to susceptible and ignorant foreigners was in fact one of Daddy's boyfriends, as Miranda called them, one of a small army of local specialists from all over the Ionian who were of use to the boat in one way or another. Sarava's log was littered with their names, numbers and appropriate references to their skills or wares; they were a gang of cronies who could spend hours gossiping with Jeremy about anything

At the helm in a thunderstorm, mid-Biscay – July 1980 …

… Louis Féraud fashion show, Nicosia Hilton, seven weeks later

Preparing for our honeymoon voyage from Salcombe to Cyprus – May 1980

Photo shoots, Cyprus – 1980

The fortified finca, La Abubilla, Jesús Pobre, seen from the casita

Spain 1988

Ashore from Seahawk at Espalmador, Ibiza

Goodbye to all that …

1997

… hello to all this

Greek Easter on the Espianada, Corfu Town

A whole lotta pot

The 'Big Episode' at Stavros, Corfu
Dinner at Porto, Kassiopi

View from The Lion House over the Corfu Straits to Albania

Sarava at Voutoumi, Antipaxos

Boarding Golden Odyssey

Her tender, Golden Shadow complete with seaplane

Rory and Miranda on watch and at the helm

Early Spring, Corfu Town …

… only a little shopping today

Sun drying tomatoes for 'Kleferti"

Burberry impatient to board the ferry from Venice to Corfu

Antonia's Baptism   *Angelos and Antonia on Sarava*

Watercolours of Caper stem and Sea Daffodil   ©Jani Tully Chaplin

Yiannis the faithful 'taxidzis'

Naughty George

A stop at Lake Garda

Sarava at Agios Stefanos

Calamitous canyon at The Lion House

The Twig Tree in spring and its first summer

Sailing to Paxos

Dressed for inter-course shopping, Gaios

Farewell

from village winemaking techniques to favoured ways of catching eels. Along with the aforementioned Andreas the Antifouling and Petros the Paint was Vangelis the Fridge, Dionysios the Slipway and Fotis the Welder. In one nameless mainland port there is Haris the Water, who dispenses brackish, brown water to any unwary boat from an antiquated green bowser truck which cruises slowly along the quayside like a kerb-crawler; somewhat disingenuously *Fresh Mountain Water for Boats* adorns the side of his truck in scruffy script.

But Kostas the Garage was an old acquaintance of Jeremy's. He was a well known member of the Kassiopi community, a local character with a thriving business and a handsome younger son the same age as Rory. Mario helped in the family firm when he was not at school, one of his tasks being to wash cars. With a dribbling hose and brush he would work at top speed in the blazing sun, as much sweat running off him as the hose; meanwhile the customers sat in air-conditioned comfort inside their vehicles, engines running, windows firmly shut, until the job was done. Because of his speed and efficiency Jeremy had christened him Super Mario, a name which really suited his short, spiky, dark hair and gleaming white teeth. The following year Mario would begin his two years of compulsory National Service on the mainland; most tragically it was his lot to be hit by a stray bullet during an exercise and killed instantly. He was just eighteen.

Jeremy made the long awaited call and arranged to meet Kostas the Garage; within the hour we were driving onto his forecourt. I had never seen a filling station that could be described as attractive, let alone pretty, but this was Corfu after all, where people usually took pride in their property whether private or commercial, mansion or maisonette. Beds of outsize exotic flowers and plants sheltered the garage from the main road; vermilion canna lilies, butter yellow chrysanthemums, stocks, red roses, scarlet hibiscus, michaelmas daisies and the bright orange flowers of campsis vine disguised the unsightly petrol company signs and lined the entrance, which could equally have been the approach to a luxury hotel. Crimson bougainvillea intertwined with sweetly scented jasmine and powder blue plumbago, covering the little shed which housed the till, formed a shady canopy under which customers in need of refreshment could sit on red plastic chairs and enjoy a cold drink from the large refrigerator cabinet.

A small, wiry man hurried across to us, his brown face lit up by a wide grin. True he could have benefited from some cosmetic dentistry, but his manner and charm belied his appearance; although sporting a two-day silver stubble, and dressed as he was for work in torn trousers and a faded tee-shirt artistically decorated with oil stains, he bowed gallantly over my hand as Jeremy introduced us, as suave and debonair as James Bond.

"Madam, I am honoured," he crooned, keeping hold of my hand. "You are most welcome."

Jeremy broached the subject of the land as Kostas' smile grew broader. He moved closer to me, still grasping my hand in his; he was thrilled we were interested in his land and was in expansive mood. It was true, he said earnestly, that many people were after this exceptional piece of land, mostly English. He only wanted English people to buy it – unsurprisingly perhaps as we were English.

"I not selling to French or Americans ... Never to Germans ..."

Jeremy tried to interrupt him from recounting his entire hit list.

"The Holland peoples I like ... But I not selling to Italians or..."

"Yes Kosta, we understand, but could you wait a few days for us to arrange for the deposit to be sent from England?" inquired Jeremy, explaining that we did not yet have a bank account in Corfu and certainly did not keep such lavish amounts of cash on board.

"Certainly, for you of course. But you musts be quick," he replied.

His arm was now around my shoulders as he leant across me at an alarming angle to shake Jeremy's hand, taking me with him. It was as hot as a furnace on the forecourt, even under the canopy, and my anti-perspirant was fighting bravely with the heat; Kostas' deodorant had long since given up the struggle. I complimented him on his flower-beds and assured him that I would try to make the land beautiful as well as taking care of the olive trees. The credit was all due to his wife, he assured me; I hoped Mrs. Kostas could give me some tips on Greek gardening.

Why do so many important things happen over a weekend? It was Friday, the banks in England would already be closed and we could do nothing until first thing on Monday morning; even then the transfer would not materialise in our solicitor's account before the following weekend. I was not entirely convinced that Kostas the Garage would be prepared to wait that long.

During supper that evening at his taverna, Kostas was eager to find out how we had got on with our negotiations; we told him about the enforced delay in obtaining the deposit, just to keep him in the picture.

"No problem. I lend-a you the money," he said without a moment's hesitation.

"Gosh, no, we couldn't possibly accept!" said Jeremy in astonishment.

"Why not? It's easys for me. I meet-a you early Monday morning in Corfu Town, say nine o'clock, I give-a you the moneys and you gives it to the lawyers. Done!" he brushed his hands together as if dusting off flour and strode back towards the kitchens.

"I think he means it," said Jeremy incredulously.

I am convinced I must have been Greek in a former life as I find their attitude and way of thinking perfectly normal and very akin to mine; I can often anticipate their words or actions and had half expected Kostas' spontaneous reaction to our problem. Although very astute most of the time, in matters of local intrigue, gossip or customs I sometimes have to explain things to Jeremy when he has not quite grasped what it going on.

"Of course he means it and he'll be insulted if you don't accept his offer. *And* we could lose the land," I retorted.

"How absolutely staggering! Can you imagine this happening in England? It's difficult enough there to get your local restaurateur to give you the time of day or even acknowledge your existence. Of course we'd be able to repay him in a couple of days … But no, I really don't think we can accept."

"Well you're *not* in England and if you're going to live in Greece you had better get used to their ways and *accept graciously*." I was getting cross again; it was such a genuine and generous offer. How could we refuse?

At nine-o-clock on Monday morning we met Kostas as arranged at Serrano, a convivial coffee shop discreetly off the beaten path beyond the old Town Hall, ordering our regular 'town' breakfast of coffee, fresh orange juice and toasted cheese sandwiches. A shabby plastic supermarket carrier bag containing fat wads of twenty, fifty and one hundred euro notes, already counted into bundles of five thousand each, was nestling on the table amongst the coffee cups and glasses. Kostas got up to leave, hurriedly draining his glass of ouzo and apologising for needing to continue with his morning's shopping for the taverna.

"Don't you want a receipt for this, Kosta?" Jeremy asked, pointing to the bag of cash; but Kostas was already half way out of the *kafenion*, waving dismissively over his shoulder. To add to our embarrassment, when our own breakfast arrived we discovered he had already paid the tab.

A short walk through the old Jewish quarter with our bag of swag brought us once more to our solicitor's office. A memorandum was drafted detailing our right to reclaim the deposit in the event of any problem with the title or building rights of the land; in the meantime we could, said Angel Gabriel, consider ourselves the proud new owners of land at Leondari. The bag of cash was handed over as our formal deposit – this time with a written receipt. As soon as we arrived back at the marina I climbed into the driver's seat as Jeremy vacated it.

"What are you doing?" he asked, "It's after one, I thought we were going to have lunch and then sail up to Othoni."

"I have something to do first," I replied, speeding away in a cloud of dust before he had time to object.

As the rest of Corfu slept, through the hottest part of the day, I followed the deserted coast road until I reached Sinies. Swinging the car off towards the village of Eleourgia I was elated at the thought that this was now the village where we would soon buy fresh bread every morning, baked by Stamos in his miniature bakery behind the *kafenion;* our milk and newspapers would come from Yiannis' little supermarket; we would collect local honey from the pastel blue painted hives of our neighbour in the olive groves.

Pulling up further down the lane, just beside the tree bearing the 'For Sale' sign, I jumped out; the fierce heat of mid-day hit me like a brick wall after the chill of the air-conditioned Jeep. Throwing caution to the non-existent wind I grabbed the sign and pulled; the higher branches of the ancient olive tree shivered slightly, but it would not yield. My next effort was more successful, wiggling the board vigorously as I tugged until the sign popped out of the trunk, nearly sending me over backwards onto the road. Feeling like a thief I hurled it into the boot, imagining someone was going to pounce and arrest me at any moment. On the way down the twisting hill to Agios Stefanos I consoled myself that the land was as good as sold now. I was perfectly entitled to remove the sign: from this day on the land was ours.

* * *

Dreams do come true, if only you wish hard enough.

J. M. Barrie

"You want I introducing you to architect friend of mine?" was a question that had followed us around like a dog's tail since word of our impending land purchase had spread at the end of that summer. The scale of Corfiot hospitality – already embarrassingly generous – reached epidemic level as friends in turn pressed *definitely the best architect on the island* upon us; we must have met partners from every practice in Corfu, as well as two from Athens and Ioannina. Cynics might suggest that motives for this show of concern were not entirely altruistic, but generally we decided, at worst, that old favours were being returned. Innocent invitations to dinner with friends in town would invariably be preceded by mysterious escorted detours along the narrow alleyways of the Cambiello or the side streets of Porta Raimonda until '*Eureka!*' some unremarkable door would miraculously swing open at our approach, revealing the swanky office of yet another architect whose vice-like handshake would drag us within. Despite our protestations lavish dinners often followed, during which the subject of our new house – a tasty morsel in the middle of the table – would be delicately sniffed at, leaving us with the twin discomforts of embarrassment and indigestion.

One evening in early September Kostas suggested he introduce us to an architect friend in his taverna. Spiro, we had been told, had offices in Thessaloniki but spent much of his time in Corfu, where he owned several substantial properties. We were slightly wary as we waited at our table for him to appear, scrutinising and dismissing likely looking, smartly dressed candidates as they approached the restaurant. Eventually Kostas ambled towards us.

" Mr. Jeremy, Mrs. Jani… here is the Spiros."

Wearing a washed-out, sludge-green sleeveless singlet, shabby maroon shorts, open sandals, sporting a walrus moustache and heavy tortoiseshell spectacles below a head of wayward greying-black hair, we took to him instantly – even if we probably wouldn't be taking any advice from him on colour schemes. Jeremy had spotted him a few minutes earlier as he got out of a battered and rusting Lancia saloon, possibly the sole survivor of an ill-judged 'eighties production run made entirely from recycled Italian olive oil tins. Conversation came easily and it soon became clear we shared a great deal in common, from mutual friends in England to a fascination with the history of the Venetian Empire. At first glance austere and even stern, his expression would flash into a broad smile beneath the soft eyes of a thoughtful and sensitive man. Here was someone we could surely have as a trusted friend, which for us was more important than a purely client orientated relationship; here was a scholar who could help us understand the unspoken mysteries of the enchanting country we so simplistically call Greece.

Although Spiro was born in Lesbos, his father was from an old Corfiot family; thus during the outrages of the civil war and the *chronia tou petrou*, the 'stone years' that followed, young Spiro was evacuated from Athens to live with an aunt in Corfu, where life was slightly less harsh than on the mainland. Like many Greeks he had been a committed Anglophile since the day the British Red Cross had delivered the first Cheddar cheese to the impoverished island, a kindness never forgotten. His father was already a decorated veteran of the battle for Crete, famous in Greece for his exploits with the British behind enemy lines, but at that time in the 1950's he was involved with the bloody battle for the soul of Greece itself. Spiro claimed to have been a champion pentathlete in his youth, only forsaking the chance of representing his country in the Olympics for an offer to study architecture – difficult to imagine now that he chain-smoked for Greece.

We had a very clear vision of the house we wanted to build; meekly we produced some plans and elevations for his perusal. Jeremy had designed three distinct structures in local village style, laid out in a shallow crescent like a triptych; the long footprint of such a plan would suit the shape of our acre of land and maximise its wonderful views. The main two-storey house was connected by a low loggia to the guest wing and swimming pool beyond; each building was of equal length, but the three roofs were set at different heights to break up the aspect of the facade.

"Of course it's only the germ of an idea ..." Jeremy muttered.

Studying it as if it were the blueprint for the Doge's Palace, Spiro frowned thoughtfully, stroking his moustache.

"*Si, nai, einai poli* beautiful." he mused.

We quickly learned that Spiro subconsciously used an interesting blend of English and Greek in the same sentence, with the odd smattering of Italian acquired whilst studying architecture in Venice during his youth; evidently he had not picked up the Italian fashion sense at the same time. Sipping black tea and smoking incessantly, Spiro pointed out the various differences between building techniques in England and Greece; the construction had to withstand earthquakes, not that Corfu was directly on a fault line, he hurriedly explained. It was important to make sure the ceilings were high enough for the air to circulate as the summers were hot; moreover much consideration should be given to verandahs and their effect upon the balance struck between light and shade within the house. I broached the subject of plumbing and drains; I did not want to employ the revolting practice of putting used paper in a plastic bin beside the loo, as was the custom in all the lavatories of Corfu, which were in the habit of blocking regularly due to poorly set pipes. I certainly did not wish to risk any repetition of the many apocryphal stories on the subject, such as the ten-year-old girl returning delightedly from a taverna lavatory to her parents' table: 'What a swish place! They even fold the loo paper and put it in a little bin for you to use!' (Believe me, it still happens, particularly when the proper loo rolls have run out.)

"*Oxi, vevaios. Aftos einai* absolutely disgusting!" Spiro agreed. "But also, let me tell you, it is most important where you decide to put the shit pit."

This uncharacteristic indelicacy – along with some others we subsequently noticed – had obviously infiltrated his vocabulary like a computer virus via some of his more down to earth English clients. It was getting late and we felt we had covered the salient points, but we were still nervous that the fees for such a distinguished architect would be beyond our means. During the conversation Spiro had mentioned the work he had done over the years for an Englishman he spoke of as a second father; this benefactor had taken him on soon after he had qualified and thereafter Spiro had worked for this man from time to time ever since. Jeremy went pale. The man to whom he was referring was Lord Rothschild, who owned a fabulous estate less than a mile from our land. I knew precisely what Jeremy was thinking: Spiro was accustomed to working for clients without budgets and where money was no object. Surely everything he would suggest for the house would be top drawer, top quality and top dollar; however we had hoped to use local materials wherever possible, not only for economy but because we wanted the house to reflect the traditional Corfiot style.

"Spiro, you must understand that our budget won't stretch to such things as elaborate imported sanitary ware, Italian marble or German kitchen equipment," Jeremy pointed out.

I had really taken to Spiro and was desperately hoping we would be able to employ his services; we seemed to be on the same wavelength in so many ways. Unlike other architects we had met, who barely deigned to speak to me, a mere woman, he appreciated my point of view and listened to my queries and suggestions intently. *Nai, nai, yes, she is right,* he would often say. If only we could impress upon him that we were not part of the jet-set who were building their third or fourth holiday villa, rather that we wanted a house for all seasons which would be our main home. As we got up from the table Spiro answered Jeremy.

"I agree, we have many good things on this island and I too like to use local materials. When Jacob Rothschild wanted Italian stone for some paths I said to him 'don't buy those which are so expensive, let me take you to see such ones quarried in Corfu; they are just as good, probably better as they are not slipping when wet.' So he came with me and bought the local stone at quarter the price. Even with so much money I do not like to waste it and he was very grateful for the saving, always asking my advice before he buy these things."

Unwittingly Spiro had just clinched the deal. He had penetrated the very core of Jeremy's being; here was a man after his own heart, not miserly but careful with finances; a practical and thrifty man who could not bear to waste money. Only much later would we discover that Spiro was a delusional fantasist.

"Let's have another drink to celebrate," Jeremy suggested. "Shall we see if Kostas has any bubbly on ice?"

"Lovely," I said, we must drink to meeting you, Spiro!"

"*Oxi efharisto*, not for me," Spiro interjected. "I do not drink. *Tha paro ena* Coca Cola, please."

That's game, set and match, I thought to myself.

Chapter Seven
Robbers, Reprobates and Rewards

Sometimes good things fall apart so better things can fall together.

Marilyn Monroe

Rory and Miranda had flown back to England ahead of us in time to begin their respective autumn terms. Jeremy and I spent the following day emptying and cleaning fridges, stripping beds, stowing the bikes, deck cushions and other paraphernalia inside; we would be back on board within seven weeks and wanted to return to a clean boat. Unluckily the weather changed just in time for our departure back to England; torrential rain hammered on Sarava's roof, waking us long before our alarm was due to go off at five in the morning. Thunder rumbled overhead and Burberry growled sleepily in retaliation from the bottom of our bed.

"Oh Lord, that's just what we need!" I moaned to Jeremy as he climbed out of bed to make tea.

"How on earth are we going to get all our luggage up to the car in this? Everything will get soaked, then it will all go mouldy during the drive back to England," I said.

"I should have taken it all up last night after we'd taken the children to the airport," he replied sullenly from the galley upstairs.

There was still the matter of a substantial quantity of cash to be resolved between us. Jeremy had drawn out seventy thousand euros the day before to cover various bills connected with the land, but he had been left with eight thousand in cash that were not required. Although usually strapped for more than twenty pounds about his person, he had become all too blasé about the necessity of carrying colossal sums of cash since our arrival in Corfu, as most bills could only be settled in cash at that time. The banks had long since closed for the weekend after his meetings with Spiro and the notary; now we were unsure whether the residual wad of notes would be safer taken home to England or left aboard Sarava. I suggested the ingenious cubby hole beneath my dressing table where I normally kept my jewellery, whereas Jeremy preferred to take it with us in his man-bag. The discussion had quickly turned into a minor domestic incident as I reminded him how often he had either driven off with his bag on the roof of the car, or had left it variously in a restaurant, train or aircraft, or thrown it away with the rubbish, or dropped it into the sea and even down a lavatory pan. Grudgingly he eventually agreed to leave the cash in the cubby hole, although still muttering that it would be safer with us.

Jeremy stuffed our holdalls into bin-liners while I dressed, first into my normal summer clothes and then into a complete layer of waterproofs including jacket, trousers, sou'wester and rubber boots; it was like being in a sauna. Despite the monsoon rain and light-ning the outside temperature was still tropical; inside the boat it was stifling, the air conditioning having already been decommissioned. I struggled across our passerelle in the pitch darkness of a power cut, momentarily illuminated by flashes of lightning, with my face-case and handbag slung over one shoulder and Burberry half tucked inside my jacket under the other arm; Jeremy followed behind, laden with canvas holdalls. Steam was literally rising from all of us as we finally reached the car. We stripped off our wet outer garments and I gave Burberry a rub down with a towel, which convinced him he had just suffered the indignity of a bath and therefore felt obliged to scuttle up and down the back seat rubbing his face vigorously on our freshly stowed luggage. Waving a sad goodbye to the security guard on night duty at the gates of the marina we headed for the port in Corfu Town.

Under a leaden dawn sky as the *Ariadne Palace* steamed serenely up the Corfu Channel, we stood on deck following the coast with our eyes and our hearts, recognising every bay, cove, inlet and prom-ontory; each tiny part of this wonderful island held its own precious memory. It was always so hard to leave.

"Look that's where we went snorkelling ... barbecued that delicious swordfish ... there's Philippos out fishing ... George's village ... that enormous house owned by the Australian lady who bought four of my paintings ... the Agnelli's villa ... St. Arsenios' Shrine where I found those fabulous pebbles ... there's Agni – let's wave to them ... the Rothschilds have gone, their flag's not flying."

Suddenly our land was in view, a green swathe of olive trees high above the sea.

"Quick, take a photo!" I said. Jeremy was already aiming the camera and waiting with the eye of a professional for a break in the clouds.

"Now!" I pleaded. The ferry was moving deceptively fast and I could see the moment being lost.

"Got it!" he said, lowering the camera and putting his arm around me tightly.

We stood side-by-side in companionable silence, Burberry cuddled in my arms, watching Leondari slip past and disappear behind the headland of Agios Stefanos as our ship headed up into the Adriatic. Without speaking we knew each other's thoughts. We were leaving our beloved Corfu once more, but this time it was different; when we next returned we would be coming home.

Twenty-four hours later our ferry glided through the lagoon towards Venice in the misty pink half light of an early September morning. I stood in front of the picture window in our cabin as I was dressing, not wanting to miss a single minute of the perfect Canaletto views sliding in and out of the frame as if in slow motion. I have always adored gondolas; first seen in paintings, on television or in films, then later miraculously in real life, they always give me goose pimples. My eyes were following the progress of the stately gondolas on the watery horizon when my attention was suddenly drawn to a commotion in the canal just below my window. Standing in three rocking gondolas were a dozen young trainee gondoliers. Waving and gesticulating in my direction with their oars held high, I knew they were apprentices as they were casually dressed in faded jeans and tee-shirts, unlike the fully fledged gondolieri who proudly sport the gorgeous, distinctive costume synonymous with Venetian culture. They were obviously shouting and laughing, although I couldn't hear them above the rumble of the ferry engines. Their white teeth flashed in their sun-tanned faces as they looked straight up at me and I waved back cheer-fully; what a charming way to welcome us to Venice I thought. At that precise moment Jeremy came out of the bathroom.

"My God! come away from the window!" he shouted. "Who on earth are you waving at?" I reassured him that it was fine, I was just waving at some sweet young lads who were learning how to gondol.

"But look what you're wearing!" he yelled. I had been so carried away by the romance of Venice at dawn and the delightful young chaps that I had completely forgotten I was only in my bra and pants. I waved a fond farewell to the lovely boys as they slipped out of sight. I threw Jeremy a parting shot, just to have the last word.

"Good job I had my best underwear on then."

Over breakfast in the restaurant, we watched the iconic landmarks glide slowly past our window table; the elegant little bridges, the rows of slim gondolas bobbing gently at their moorings, the fairytale façades of the Doge's Palace, the tall column from which the winged lion guards St. Mark's Square, the ornate pearl white Basilica di Santa Maria and the glowering Chiesa dello Spirito Santo.

By ten-o-clock we were speeding up the motorway towards Milan and the Swiss border, but it was not long before I felt the need for a comfort stop; thus it was at the Liminella service station, near Padua, that Jeremy waited in the car for me. Our Jeep was often prone to overheating if the air conditioning was kept running whilst stationary; the September sun was by now blazing through the windscreen and soon Jeremy needed to open his door. Moments later a smartly dressed man approached him and pointed to the rear window, where Burberry was asleep on top of our luggage. Beckoning Jeremy towards the boot he enquired in broken English about the breed of our dog; but having taken two paces towards the man Jeremy smelt a rat and quickly got back into the car, locking the doors as he did so and feeling rather pleased with himself to have foiled the scoundrel. Meanwhile a group of youngsters had been playing in the car park and when a scruffy urchin with a football momentarily appeared at the passenger window Jeremy took no account of it; indeed he thought too little of the entire incident to mention anything to me when I returned to the car.

Three hours later, well on our way to the Gotthard Tunnel, we stopped for fuel and a late lunch in Switzerland. But where was Jeremy's man-bag? A long and thorough search of the car revealed nothing; our passports, driving licences, bank and credit cards had vanished with it.

"What have you done with it this time, Jeremy?" I asked icily. "Think!"

"Well, there was this man," he began hesitantly. "He distracted me … But I was only out of the car for a couple of seconds and then …"

"So that's it I suppose; our passports and credit cards all gone. How could you be so idiotic!"

"It's worse than that, darling," he replied, staring wistfully through the window at distant patches of tranquil, emerald green pasture where cattle grazed contentedly high on the mountainsides above us.

"Oh no, no. Oh God, please tell me we haven't just lost eight thousand euros … Tell me you left the cash on Sarava, Jeremy! AS I TOLD YOU TO!"

Gradually the events at the service station dawned on Jeremy. He slowly explained how the Italian spiv's practiced eye must have spotted his man-bag in its usual place beneath his knees in the footwell when the door was open. Then, instructing a young accomplice to crawl underneath the Jeep, the rogue had managed to divert Jeremy's attention for the pair of seconds needed for the young rapscallion to hook his arm over the door sill, snatch the bag and roll swiftly to the other side of the car. Jeremy had spotted the child as he got to his feet by the passenger door, but had blithely assumed he was fetching a stray football. How simply and perfectly he had been hoodwinked!

Oblivious to the robbery until this moment, we had been waved through the border control into Switzerland without being required to show our passports – thanks to the annual Swiss road-toll carnet attached to our windscreen. Now we found ourselves in the only extra-Schengen country in western Europe, a hundred miles shy of the French border where our passports would undoubtedly be requested by the douaniers. Furthermore we had no money apart from an ash-tray full of coins in several denominations, no bank or credit cards – all our shared cards having been cancelled by one call to Sentinel – and, with the exception of Burberry's pet passport and the Jeep's documents, no identification of any kind.

Then out of the blue we were thrown two lifelines by the Fates. First, Jeremy remembered the two hundred-euro note kept for emergencies in the windscreen visor, while I extricated the fifty-euro note I always kept tucked in my bra for emergencies – something my mother had taught me to do when I was a teenager, albeit with a ten-pound note in those days which would get me safely home from anywhere in England. Since this burglary I have always kept my credit card inside my bra – something my closest girlfriends will confirm. A robber would have to wrestle me to the ground to get it, moreover on a chilly day it is lovely and warm when I use it.

With the Jeep's tank once more replenished we set off for the border with sweaty palms and racing hearts, certain we should soon be interned in Basle as illegal aliens. My primary concern was whether the Swiss prison authorities would allow Burberry into my cell: I would just have to threaten to telephone the Queen if they objected. Our combined heart rates scaled new heights as we gradually edged up the queue in the tunnel beneath the Rhine towards the frontier control. I hastily covered Burberry with a blanket as he snored contentedly in the footwell, just in case his presence attracted the unwanted attention of the guards, who would then discover we had no passports and, in Jeremy's case, no driving licence. At this point we could barely breathe, but our second pardon was about to be granted. The car in front of us, a scruffy hatchback with six swarthy gentlemen crammed inside, was summarily flagged to one side and immediately pounced upon by every guard and customs officer at the border. Miraculously the barrier opened in front of us. Pedal to the floor we accelerated into France, anxiously scanning the car's mirrors for the blue lights of pursuing gendarmerie and fervently praying there would be no road block awaiting us at the next toll.

Our leisurely itinerary through France – a stop in a delightful *pension* set in the medieval charm of Riquewhir, a second night at Monsieur Chandon's former mansion in Epernay, where Burberry would always be spoilt with tasty morsels from the kitchens, and a further night amidst the Toile de Jouy and genteel dilapidation of a chateau near Recques-sur-Hem – had turned into a headlong dash towards the English Channel. By ten in the evening we could drive no further and decided to stop in Reims, stupidly forgetting the *vendange* was in full swing. There was not a room to be had at any price; even the Go-hotel website was telling us to go to hell. We pressed on gamely until matchsticks would no longer support our drooping eyelids, eventually swerving precipitately off the road at the sight of distant bright lights on the outskirts of some nameless, drab industrial zone beside the A26.

The lights, we soon discovered, belonged to a roadhouse by the name of Mr Bed. Delirious with drowsiness by this time, it took a few minutes in the rain to work out that Mr Bed did not boast a night porter; indeed it surely did not boast a day porter. Instead a pre-payment machine in the wall beside the only door in the building obligingly swallowed a fifty euro note and regurgitated some change and an entry code for our room. The hermetically sealed building gave a faint shudder as the door hissed opened automatically, introducing us to the overpowering stench of world-class body odour, stale tobacco and sweaty trainers. Faintly luminous signs directed us over sticky corridor carpet to our room; mercifully we never would see the place in daylight.

One glance around the bedroom, dimly lit by a pair of glow worms with libido issues, confirmed our worst fears. Too terrified to turn down the beds, for fear of what might be lurking on the sheets, Burberry and I collapsed painfully onto the shabby coverlet on one of the metal-framed beds as Jeremy inspected the bathroom; it consisted of a freestanding, moulded plastic cubicle barely more accommodating than a telephone box. Within this portaloo lurked a shower with no rose, a minute folding basin scorched with fag end burns, a seatless lavatory pan bereft of loo paper and one grimy towel the size of a pygmy's modesty flap.

Fully dressed, the two of us slept fitfully for an hour or so until our aching joints lost the battle with the boilerplate mattress. Long before daybreak we skulked out of Mr Bed and started northwards once more, wishing we had never vacated the comfort of the Jeep's deep leather seats. Somehow we needed to obtain temporary passports before we could cross the Channel; we knew Lille slightly and decided to try our luck with the British Consulate there. It was an inspired choice. The Vice Consul was a charming, educated lady who sized up our situation in a flash; ignoring the various proscriptive signs she ushered us through the grilled security doors into her fragrant, elegantly furnished inner sanctum, where we could wash and freshen up. The ladies loo contained every item of feminine toilette a weary traveller might need, nevertheless she asked me if there was anything else I needed. Soon her assistant brought a tray of tea and biscuits for us and a bowl of water for Burberry to an antique coffee table adorned with a crystal bowl of fresh flowers, set beneath the comforting radiance of Her Majesty's portrait. After a quick phone call to the Home Office in London, our repatriation passports, resembling nothing so formal as a chit for the school uniform shop, were speedily issued and ferry tickets booked with the last of our euros. By the end of the day we were once again on British soil. Weeks and months later I could still catch Jeremy distractedly muttering 'eight thousand sodding euros ... the thieving bastards!' between gritted teeth.

Our journeys across Europe took a different pattern from that day on, spending the shortest possible time on Italian roads and keeping doors permanently locked whilst driving through Northern Italy. Despite all our precautions we still managed to suffer two further attempted robberies – well, three actually, if one were to include the king's ransom extorted in Venice for a 'luxurious room overlooking the canal', which turned out to be a superficially plush, dark and musty cupboard overlooking a mosquito infested ditch.

The first attempt was merely a jemmied window, which succeeded only in breaking the winding mechanism. However it forced us to crawl the remaining two hundred miles along the lorry racetrack from Milan to Venice – think Ben Hur with juggernauts – with a fully open window in thirty-eight degrees of exhaust laden heat. This particular trip was precisely five weeks after I had endured an emergency hysterectomy in Devon; without any possibility of any comfort stop for over five hours in such heat and fumes, I really thought I was going to collapse and die beside that ghastly Italian road.

The second attempt was rather more sinister. Jeremy had left me in the car with Miranda at one of the vile service stations along the road between Milan and Venice, while he bought some Prosecco and olives to enjoy in our cabin on the ferry to Corfu. Our Jeep was nosed in to the busy shop forecourt and it was only a matter of moments before a shiny, blacked out Mercedes drew up directly behind us, blocking any possibility of escape. Two suave miscreants got out and moved either side of the Jeep; the man on the passenger side put a fresh cigarette between gleaming teeth and signed to me that he needed a light. His casual manner quickly turned ugly when I refused to open the window and he immediately began to tug at the door handle; thankfully I had remembered push the central locking button as soon as Jeremy had got out. Petrified as the car rocked to the insistent tugs, I had ferreted in my handbag for anything to use in self-defence, but at that moment Miranda – whose capacity for sleep as a teenager merited a paper in The British Medical Journal – awoke from her slumbers in the back seat. Finding the other crisply besuited reprobate heaving at her own door, and quickly disabusing herself of any notion that Two Gentlemen of Verona had come calling, she coolly reached over the seat and leant on the horn until the scoundrels scampered back to their car and sped away. Oblivious to the entire episode, Jeremy had returned moments later to find me still tightly gripping my Calèche atomizer with which to perfume the hijackers into tearful submission.

Our indiscriminate contempt for Northern Italy, in particular those infamous provinces of Larceny and Perfidy, knew no bounds and made even less allowance for the many mishaps which fate bestowed so readily upon us wherever we ventured. Perhaps our scorn was further magnified by such fond memories of Calabria, San Pietro and even Sicily, where, contrary to all expectation, we had always felt heartily welcome and utterly unthreatened. These days we enter Lombardy and the Veneto with empty bladders and a brimful petrol tank.

* * *

If you decide to become a veterinary surgeon you will never grow rich, but you will have a life of endless interest and variety.

James Herriot

A new summer was upon us and another long list of friends were waiting eagerly to keep us on our toes for most of the next eight weeks. Sue, my best friend from schooldays, and her husband John were the first to arrive. They lived on a picturesque farm bordering the edge of Dartmoor, where John was a highly respected veterinary surgeon. Over the years he had diligently looked after my Yorkshire Terriers Pushkin and Chekhov, and my beautiful young Palomino Adonis, who he had miraculously brought back to soundness against all odds and all other professional opinion. Needless to say John became my hero from that moment on; Adonis continued competing successfully with me for the rest of his life. In the years left to John, no other vet was ever employed to treat any of our animals.

Sue and John were the delightful sort of guests who loved Corfu from the moment they stepped off the plane. Everything was appreciated and commented upon: the warmth, the greenness, the flowers, the people, the food and of course Sarava. It was a joy for us to show them our island. The first stop after collecting them from the airport was the open market in Corfu Town, where I needed to buy fresh supplies for the boat as we intended to head south that morning. Despite their overnight flight our friends were delighted and intrigued by the colourful array of fruit, vegetable and fish stalls, each one shaded by a small, gaily striped awning. They moved from stall to stall admiring every type of produce, exclaiming in turn at the size of the tomatoes and lemons, the vast selection of olives, the abundant fresh herbs and the unfamiliar varieties of fish. If the name of something could not be gleaned, John reverted to latin, which often had enough of a Greek root to be understood. Similarly Sue would listen intently to the Greek word for something and repeat it over and over until she had it.

With a large pot of growing mint for our Pimms, two baskets full of fruit and vegetables, some giant prawns and sea bass from the line of wet fish stalls we had nicknamed 'Fishermen's Roe', we drove back along the coast road to the marina, stopping to gather some wild jasmine on the way. As we walked down the pontoon I pointed out Sarava; they had seen photographs of course, but nothing truly compared to seeing her in the flesh, especially when Rory and Miranda had spent a day washing and polishing the salt off her. She usually managed to make quite an impression on our guests as soon as I pointed her out, although one friend had simply commented 'I gathered that'.

Our sail to Gaios was particularly special; Sue and John stood on the webbing trampolines between the bows with the children and me, hoping to catch any drops of welcome salty spray. To everyone's delight a pod of dolphins joined us, shooting alongside, leaping out of the water and criss-crossing Sarava's bows just a metre below our feet. A few nautical miles further on towards Lakka, a shoal of flying fish leapt out of the sea and flew across the surface immediately in front of the boat, their iridescent wings gleaming in the sun. This couldn't have been better planned for a visiting vet and his wife; it was as if we had personally choreographed this whole enthralling aquatic display. A couple of hours later we motored slowly and sedately into the narrow channel which winds its way from the open sea into the harbour at Gaios.

"This looks just like the River Dart," Sue remarked, pointing to the banks on our port side which were thick with oak trees, their lowest branches mirrored in the glassy surface of the tranquil water. Tiny fishing boats, painted gaily in all colours of the rainbow, were moored along the wall on the opposite side, gradually increasing in size as the depth of water allowed.

Niko, the waiter who always served us at Pan & Theo's taverna, came running across the road to the quayside. Sarava was very distinctive, even amongst the hundreds of boats that plied the Ionian.

"*Yiassas*! Welcome back!" he shouted. Niko had an engaging, impish grin to match his effervescent personality. He caught our stern lines and secured them to mooring rings exactly and conveniently opposite his taverna. We were usually able to secure this position but in August, when the Italian owned motor boats came in and filled every spare berth, we could be unlucky and have to drop anchor in the roadstead outside the harbour. If ever I telephoned him from Sarava to reserve our favourite table, faithful Niko would tie a couple of wooden chairs over the mooring rings we always used, although Italian boats would often pay no notice or attempt to squeeze themselves in where there was no room – much as they tended to park their cars.

The irresistible aroma of baking bread, vanilla, cinnamon and freshly brewing coffee wafted across to us as we made fast by the quayside. After a swim from the tender at a nearby cove, everyone except Jeremy wanted to go ashore for some retail therapy. He loathed shopping and much preferred to stay on Sarava and fiddle around with the numerous odd jobs that always needed his attention. We quickly showered and changed and headed for the shops. Miranda and her friend from Millfield clutched miniature handbags containing their pocket money for the week.

The girls couldn't wait to buy some of the local costume jewellery, hair clips, sarongs and ice creams from the Italian ice cream shop. Sue and I were after pashminas; I knew a little boutique in the back streets which sold the biggest selection of colours I had ever seen, made in Kashmir from the finest, softest cashmere. I am allergic to sheep's wool, although pure cashmere and pashmina suit me, no doubt because neither are actually wool but shorn from the softest under-hair or pashm, of the respective breeds of Himalayan goats. It also has the advantage of being eight times warmer and considerably lighter than sheep's wool.

Rory had done well in his last term in the Upper Sixth at Millfield, gaining a much coveted scholarship to the Bristol Old Vic Theatre School. Jeremy and I were very proud of his achievement and wanted to buy him a special present while we were in Paxos. We knew the eclectic selection of shops which line the harbourside and fill the narrow winding streets of the tiny village would definitely produce something Rory would like. In a jewellery shop on the quayside Rory selected a very distinctive silver identity bracelet.

"We can have your name or initials engraved on it," I suggested, although it was much too large for his wrist.

"No problem," said the assistant. "We can take out a few links so it will fit him."

I explained that we were only in Paxos for the night and would be leaving the following morning.

"No problem," she repeated, "I will send it by water taxi to Corfu Town where someone in our jewellery workshop can engrave and alter it. Then the taxi will bring it back later this evening."

Sue and John stood there listening with their mouths open like goldfish. But this was Greece and, as we had discovered many times before, anything is possible. Rory nudged me and whispered; "It'll cost a fortune Mummy! I know how much the water taxi charges!"

"How much will it cost to send it by water taxi?" I ventured, suddenly thinking it prudent to enquire.

"Nothing, Madame, it is a free service and we will not charge for the alteration either. If you can come back after nine this evening it will be here for you."

"I'll believe that when I see it!" Jeremy grunted with his customary cynicism when we told him.

He had to eat his words with his *marides* later that evening when Rory went into the shop again. He came out proudly wearing the bracelet, duly engraved and fitting perfectly. Supper in Paxos lived up to all our expectations, except that we couldn't have our favourite table at the front of the restaurant as we had finished shopping so late. Niko was most apologetic but the taverna was full to bursting with Scandinavian customers who dined earlier than we normally did and tended to make their meal last for the whole evening. We had to make do with a table at the back, near the kitchens, which would have been fine except it was impossible for Jeremy to keep a weather eye for clumsy charter boats from there. Unable to relax and certain that Sarava was in mortal danger from the visiting Italians, he would leap up from the table every ten minutes and go to the quayside to check, resulting in giving himself and the rest of us a serious dose of indigestion.

Next morning as we were sitting down for breakfast in the cockpit, Niko appeared across the road carrying a tray of coffee. He wobbled across our passerelle and set the tray on the table.

"On the house," he announced, smiling broadly.

"Why have we deserved this, Niko?" Jeremy asked.

"Because you could not have our best table last night," he answered. "You can bring the tray and the cups back next time you come!" he called over his shoulder as he trotted back to the taverna.

A week later I returned the tray and cups, adding a small gift of prettily wrapped pairs of tiny cotton socks from Marks & Spencer;

unlike us, I knew he would appreciate something from an English shop. Niko's wife had just given birth to their first, long awaited baby and I knew they would be delighted with a daughter. I hoped their friends and relations would not greet the news of the arrival of a baby girl with the traditional Greek response of 'commiserations'.

A couple of days later we were back in Kassiopi harbour. There was washing to be done; salt-soaked beach towels and swimwear would be needed next day. From the machine housed in a cavernous locker on the aft deck, the washing was all hung on lines over the foredeck, despite Miranda's protestations that no laundry should ever be seen when we were in port. It was bone dry in half an hour and I asked Rory to bring it in for me. I had been showering in our bathroom and had just put on clean white underwear when I heard a thud on deck, followed by a cross between a loud yell and a groan. I ran up to the saloon, from where I could see the foredeck through the window. A figure was lying curled up on deck, clutching his chest with both arms. 'Oh my God, Jeremy's having a heart attack!' was my immediate thought. I ran out on deck to discover it wasn't Jeremy, but Rory. Garments from the washing line were scattered around him and he was still groaning, obviously in a great deal of pain.

"What happened darling?" I asked as I knelt beside him.

He could only gasp and groan. I called Jeremy who was doing something on the quayside and hadn't heard the commotion. Rory just managed to say he had stepped back with an armful of laundry without noticing the large open hatch above the guest cabin; usually the glazed hatch was fixed half-open at an angle for safety, but instead Rory had stepped into a three foot square void. His ribcage had taken the full force of the fall against the aluminium frame. John was immediately beside Rory, promptly sticking his forefinger into Rory's mouth and feeling his gums – much to Rory's surprise and ours.

"I'm testing the temperature of his gums," John explained. "If they're cold it means he has gone into shock and we'd need to get him to hospital."

We watched in silent admiration as our vet took charge, calling for two paracetamol and a glass of water.

"Rory, stay still!" he commanded, as Rory tried to sit up.

Miranda ran to get a blanket, despite the warmth of the early evening, as John was worried about Rory getting cold through shock. Rory swallowed the pills and lay motionless, wrapped in a blanket, while every few minutes John put his finger back in Rory's mouth.

"It's what I have to do with animals," John explained.

"Good job it's not what you have to do at the other end of cows!" joked Jeremy.

"Daddy, don't make me laugh," groaned Rory. But he was smiling bravely and I knew then that he would recover, I have always had more faith in vets than doctors. After half an hour or so John said we could help Rory to his cabin to lie in more comfort. Taking me to one side John urged me stay with Rory through the night to make sure he didn't move; he was worried that if a rib had splintered there was a danger of it piercing a lung. It was only then that I realised I was still only wearing my bra and pants.

The others went off to our usual harbourside restaurant for supper that night while I stayed with Rory in his cabin. He was dozing on and off and seemed to be in slightly less pain, thanks to the painkillers; I made us some Marmite toast, the family staple when anyone is feeling under the weather, but I needn't have bothered. When Daniel, the owner of the restaurant, inquired where Rory and I were, Jeremy explained about the accident. Daniel went to the kitchen and returned after a few moments with two plates of hot food covered in tin foil for us, with his compliments.

I sat next to Rory all night and he slept reasonably well, but although John had assured us that Rory was out of danger, the pain was still there two days later. Once back at the marina I drove him to the nearby Kontokali Bay Hotel where a physiotherapist from Athens came for the summer months to give massages and other alternative therapies to the guests. I had been to Fragiskos several times for a back massage and found him excellent; I had also tried acupuncture but the needles kept popping out of my skin, much to Fragiskos' surprise as he had never witnessed this before. Jeremy and Rory were sceptical of course, but I convinced Rory it was worth a try and might just help his pain. On the couch in the little treatment room by the swimming pool, Fragiskos administered the hairlike acupuncture needles; Rory was astonished he could not actually feel them going in at all. He lay quietly for about twenty minutes, the needles were removed and he was told to sit up slowly. The pain had completely gone, never to return.

If the accident had cast a small shadow over the end of our friends' stay, they had certainly come to see why we were so very fond of Corfu and its wonderfully generous and hospitable people. They promised to return the following summer, having first read up on Greek mythology and history.

* * *

Our delightful week with Sue and John was followed by a hellish seven days. Teenage guests on board were always a potentially dangerous hazard, as soon became crystal clear. Miranda and Rory had invited a pair of American cousins to stay for a week; they were friends from Millfield who lived in the Hamptons, from where the girl's mother had written to inform me she was very worried, as her daughter was not a swimmer. Miranda had told Renée about the great nightlife in Kassiopi, so Renée's poor mother was obviously imagining the tiny village was more akin to Miami's South Beach. Consequently she asked me if we would stay up whenever the youngsters were out, making sure Sarava's door was locked when they returned on board, thus preventing any possibility of the girl ending up in the water after a few drinks. But on the cousins' last night in Corfu the four teenagers had left us after supper and headed for one of the music bars. Jeremy had asked them to be back on board by midnight, as we all had an early start for the airport next morning; Rupert and Renée had a long journey ahead of them, a flight from Corfu to Amsterdam before joining their connection to New York.

It had been a very busy week, sailing down to Zakynthos and back, visiting as many of the Ionian islands as possible along the way. Jeremy and I were longing to go to bed but kept ourselves awake with coffee and chocolate biscuits, knowing we were obliged to keep our promise to see Renée safely locked on board, despite finding the pair of them rather obnoxious, unrewarding guests. Midnight came and went with no sign of the young, until Rory and Miranda returned a little later saying they couldn't persuade the others to leave the bar.

"Give them another half-an-hour," said Jeremy, not wanting to be a spoilsport.

By two in the morning we had lost all patience; Miranda and I went to bed while Jeremy got dressed again and went with Rory to the bar. About ten minutes later we heard the passerelle rattling and disgruntled voices raised in anger. Jeremy stormed into our cabin looking shocked and furious.

"Whatever's the matter?" I asked, sitting up in bed and squinting against the light he had switched on.

"Rupert flatly refused to leave the bar," he said, "and when I insisted he took a swing at me!"

"Crikey! Are you all right?" I searched his face for signs of damage.

"Yes, I'm fine. Luckily he's very drunk and I was able to duck."

"Where's Renée? Did she come back with you?" Frankly I couldn't care less where Rupert was now.

"She's back, in bed and I've locked the door." He looked exhausted and very shaken.

"What about Rupert?"

"I told him he could find his own place to sleep tonight, the ungrateful brat."

At five o'clock that morning we told Renée to call Rupert to tell him to meet us in the village square for the trip to the airport. He arrived looking decidedly hungover and dishevelled but not as shame-faced as

I had hoped; I think he may have slept on the beach. He didn't speak to either of us, nor even to Rory and Miranda who had come to see them off. Rory had packed up Rupert's things on Sarava and Miranda had helped an ashen-faced Renée to pack hers. Halfway along the coast road to the airport Miranda tapped me on the shoulder.

"Renée hasn't got her passport!" she suddenly announced.

"What? Where is it?" demanded Jeremy, slamming on the brakes.

"I think I left it in my cabin." Renée replied nonchalantly.

"Oh God," exclaimed Jeremy, horrified. "That means you're going to miss your plane!"

The thought of having the teenagers from hell for another week on the boat was more than we could bear. Jeremy swung the Jeep around and raced back to Kassiopi; Miranda boarded Sarava with Renée to help her look for the missing passport, which was found in seconds. It was only on the return journey from the airport to Kassiopi, after the cousins had caught the plane by the skin of their unbrushed teeth, that Miranda admitted Renée had left her passport behind on purpose, hoping for another week's holiday. Renée had whispered this to Miranda in the car and thank heavens, Miranda had endured more than enough of her selfish friend by then and had the good sense to sabotage the plan.

On returning to Sarava, Miranda and I went below to the guest cabins to strip the beds and gather up all the grubby wet towels that our young visitors had thoughtfully dumped on the carpet in their cabins. In Renée's bathroom was evidence of the previous night's heavy drinking and eating; what I can only describe as a scene from a horror film met my eyes, the smell making me retch. The loo was full to the brim and blocked, the wash hand basin was overflowing with vomit, every variety of excreta was spread on every surface, splattered halfway up the padded cream walls and still dripping slowly towards the floor. I tied a scented scarf around my nose and mouth, put on an apron, donned my trusty rubber gloves and, with disinfectant, plunger and kitchen paper in hand, stepped into the breach before the heat of the day dried the excrement to a crust. Needless to say these two were never invited again.

∗   ∗   ∗

After women, flowers are the most lovely thing God has given the world.

Christian Dior

The summer was proving one of the hottest we could remember in Corfu; each day we awoke before dawn to a stifling heat which intensified inside Sarava as the morning progressed. Although we had mosquito screens over all the windows and hatches, the night air that filtered through them was often too warm to be refreshing. Unable to sleep after the first two or three hours, I would get up and make tea, taking it out into the cockpit where it was much cooler. Sitting at the table with a cup of tea I could draw and paint, read, write, or simply watch the sunrise over the hills of Albania across the straits. Sometimes, if we had a boat full of guests, I took the opportunity to prepare lunch while all was quiet and peaceful; I don't enjoy cooking at the best of times, particularly when the temperature in the galley began to soar. So on this particular morning I decided to make a simple tabouleh, the delicious North African salad of couscous, finely chopped tomato, sweet onion and flat leaf parsley, dressed with virgin olive oil, salt, freshly ground black pepper and lots of lemon juice. This useful accompaniment to any dish was always a great favourite with family and friends. As I boiled the kettle, I noticed it was only three in the morning, but as I reflected, I could always have a siesta after lunch – or even a *fiesta*, as five year-old Rory called it when we lived in Spain.

Footsteps on the passerelle signalled the arrival of a late night visitor; looking out of the door I saw Rory kicking off his flip-flops and tip-toeing across the aft deck. He had been at his usual haunt, the Harbour Bar, a popular meeting place for all the youngsters who congregated there each summer. Lifetime friendships were formed there, romances were begun and Rory became resident DJ as a holiday job. The Greek owner of the bar was delighted that Rory brought all the latest music with him from England each year, attracting a large following of club goers and young ladies, so essential for the success of nightclubs the world over. This summer Rory had been given use of the apartment above the bar, its wide French doors opening to a balcony which boasted the best view of the harbour and sea beyond. He only came back to the boat for the occasional night Sarava was in harbour if he wanted a bit of peace and quiet, as well as to get his washing done.

"Golly Mummy, what on earth are you doing still up at this time of night?"

"Actually it's morning and I've just got up; it was too hot to sleep," I answered my bewildered son. An understanding grunt followed; he was rarely surprised by my eccentricities.

"Well I'm off to bed. Night night!" He kissed my cheek as he dumped a bag of washing in the cockpit, which he said he would put into the washing machine when he woke up … or I would do it because I'm a softie and I love him.

I peered at the couscous which had finished steaming under a clean tea towel. It looked rather peculiar under the dim lights of the galley. I tasted a spoonful: no it definitely wasn't right, it was jelly-like and distinctly slimy. I picked up the empty packet and inspected it more closely, quickly identifying the label as ταπιόκα – tapioca. I remade the tabouleh with the correct durum wheat semolina and then mixed a tapenade with plump, organically grown Kalamata black olives, capers, anchovies and olive oil. Tapenade was used by the Romans as an appetite stimulant, but I hardly think this was necessary given their well documented fondness for gorging themselves until they were sick at gastronomic orgies, which enabled them to start eating all over again. This recipe from Provence (Tapeno being Provençal for caper) uses the marinated, unopened flower buds of the plant rather than the caper berries, which look like hard green grapes; some of you, dear readers, may remember the disastrous, bright blue caper berry gravy incident in the film *Bridget Jones' Diary.*

The caper plant can be found growing wild on the cliffs and beaches around the coast of most Greek Islands; above the tiny pebble coves around Corfu they spring out of the sheer rock face and cascade downwards like a waterfall. Their dark glossy leaves are prettily heart-shaped, the profusion of palest pink flowers with clusters of long, dark pink stamens resemble a stunning combination of wild roses and hibiscus blooms. They could easily be mistaken for the most exotic tender houseplants to be found in the climate controlled indoor plant section of any English garden centre; yet here they thrive, enjoying the extreme heat of summer and the refreshing salt spray from the sea.

Having put my dishes in the fridge, I went off for a swim. I revelled in these pre-dawn dips in the little cove beyond the harbour, quite alone apart from the nut brown villager who owned the sunbeds; he would arrive soon after me, offering a nod and a polite *Kalimera Kyria* as he arranged the beds in neat rows on the pebbles. During these quiet early mornings when the island was just waking up, I frequently spotted kingfishers and dolphins, swallow tail, peacock and other butterflies, or an occasional flamboyantly plumaged hoopoe perching briefly on top of a Cypress tree. Emerald green lizards were common, lying motionless on the rocks like shiny plastic toys, waiting for the first rays of sun to warm them. Tiny swallows glided overhead, swooping to skim flies from the surface of the water as I returned to Sarava, refreshed and ready for the day. Before long the family stirred and appeared bleary-eyed from below decks.

"It's *so* hot!" moaned Miranda. "Can't we go to Ereikoussa today?"

Ereikoussa is a small, virtually uninhabited island which is one of three known collectively as the Diapontia Islands; belonging to Corfu's prefecture, Othoni, Ereikoussa and Mathraki lie between two and a dozen nautical miles to the north-west of Corfu. The sapphire blue sea surrounding Ereikoussa was cooler than anywhere else, due to a profusion of cold subterranean fresh springs and the deeper, open waters surrounding it.

"Actually we're going this morning," I replied. "So please help Daddy get the boat ready. Spiro and Androula will be here in a minute."

We had invited our architect and his wife to join us for a trip to Ereikoussa where we would have a barbecue lunch on board.

"Oh great. Old people!" groaned Miranda. "You might have invited somebody for Rory and me."

"Actually Simos is coming too," I said, pleased to surprise her and see her beaming smile.

Everything was ship shape and Bristol fashion as Spiro and Androula eventually crossed the passerelle, their arms laden with fresh horse mackerel from a local fisherman in Acharavi early that morning. Knowing we would be a party of seven, Androula had purchased ten of the most enormous fish and brought a dozen huge lemons from her garden; Spiro clutched a basketful of bottles of local wine and I set about finding space in our galley and fridges for this bounty. Our other guest, Simos, a waiter we had befriended, was nineteen and studying at university in Athens; during the long summer holidays he worked in Corfu to pay his fees.

Born in a hill village in southern Albania, once part of Greece, he and his older brother had found their way to Athens, where the two young boys had managed to earn a few drachmas each day washing windscreens at traffic lights in the busy city. Somehow Simos had found a place at school and continued to learn languages and other subjects by borrowing books from the library and teaching himself. We were full of admiration for his tenacity and determination, which eventually earned him a place at university. Each time I saw him sweeping dry leaves from the terrace of the restaurant, or laying tables, I felt the sharp contrast between his situation and that of my son; Rory had been given the best education and a happy, carefree and secure childhood where he wanted for nothing of importance. A few years later we would attend Simos' wedding in Athens; his lovely

Norwegian bride Anita, who he had met one summer in Corfu, and their two beautiful children now live happily and very successfully in Oslo, but at the time we felt he deserved his day off in Ereikoussa.

Schools of dolphins appeared on all sides as we reached the open sea between Corfu and the islands, thrilling our guests as they munched on Miranda's home made brownies and sipped iced coffees. We dropped anchor off a long stretch of dazzling white sand, backed by dunes where the highly fragrant white sea daffodils, *Pancratium maritimum*, grew in abundance; until I was able to identify them in my book of Mediterranean wild flowers, I thought they must be a variety of sand lilies. Sadly the large sand dune which divided the Corfiot bay of St. Spyridon from Antiniotissa lake, described so eloquently by Gerald Durrell in *My Family & Other Animals*, has been gradually eroded by prevailing winds and the tread of tourism until it is now little more than a small mound.

> *The curve of pearl-white sand was backed by the great lily-covered dune behind, a thousand white flowers in the sunshine like a multitude of ivory horns lifting their lips to the sky and producing, instead of music, a rich, heavy scent that was the distilled essence of summer, a warm sweetness that made you breathe deeply time and time again in an effort to retain it within you ... the scent of the lilies came out over the water to greet us.*

Despite their rarity, I have found a few stray clumps of Sea Daffodils still growing under the eucalyptus trees which border the same beach, beside which sits the miniature church dedicated to St. Spyridon. Home to a varied selection of aquatic and water-loving wildlife, including wading birds, terrapins, frogs and toads, the nearby brackish lake has a tragic heritage which is reflected in its name. Literally translated, *Antiniotissa* means enemy of youth. In times past the lake was infested with malarial mosquitoes; so many children died of the fever that the lake was given this unfortunate name. As soon as aerial spraying of insecticide was instigated, most of the mosquito population of the lake and the rest of Corfu was annihilated; the spraying continued for many years after the malarial mosquitoes were destroyed, thus keeping the whole island virtually free of these infuriating insects at an unknown cost to other wildlife .

During the first few years we spent in Corfu we were never bothered by mosquitoes. However, until a decision was made to suspend aerial spraying of the olive crop with the insecticide that killed the olive fruit fly, most Greek olive farmers regularly had their groves sprayed by small planes or helicopters. During the spraying season, whenever Sarava was at anchor in a bay somewhere, I would drag our crew inside if ever I heard the drone of the little planes' engines as they approached the groves nearby. I knew instinctively that we didn't want any of the chemical – a particularly toxic substance called Fenthion – entering the boat or landing on us.

Miranda was particularly susceptible as she suffered from allergic asthma, as we found out to our cost when she was eleven. We had flown with Quantas to Australia and as the plane touched down at Sydney, before we had unfastened our seatbelts, the cabin crew came down the aisles spraying some vile insecticide all over the passengers. The stewards carried a large aerosol can in each hand, like cowboys with a pair of pistols, spraying continuously over our heads as they walked. No warning or explanation was given but as soon as I saw what was happening, I took off my large silk scarf and threw it over Miranda's head. As we left our seats to disembark, Miranda complained of feeling ill and being unable to breathe properly; a few seconds later she was violently sick. This sickness and shortness of breath continued for the first two days we were in Sydney. Rory managed to escape this chemical dousing; it was his seventeenth birthday and as a surprise the Captain of our 747 had invited him to sit in the cockpit for the landing. How times have changed.

The Greek Ministry of Health recommended that spraying should only be carried out from ground level to protect public health, pollution of ground-water and disturbance of the ecological balance. Nowadays pheromone traps are a worldwide alternative, but they are not considered an affordable, practical or effective solution by most Greek farmers. Some years ago I was told by a renowned Corfiot scientist that the Greek Government had been offered a free trial of an American organic pesticide based on citrus oils, but strangely the offer was declined; one can only surmise that the big boys of the chemical pesticide industry would be more than a little upset if this had proved successful. But Greeks are an indomitable force of nature, who my family and I admire tremendously; when it comes to bureaucracy and red tape they simply carry on in their own sweet way if they believe something is unfair or unnecessary. I knew of at least one helicopter still spraying illegally, if rather less admirably.

* * *

A rather more amusing example of Greeks taking the law into their own hands happened at Agios Stefanos. As we brought Sarava into the little horseshoe bay one evening, we were shocked to see a huge, bright green pantechnicon sitting atop the promontory. Having somehow steamrollered its way over the narrow footpath, it made an incongruous blot on the unspoilt landscape, an ugly metal monstrosity amongst the pretty maquis of sunshine yellow Spanish broom, myrtle and virgin's bower vine. Once ashore we asked Kostas what on earth it was doing there.

"For the communications-a mast. You know, big mast for the *kinita*, the mobile phones," he answered.

"But that's outrageous, Kosta! A phone mast will completely desecrate the bay!"

"But what-a can we do?" he replied, shrugging before giving the hint of a conspiratorial wink.

I took a photograph of this unsightly intruder, certain I wanted evidence for some reason; perhaps I could send it with a letter of complaint to the local mayor, or the Tourist Board. Early next morning I was first out on deck and could hardly believe my eyes: the pantechnicon lay forlornly on its side, almost at the bottom of the cliff, as if a hunter had shot it stone dead.

"Jeremy, come here quickly!" I called into the saloon.

"They won't retrieve that in a hurry!" he laughed.

"But how did it get there? Could there have been an earthquake during the night?"

My suggestion was not so fanciful; we had experienced several earth tremors in Corfu, one of which shocked me underwater when I was snorkelling, sounding and feeling like a mine exploding under the sea. A little later that morning we sat down for our customary coffee at one of the cocktail bars. We asked our young friend who owned the bar about the sudden relocation of the lorry. His sheepish grin could not conceal a certain amount of pride.

"Nobody wants a phone mast here; it is too much ugly and spoils our bay. So last night fifty or so people walk up there and feels the lorry – just to see how heavy it was, you understand," he continued, his grin broadening. "But it was much lighter than we thought, so unfortunately … over it go!"

A few weeks later an enormous crane was brought over from the mainland to remove the offending wreck from the rocks below the headland. To this day Agios Stefanos is not blighted by an unsightly phone mast. Hip hip hooray for hands-on Greek democracy!

* * *

It seemed the entire eastern side of Ereikoussa was deserted, its long stretch of golden sand without a single footprint; feeling like Robinson Crusoe, I was eager to explore this solitary paradise. The sea was as cool as promised, the streams of fresh water bubbling up to the surface clearly visible for all to see. Swimming towards the beach, the heady scent of the sea daffodils drifted over the water to meet me, carried on the warm airs from the island. As the others caught up we strolled along the sand picking up shells and heart-shaped pebbles; I picked a bunch of sea daffodils to take back to the boat. How they grew straight out of the fine dry sand was baffling, but their bulbs, only partially buried, were enormous, so obviously these stored water from the heavy rains of winter. I hoped to complete a watercolour of these gorgeous flowers before they faded, although I needn't have worried because the exquisite blooms are ephemeral, their glory lasting only a day before the next bud opens. Miranda and I had to use her lilo as a float which we paddled back to Sarava, Miranda clutching the flowers to keep them above the salt water.

Rory lit the barbecue which was attached to a platform over the davits, well out over the water – red hot charcoal and fibreglass being dangerous bedfellows. The ample mackerel were wrapped in tin foil and placed in a row on the grill, looking like pelagic, silver Egyptian mummies. Simos and Rory kept watch over the barbecue while Miranda and I prepared salad in the galley and Jeremy kept everyone's glasses charged with chilled white wine or delicious *Mythos* beer. We made a jolly party as we sat in our swimming things in the shady cockpit feasting on starters of nutty houmous, cool tsatsiki, glossy black tapenade, fiery orange hiti-piti and fat, juicy Kalamata olives with thick slices of crusty bread, fresh from Stamos' bakery that morning.

Stamos the Baker was a staunch communist, probably one of the last of his kind surviving on the island after the troubles of the early 1950's, but his bread was delicious. His bakery was a minute white-washed stone building, once a goat shed, tucked away in the bushes behind the little village stores in Sinies; the traditional bread oven was fuelled with olive wood, imparting the most glorious flavour and texture to the loaves. A rough wooden sign lopsidedly nailed to his whitewashed wall advertising BAKERY, painted in pillar box red wobbly capitals, was invisible from the road; nevertheless his reputation was such that people came from miles around to buy bread from him. He employed a young lad to deliver loaves all around the area on an ancient, spluttering moped. Each morning, at every house within a six mile radius of the bakery, you could see white plastic bags containing Stamos' loaves hanging from gateposts, bushes or branches of trees in the gardens, or simply tied onto door handles. A few years later Stamos retired and sold the tiny bakery in the hamlet to his young assistant, who immediately became Yianni the Baker.

When our leisurely lunch was eventually finished, I took out my sketch book and started to draw the Sea Daffodils. The heady scent of the flowers, now safely enjoying a drink of mineral water from a pretty vase in the saloon, pervaded the whole boat. It is hard to capture the delicate snowy whiteness of any such flower; even the whitest gouache paint looks cream as soon it dries on paper. The most accomplished watercolourists leave spaces on the paper where anything white, including highlights should be, but I am not clever enough to do that. So I use gouache, a water-based opaque paint which has two shades of white in the palette, zinc white and permanent white. Unless one paints on coloured paper, any attempts to define white flowers on a white background result in the petals looking too heavily outlined, or not showing up at all.

For my future book, *A Greek Island Nature Diary*, I had resorted to painting jasmine blossoms on a piece of rather crumpled brown paper saved from a parcel; it actually looks rather effective but the creases still show when printed. Later I managed to find some coloured drawing paper in a marvellous bookshop in Corfu Town which also sold art supplies. One of the smokey blue pages of illustrations for the book contains only white flowers; I entitled it *A Whiter Shade of Pale*, after the enigmatic song by Procol Harum ... Incidentally I wonder if I am alone in being so baffled by the words of that song; I knew *Skip the Light Fandango* referred to a dance. But who was the Miller? Was he Chaucer's? And who were the sixteen Vestal Virgins and why were they heading for the coast? Perhaps it was a reference to the amusing painting 'At the Beach', by the Italian artist Carlo Canevari ...

The sunset cast its magic pink glow over us as we sailed back towards Corfu. During the heat of the day the sky had been drained of its usual vivid cerulean to a washed out blue that was almost colourless; now it glowed with colours that graduated from pale lilac to blush pink and rose gold, then to flame red as the sun's crimson orb touched the sea on the horizon. High above an ethereal layer of palest duck egg green only lasted for a few moments before dissolving into the soft grey of evening. Munching roasted pistachio nuts and plump green olives, we clinked our glasses of chilled retsina together and wished each other, '*Yiammas*', 'to our health'. I wondered how we could feel anything but healthy on such an evening and after such a day.

During the sail homewards Androula related two extraordinary stories attached to the island of Ereikoussa, one tragic, the other telling of extraordinary courage and kindness. The first occurred when twenty-two of the island's population of five hundred embarked on a sea passage bound for Corfu aboard the *Ayios Nikolaos*. Halfway across the water a storm arose and all were lost without trace. To commemorate the disaster John Manessis Kalogeros wrote the poem, '*In Memory*', which I have since discovered in translation.

If you should walk the shore at evening time when calm prevails,
And wish to let their presence be,
One by one recite the names
And the sea will share its mystery,
Those echoes rising from the deep.

The other story Androula told us was kept secret for many years. During the German occupation of Greece in the second world war, when the Jews of Corfu were sent to concentration camps, Savvas Israel, a tailor from the Jewish quarter of the town, managed to escape by boat with his three daughters to Ereikoussa, where they took refuge. The islanders hid them, shared their meagre food with them and gave them clothes. The island's priest even gave up his own house for Savvas and his daughters, having burnt all the church records to confuse the Nazis further. The island was searched regularly but the family were never discovered. After the war ended Savvas continued to live on Ereikoussa until he died some years later; his descendants now live in Israel but some have been back to Ereikoussa for an emotional reunion on the island whose inhabitants had saved their forebears without a thought for their own safety. More recently the islanders were presented with an award from the Raoul Wallenberg Foundation for these heroic wartime efforts.

Delightful as our day at Ereikoussa with Spiro and his wife had been, it would turn out to be the last time our paths ever crossed socially. A month later work began on the foundations for the house. A team of Albanians had been employed by Spiro to level the steep slope of our land, in order to create a base for the raft and pile platform; but instead of solid, rocky ground they had discovered rich, loamy soil that had a certain value. Unfortunately Spiro, who was supposed to oversee their work in our absence, had chosen to disappear on holiday at this crucial moment. Seeing an opportunity the Albanian crew continued to dig with great enthusiasm, selling lorryloads of prime topsoil in the process, until a canyon five metres below the top levels had been excavated. Jeremy and I had returned at the end of October to discover this rift valley smack in the middle of our land.

Knowing a thing or two about construction, Jeremy immediately came to the conclusion that our building costs had doubled in a flash. It was neither safe nor possible to replace the earth and build on top of it; instead the foundations would have to be laid at the bottom of the chasm, which in turn meant that colossal quantities of reinforced concrete would be required to reinstate the levels – for we certainly didn't want to enjoy the fabulous views from the ground floor windows of our new house through a periscope.

After some quick calculations it was painfully obvious that our elegant tryptich design was no longer viable, unless we were willing to spend hundreds of thousands on buried concrete which nobody would ever see. Reluctantly we decided to build a single structure instead, a house with six bedrooms, two of which would be at lower garden level; beneath all this stood a completely buried basement atop two-metre tall foundations. Jeremy's new design, now entirely constrained in shape and scale by the excavations, was pleasant enough, but it lacked the style, proportions and practicality of the original concept. We decided the only way to redeem the structure slightly was to include detailing from the stylishly elegant Venetian houses to be found in Corfu. In retrospect we rather lost our enthusiasm for the house at this point, particularly as we realised our faith in Spiro had been so utterly misplaced.

Chapter Eight
All That Glitters

There are rich people, and there are those who have money. They are not the same people.

Coco Chanel

Corfu attracted a diverse and interesting range of visitors; some were easily forgotten, but a few stuck in your memory like glue. Such a person exploded onto the island that summer like a diminutive, platinum blonde firework. Clarissa lived in a fashionable part of London where she spent her days shopping, having first spent a gruelling hour under the watchful eye of her personal trainer; this daily exertion would be followed by a massage and beauty treatment at an exclusive Chelsea health club to recover from her ordeal. We first met at a drinks party given by friends of ours whose villa overlooked a small, secluded bay on the north-east coast; Clarissa had come along with Amanda, who owned the travel agency in Chelsea through whom Clarissa had booked her holiday. In the 1960s, Amanda first discovered the potential of Corfu and, with impeccable taste and imagination, had converted an old seaside olive press into a glorious holiday home which she let for a small fortune during the three months of high season.

Clarissa had been assured by Amanda that she would be invited to a clutch of cocktail parties and dinners where she would meet the cream of Corfu society; this suited her perfectly as she would be coming alone. Clarissa would then decide if it was worth bringing her husband for a longer stay later in the summer. True to her word Amanda had secured an invitation for Clarissa to the small gathering where Jeremy and I somehow found ourselves.

"Oh, you're wearing your *real* jewellery!" gasped Clarissa in an over-excited, breathy voice as we were introduced. "I left all mine at home; it's far too valuable to risk out here."

I was muttering something about not liking to leave it at home as we were in Corfu for the whole summer, but she wasn't listening. Instead her attention immediately reverted to the person she had been questioning about luxury villas that might be available during the height of the season.

"Yes but when do the Rothschilds and all the *beautiful people* arrive?" I heard her ask as I moved away to talk to someone less distracted.

The following day I spotted her in the village, where Sarava was at her usual berth alongside the harbour wall. Clarissa was sitting at a bar and stopped me as I walked past.

"Oh hello, I expect you remember me – most people do."

"Of course, hello, how are you enjoying Kassiopi?" I replied.

"Oh yes, it's lovely," she answered distractedly, glancing over my shoulder in search of someone more interesting. "But where are the best shops?"

I explained that this was a village which catered for locals and tourists; the sort of shops I was sure she meant could only be found in Corfu Town.

"Can you take me there this week?" she asked breathlessly, her blue eyes twinkling with excitement.

"Well I would love to but....."

"Super, can we go tomorrow? I am desperate to buy some holiday clothes. My sister is arriving here in a couple of days and she's *even* more glamorous than me, so I need something new."

I was about to explain that Jeremy and I were thinking of sailing down to Ithaca for a couple of days before it became too busy. Still, I thought, we were there for the whole summer, so I should really help a newcomer to the island and I relished any excuse to go to town. I was certain Clarissa would appreciate the exquisite town, with its Venetian architecture and polished stone streets, which had recently been honoured as a UNESCO World Heritage Site. I knew the town so well; from the Palace of St. George, summer home to the exiled King of Greece and now the Museum of Asian Art, to the Old Fort which houses the Corfu Public Library and an armoury in the English barracks. I thought she would be interested in the Archaeological Museum displaying treasures from the Temple of Artemis and the Art Café with its exhibitions of work by local artists. We could visit the exquisitely ornate St. Spyridon's Church and admire the pretty, flower filled park overlooking the sea, dedicated to Lawrence and Gerald Durrell. Surely she would appreciate every fascinating back street and hidden architectural gem the town had to offer.

"But there must be somewhere here in the village I can buy some jewellery today?" she asked hopefully. "I left all mine at home because it's far too ..."

"Ah, yes, there is one small shop over there," I interrupted, knowing what was coming next and pointed to the tiny harbourside jewellery shop belonging to a local friend.

"Super!" she said as she grabbed her outsize designer handbag and strode off at a pace I could hardly match. Clarissa was in the shop before me, so I followed her and introduced her to Marietta. Clarissa's eyes were busily scanning the glass cases like a voracious magpie, scarcely noticing me as I took my leave and carried on with my more mundane shopping for provisions. An hour or so later, as I passed Marietta's with my bulging trolley, she came out to thank me for the introduction; Clarissa had bought the most expensive necklace and bracelet in the shop.

As I walked back to Sarava I formed a mental picture of Clarissa's lonely, unloved husband in rainy London, a bank account on legs working his socks off to pay for his wife's extravagance. Little did I know the dizzying heights to which her spending would soar on her next visit to Corfu.

Our morning in Corfu Town was great fun; whatever else, Clarissa was good company, always energetic, vivacious and very amusing. I had never met anyone quite like her before; my Devon friends were country people on the whole, educated, cultured and well travelled, but usually more at home in a pair of wellies than high heels. She was like a glittering butterfly, leaving me feeling like a dowdy moth in comparison. I was a little disappointed that Clarissa didn't enthuse over the Palace and refused to look at the art exhibition inside; nor was she the slightest bit interested in the history of the town as we walked briskly along the sunlit Espianada towards the shops. Even at that early hour the morning was still and hot; I had left my sun hat on the back seat of the Jeep, which was parked under a shady tree by the cricket pitch, several hundred yards away. These few shaded spaces were always taken by nine o'clock, so it was essential to arrive in town very early or you would return after a couple of hours shopping to a car that was like a furnace, the leather steering wheel far too hot to touch.

"Oh blast, I forgot my hat," I said to Clarissa.

"Why do you need a hat?" she asked, bare headed as usual and taking every single opportunity to get a real tan to supplement the spray-on version she had bought in London.

"Well, my face freckles so badly if I don't wear one," I replied practically.

"But you're *completely covered* in freckles anyway!" she said as she strode off purposefully towards the shops, leaving me trailing rather dejectedly behind her.

I have always hated my freckles, so this blunt remark gave me quite a jolt; I had got used to them over the years and imagined they hardly noticed. When I was about twelve I had read in a girls' magazine about a cure for freckles; the glutinous mixture of honey, glycerine and lemon juice was supposed to miraculously remove them while you slept. Those awful, sticky nights I spent with my face liberally plastered with this concoction did absolutely nothing to the freckles, but my poor, uncomplaining mother had to wash the congealed mess from my pillowcases every morning. So I tried to ignore this latest comment; at least Clarissa spoke her mind and it was refreshing to know she would always give me a straight, possibly brutal answer if ever I sought her opinion. I tried to see it as an attribute, stingingly hurtful though it might be on those occasions when one doesn't really want to know the unvarnished truth.

"Shall we stop for a coffee?" I asked hopefully as we reached my favourite café under the lime trees dripping with sweetly scented cream blossom, which divided the cricket pitch from the shiny, smooth paving stones of the Espianada.

"I don't drink coffee, let's just go to the shops. Take me to the ones that sell designer clothes."

"You could have tea or orange juice?" I suggested, but she wasn't listening. She was on a mission.

Lovely as I thought the boutiques and small shops of Corfu Town, I feared my cosmopolitan companion would be disappointed by the lack of Lacroix, Prada and Versace. Clarissa was pleased with the plethora of shoe shops however, as well as those selling handbags and luggage. I am pretty good at buying shoes – Jeremy had been horrified to discover over forty pairs squirrelled away deep in one of Sarava's cavernous lockers – but Clarissa knocked spots off me; her dainty, tanned feet, with professionally pedicured toe nails, looked wonderful in the numerous pairs of pretty kitten heeled sandals she bought. Handbags and beach bags were rapidly purchased along with several pieces of 'holiday clothes'.

"I'd *never* wear these in France or Italy," she carefully explained, in case I thought she would normally consider wearing any garment with less than three zeros on the price tag. "But they'll just about do for Corfu."

My head was spinning at the speed with which her credit card was swiped in these shops; within a couple of hours she had gathered so many smart carrier bags that a suitcase on wheels had to be bought to haul them back to the car.

But despite all efforts to be irresistibly attired, and to her intense chagrin, Clarissa did not manage to secure an invitation to the Rothschilds; for the time being she had to curb her social aspirations and content herself with lesser mortals like us. Instead she took windsurfing lessons to pass the time, sometimes venturing out from the shallows whenever Sarava was at anchor in the bay. On one occasion she circled the boat in a particularly wobbly fashion, wrestling with the sail and calling out to us that she couldn't get back to the beach. I thought it was uncharacteristically callous of Jeremy to shout a few simple instructions back at her.

"Why didn't you ask her to come aboard?" I asked testily. "You could easily tow her board back to the beach with the tender."

"That's exactly what she wants. If she comes aboard we'll never get rid of her!" he replied.

Jeremy had got the measure of Clarissa from his very first meeting; he was more astute than me and often a better judge of character, whereas I tended to like everybody and think the best of them until, in some cases, I was disappointed. To assuage my pangs of guilt at letting my new friend find her own way back to shore that day, I invited her to a drinks party we were giving on Sarava. There the following evening, her last night on the island, Clarissa met several of the more established villa owners who convinced her that Corfu was *the* place to holiday.

A couple of weeks went by before Clarissa returned to Corfu, newly tanned, toned and waxed to within an inch of her life. Jeremy was curious to understand why her face was always so shiny; Miranda, wearing her Champney's hat, attempted to explain to him that as well as all her other body parts, she regularly had her face waxed, giving it the appearance of new skin. He remarked that he found it slightly disconcerting, reminding him of a naked hermit crab transferring to a larger shell, or a snake that had just shed its old skin. I thought, rather more sympathetically, that it was like a damp butterfly emerging from a chrysalis.

Clarissa had made up her mind that what she needed in Corfu was a boat and a villa, which she always referred to from then on as MY BOAT and MY VILLA. The first task was easy; she asked the owner of the boat hire company to sell her one of the little motor boats that he rented out to tourists. Clarissa assured Makis that she had a proficiency certificate for driving small motor boats, which she had been awarded after a day's course on a reservoir just outside London; taking her word for it, he sold her the most expensive little boat in his fleet. However, tales of her first foray to sea in the new boat spread like wildfire through the village and soon became legend. Having launched the anchor overboard she had fallen asleep whilst frying her skin to a crisp on deck, only to be awakened by the bows of the boat bumping noisily against some rocks. Panicked because the engine wouldn't start – having forgotten to reset the 'kill' switch – she called Makis on her mobile phone, furious with him about the anchor that didn't work and engine that wouldn't start. A few minutes later Makis' son appeared around the headland in a speed boat and began to investigate the problem. After retrieving her anchor from the seabed, the young lad gently gave Clarissa some sound advice: in future she should tie the end of the anchor rope to her boat before throwing the anchor overboard.

Every morning thereafter she could be seen rushing to the harbour, clutching a beach bag, announcing loudly to all and sundry that she was on her way to MY BOAT. Once back at her London home she had instructed Vassili, a Corfiot businessman who doubled as an estate agent, to find her a suitably impressive piece of land. It had to be on the north-east coast and within olive pip spitting distance of the Swiss couple's villa where she had attended her first party. Money, naturally, was no object.

Unsurprisingly this was executed swiftly and the piece of land was bought and paid for by Clarissa's husband before he had even set foot on it. James was only able to leave his work for a few weeks' holiday each year, but his wife was planning much longer vacations for herself; the long suffering husband would have to work even harder now to finance Clarissa's Costly Corfiot Venture. Her plot of land was exquisite, covered in wild flowers beneath ancient olive trees and perched above a small, tranquil bay with water so clear you could see the minutest fish flitting in and out of the weed on the sea bed. A narrow pathway meandered between overgrown olive and stately cypress trees down to a private, handkerchief sized patch of sandy beach. As with the land we had bought, the distant coast and mountains of Albania beyond the sea provided a stunning, ever changing backcloth. The only drawback to Clarissa's land was its exposure to a beach bar across the Corfu Straits near Sarande; it played very loud, thumping, Albanian pop music all day and every day into the early hours of the morning during the summer months. The sound travelled easily across the four miles of water to bounce around the rocks and cliffs of this particular bay and reverberate with the perfect acoustics of an amphitheatre.

However an architect was instructed and Clarissa was confident that all her ideas for the perfect villa would swiftly be executed, accurately and without fuss. She had forgotten that she was in Greece, where nothing ever goes quite to plan. Cheerfully and blissfully unaware of this, and accustomed to getting exactly whatever she overpaid for, Clarissa would jump aboard MY BOAT and tear out of the harbour at high speed to go to MY BAY, overlooked by MY LAND, where MY VILLA would soon be built. As soon as she was on board the little craft she would whip off her flimsy sarong to reveal the skimpiest flame red bikini, which barely concealed the smallest and most private portions of her nut brown body. This was a daily delight for all the lads in Kassiopi, young and old, who were in turn bemused and amused by this middle aged Englishwoman exposing the expert handiwork of her Harley Street surgeon for all to admire.

Progress on the villa was painfully slow, much to Clarissa's annoyance. As she explained to me on one of our numerous visits to inspect the building work, she had already bought most of the fixtures, fittings and even furnishings and paintings for her villa.

"MY BEDROOM will be a spacious suite on the top floor with its own balcony and will be painted pale pink throughout," she waxed lyrical.

"Every woman should have a pink boudoir. My grandmother told me."

"What does James have to say about that?" I asked innocently and rather wistfully envious. I had loved the pale pink bedroom of my childhood, leaving it unchanged into my teens and twenties, so it had always rankled that Jeremy would never agree to a pink bedroom at any of our marital homes.

"Oh it's not for *him*," she explained loftily, dismissing me as frightfully provincial. "We don't *share* a bedroom! He can have one of the others when he comes to stay; after all there will be seven or eight to choose from."

To complement the pink suite, Clarissa had asked her architect to find her some pink marble. Most of the marble used in Corfu came from Italy, but it wasn't pink and only pink would do. Clarissa had seen some in a French interior design magazine at her hairdresser's in Knightsbridge, so it obviously had to be available in Corfu too. One hot morning she asked me to meet her at MY LAND where she could point out where MY GARDENS and MY POOL would be as we walked around. I suggested that she brought Wellington boots.

"What on earth for? It's not raining!"

I told her that most of her rocky land was still covered in dense undergrowth, where snakes would certainly be thriving.

"Oh no," she insisted. "There aren't any snakes there. And anyway the ones on Corfu are all completely harmless."

"Really?" I said, "How do you know?"

"Because they only live on the roads. Haven't you seen them, Jani? They're all flat snakes."

Once at the plot it was worrying to see how little had been done in the months following the purchase. Many of the lovely old olive trees had been cut down and piles of roughly cut stone littered the ground, but Clarissa had been distracted from the delays by a marvellous discovery.

"Look! They've found me some pink marble! It was dreadfully

expensive because it's the very last on the island," she exclaimed, pointing to a cluster of pale pink slabs in the area which would soon become her sitting room.

It was indeed very pretty and I was glad the last lorry load had been secured for her. A week later Jeremy and I were driving up into the hills with some Greek friends for lunch at a little known taverna. I had just been telling our friends about Clarissa's great find when we rounded a bend in the narrow track and drew to a sudden halt. Pointing at the quarry in the hillside right next to us, Jeremy asked me if the rock face bore the same delicate pink shade of stone that I had seen at Clarissa's land. Sure enough, lying amongst the idle machinery were towering piles of this rare marble, sorted and stacked at the ready for the next gullible customer. Naturally we never had the heart to tell her.

Another of her purchases was an L-shaped sofa, bought on a flying visit to Rome. She pointed out where it would sit within the cavernous shell of concrete, which after many months was starting to take shape as a house.

"It will go just there," she said, pointing to a dark hole where the fireplace would be.

"My girlfriend in Rome says that L-shaped sofas are common, but I don't care. I'll just put it the other way around, then it won't be vulgar any more."

"But then its back would be towards the fire," I pointed out, "and it would still be L-shaped!"

"I'm not having *any* curtains," she continued, ignoring my observation and waving her arms expansively in the direction of the vast openings in the concrete shell that would one day be glazed.

"But won't you need them with such big windows?" I questioned, imagining stormy winter evenings before suddenly remembering that Clarissa would not be in Corfu at such unfashionable times.

"Oh no, I'm just going to hang muslins everywhere."

Instantly my furtive imagination drew a ghastly, grizzly scene of carnage in my mind's eye of a group of wretched corpses dangling and swaying gently to and fro in the sea breeze. I simply couldn't resist.

"Won't you find it difficult to get enough muslims?"

"Of course not," she answered innocently, turning her big blue eyes on me. "They're two-a-penny in Peter Jones."

Entertaining and infuriating in equal measure, at once an invigorating tonic and a bitter medicine, Clarissa breezed out of our lives as abruptly as she had arrived. Shallow and manipulative she might have been, but nobody could ever accuse her of being dull company. Nevertheless, as during our year in Spain, Jeremy and I had been reminded why we were often pleased to avoid the English abroad.

* * *

Rory's second accident on Sarava happened near Kouloura. Jeremy had always warned us never to put our hands or feet anywhere near the anchor windlass or its chain. Safely tucked deep within its own deck locker, the powerful electric winch was operated by buttons on the foredeck and at the helm. I could do this with my big toe, which saved me bending over with my dodgy back. Very occasionally, if a lot of chain was being veered too fast, the links of heavy chain would tangle into a riding turn, which could usually be freed safely by deft use of a boat hook.

We had just arrived for an afternoon swim before supper and to spend the night; it was a firm favourite with everyone and the only place we had seen seahorses living in the seagrass. Once Jeremy had spotted a tiny seahorse clinging to a link with his tail as the chain was raised. He called me and the children; I gently uncurled the seahorse's tail and placed it tenderly in a bucket of sea water for a few minutes while I took a photograph. When I tipped the water over the side, the little seahorse unfurled himself until he was as straight as a pencil and shot down into the weed like an arrow, leaving a trail of tiny bubbles to mark his dive.

As we entered the bay we gasped at the sight of an enormous, gleaming white superyacht which lay at anchor in deeper water. A short distance behind the white yacht was another of about the same size but it was dark blue and rather more workmanlike. We had become rather blasé about these great white giants during our years sailing in the Ionian, but this one took the biscuit. I called Nathan to book a table at Agni for supper that evening.

"Who does the gin palace belong to, Nathan?" He was a veritable encyclopaedia when it came to anything or anyone on the island he had made his home. And if he didn't know, one of his extended Corfiot family would.

"I thought it was your new boat!" he joked. "Actually we have all been wondering and trying to find out, nobody seems to know. Some holidaymakers think it's Nicholas Cage," (famous at the time for his starring role in *Captain Corelli's Mandolin* and a double for Nathan's brother-in-law, Theo). "Eleni thinks it's Bill Gates and my mother-in-law thinks it's George Clooney, but that's just wishful thinking!"

"Jeremy's looked through his binoculars at the house flag and says it carries a Middle Eastern emblem, as far as he can make out," I said.

"Ah yes, it could be one of the Saudi royal family, there are so many of them, they all love Eleni's cooking," he joked.

We were all well aware that these superyachts carried their own chefs, usually several of different nationalities so their cuisine was varied. Fresh delicacies would be flown in from all corners of the globe every couple of days to wherever the yacht was based; we knew of one superyacht that employed an Austrian chef especially to make cakes for tea each day. The owners, charterers and their guests on these gigantic yachts rarely ventured ashore to sample the local food and atmosphere, which seemed more than a terrible shame.

"Miranda is hoping it's the 'Spice Girls' on vacation!" I replied.

"Well do tell us if you find out. See you about eight-thirty my lovely."

Jeremy was at the helm, manoeuvring Sarava into a position where he could signal Rory to let go the anchor. Rory pressed the button and the familiar clatter of chain over bow roller began. When it suddenly ground to a halt, Rory reached down into the hatch and tried to loosen the heavy chain by hand. Unfortunately he was successful, his screams bringing everyone running to the foredeck where Rory was clutching his hand, a stream of blood running down his arm.

Jeremy had a good look at the wound, a ragged tear deep in the skin and muscle between thumb and forefinger; other abrasions showed that Rory had almost lost the entire thumb when the chain had suddenly run free. Rory turned the colour of Greek yoghurt as Jeremy applied antiseptic spray to the wound before bandaging the hand. Remembering it was good for shock, I made Rory drink some sweet tea, which he hated, with a couple of paracetamol for the pain. Jeremy was unsure if the gash would need stitches; we were at least an hour and a half from the hospital in Corfu Town and in any case I was loathe to take my son anywhere near the place after visiting a friend there.

"Mummy, go inside and sit down. I'll be fine," Rory added bravely, seeing my ashen face and knowing how ridiculously squeamish I am whenever my children are injured.

He lay on the cushions in the shady cockpit with his arm propped up on pillows. As he was not in too much discomfort, we decided to leave it for an hour to see how he was, knowing we could still make Corfu Town before dark if necessary. I went below to my bathroom to take a quick shower and splash my face with cold, refreshing water. Just then I heard the roar of a powerful engine alongside. Peering crookedly out of the porthole, I could see an expensive looking tender driven by a crewman wearing a smart white naval uniform. Another man beside him wore the same uniform bedecked with slightly more gold braid.

"Ahoy Sarava!" came a cheerful English voice. "Permission to come aboard?"

I heard Jeremy invite them to tie up alongside and join us for a beer. The two visitors sounded delighted at the prospect and hopped on board with enthusiasm.

"That would be wonderful, we're on a dry ship! Our Captain sends his compliments, by the way."

Surely, I surmised, these visitors were from the superyacht we had been admiring; moreover, as Jeremy had suspected, that it was Arab owned and therefore alcohol free. Not wanting to miss anything I threw on a swimsuit and sarong, arriving on deck in time to hear one of the men telling Jeremy how their captain had sent them over to investigate Sarava; he knew her builder and wanted a catamaran exactly like her for his retirement.

One of the men was the First Engineer and the other was Dr John, the ship's surgeon, who explained there were two doctors permanently on the *Golden Odyssey* whenever her owners were on board. I didn't hesitate.

"Could you please take a look at my son's hand?"

He put his beer on the table and carefully removed Rory's bandage.

"I'd like to examine this more closely," he said, "I'll just radio the Captain to ask permission to bring Rory on board."

The good doctor took a walkie-talkie from his belt;

"Permission to bring a young man aboard Sir, he's injured his hand quite badly and I want to treat it."

"Granted," came the crackly response.

Dr John explained that the owner of the yacht had often helped fellow mariners in this way, relating an incident in a remote part of the southern Caribbean when a sailor had fallen between two boats and had crushed his leg. His injuries were severe and needed immediate treatment. Golden Odyssey happened to be nearby and the doctor had brought the unfortunate man aboard to see what he could do. Realising the extent of the injuries that would necessitate several operations and a prolonged period in hospital, he received permission from his employer to have the man flown to the nearest hospital in the private seaplane. Rory was on his feet in a flash, his pain unnoticed at the thought of seeing this superyacht and its interior.

"May I come too?" I asked the doctor.

"Of course," he replied.

"Can I come?" asked Miranda hopefully.

"I'm sorry young lady, we can't take the whole family! Just Rory and Mum I'm afraid."

Miranda watched enviously as we climbed into the tender, which was almost as long as Sarava. Jeremy, who could have happily talked about marine subjects to the two men all evening, asked a final question.

"What is the large yacht lying behind Golden Odyssey?" It was virtually the same size as Odyssey but far more utilitarian in design.

"Oh that's *Golden Shadow*," Dr. John replied, "She's for the extra crew and company; we have about a hundred all told. She also carries our seaplane, *Golden Eye*."

The tender sped across the water to Golden Odyssey, where some of the armed security guards on the bridge deck briefly lowered their binoculars from scanning the hills of Albania to scrutinise our approach. A group of Filipino crew in pristine tropical kit helped us onto the landing platform at the stern, from where we followed Dr. John up a few steps onto the vast lower aft deck. In front of us rose wide, gracefully curved port and starboard staircases, the top bannister of each one embellished with an enormous golden orb. Rory nudged me as if I hadn't noticed.

"Crikey!" was his whispered comment.

"Great balls of fire!" was my whispered response.

Entering the cool, luxurious interior Rory and I started shivering in our swimwear; our bare feet padded on velvet soft navy blue carpets through what seemed like miles of subtly lit corridors. Everything had the look and feel of a *James Bond* film. How I wished I had found time to change into something a little more formal than my swimsuit and sarong. But had I worn shoes, I would have had to remove them anyway.

"Great lighting!" Rory said, with all the admiration of a student of theatre lighting.

Along the sides of the floor were strips of miniature blue LED lights, which presumably would guide the owner, his guests, staff and crew to the upper decks in case of an emergency. In this maze of passageways and mirror-finish lacquered doors I had to try hard not to think of the film *Titanic*. Eventually Dr. John stopped in front of a frosted glass door and placed his hand on a panel at the side.

"Wow!" said Rory, as the door opened with a swish.

"I always have the urge to say the magic words; 'Open Sesame!' when I do that," joked the doctor.

"Come in and sit there, Rory," Dr. John pointed to a black leather covered reclining chair. This room was something between a consulting room and a surgery; locked, glass fronted cupboards lined the walls and trolleys filled with all kinds of medical equipment stood on the highly polished floor. I marvelled at this surgery which would not have looked out of place in the best private hospital.

"If you think this is good, have a look in there," continued Dr. John, placing his hand on a panel beside another door, which opened at his touch to reveal a complete, state of the art operating theatre.

"Does the owner of this yacht get ill very often?" I gasped.

"No, but we often have very high profile guests on board; royalty, statesmen, Hollywood film stars and the like, so we have to be prepared for any medical eventuality in all corners of the globe," he answered as he cleaned the wound and pulled the skin together with butterfly plasters.

"No stitches necessary, but I'm giving you a course of strong antibiotics, Rory, just to be on the safe side. Take the whole course and I'm afraid it means no alcohol for a week, old chap!" Rory's eyes widened.

The prospect of an alcohol-free week in Corfu was worse than a prison sentence for this 18 year-old, but he nodded obediently. We were escorted back to the waiting tender where I asked if I might have the name of the yacht's owner so I could write to thank him.

"Awfully sorry," he replied, "but that's classified; we're not allowed to tell anyone."

"Cool!" said Rory, "Wait 'til my friends at the Harbour Bar hear about this."

If only mobile phones had built in cameras in those days, but I dare say mine would have been confiscated by one of the black-clad, heavily armed security team as soon as my bare feet had touched the aft deck.

Dr. John and Mike the engineer took us back to Sarava and continued their chat with Jeremy about the benefits and joys of catamarans. As more beers were produced I went into the saloon and found a spare greeting card I had been commissioned to design and produce for Glamis Castle the previous year, intending to express my gratitude for Rory's treatment. But how was I to start this note of thanks to the unknown owner of the yacht? I went into the cockpit, card in hand.

"How shall I address the owner if you can't tell me his name?" I asked Dr. John.

"Oh, just write Your Highness," he said casually, continuing his conversation with Jeremy.

So I did just that and hastily wrote how very kind it was of him to allow us on board for Rory to be treated. I put it in an envelope and handed it to the doctor.

"Please give this to His Highness." I said, feeling like Anna Leonowens referring to Prince Chulalongkorn in *The King and I.*

"Of course," he replied. The two men climbed into the tender and set off for their alcohol free yacht, waving to us cheerily as they skimmed away across the water.

We were all very relieved that Rory's hand would make a full recovery, consoling him with a supper that night at Taverna Agni. Nathan was intrigued to hear about our visit to Golden Odyssey.

"So did you find out who owns it?" he asked eagerly.

"Awfully sorry, Nathan," Rory replied with a perfectly straight face. "That's classified; we're not allowed to tell anyone."

In fact it was only when we were back in Devon at the end of the summer that we finally discovered the identity of this benefactor and very good samaritan. He was Prince Khalid bin Sultan al Saud of Saudi Arabia; at that time Prince Khalid, a former Sandhurst Graduate, was Assistant Defence Minister.

Chapter Nine
Winds of Change

When things go wrong, don't go with them.

Elvis Presley

The Greek word for wind is *ánemos*. I am convinced there should be a connection between this and the English word *animosity*; surely it ought to be a derivation. Throughout the world humans and animals have reacted badly to strong winds, particularly those of long duration. For hundreds of years in Provence the Mistral has been blamed for practically everything, from irritability to madness and suicide. The fierce Etesian, annual winds such as the Ionian Maestro or the Aegean Meltemi have a similar reputation, as does the hot, dry Sirocco which blows from the Sahara to the Mediterranean carrying with it clouds of fine red sand. Argentina has the Zonda; Mexico the Tehuantepecer; the Williwaw blows down the mountains of Alaska. Siberia and the plains of Central Asia are blasted by the strong, north easterly Buran. The Simoon, from the Arabic word for poison, reshapes sand dunes in the deserts of Arabia. Herodotus wrote of the extinct North African tribe, the Psyllians, who took up arms and marched to war against the south wind, probably the Simoon, never to be seen again.

We had arrived for this summer in Corfu much earlier than usual, relishing the prospect of an even longer holiday. However things began to go awry from the outset; at first trivial, they soon began to develop into a worrying pattern. Unseasonal and unusually strong winds buffeted and howled around the island from all directions, ruffling the sea into confusion by day and fraying nerves at night, when the frantic clanging of the rigging on every other boat in the marina mimicked an exceptionally enthusiastic Caribbean steel band. Rory and Miranda flew to join us as soon as they had attended her graduation from Champneys International College of Health & Beauty; naturally they were keen to escape the confines of the marina. Each evening we would plan a short excursion away from Corfu to visit Sayiada or Sivota on the mainland, or perhaps the nearby semi-deserted island of Ereikoussa with its cooling springs that bubbled up from the sand like Perrier; but the following dawn would unfailingly bring lurid skies and unruly, cyclonic winds to spoil our plans. For the first time in seven years Sarava spent more than two consecutive summer nights on her berth at Gouvia; nevertheless this wonderfully picturesque and sheltered natural harbour was the only relaxing place to be in such conditions, for we certainly had not come on holiday to spend long nights awake on anchor watch.

One evening when the weather seemed slightly more settled we hosted a drinks party on board while at anchor in Kassiopi. Many of our guests were from the English fraternity of villa owners, who we only saw occasionally during their briefer stays on the island; about twenty of them were happily lounging on the decks and in the cockpit enjoying wine and canapés, when an unusual southerly breeze began to pick up halfway through the evening, causing Sarava to strain at her mooring warps and anchor like a dog pulling impatiently on the lead. Before long the unmanned yacht next to us began dragging her inadequate anchor, leaning on Sarava with all her weight. Jeremy rapidly started the engines in order to keep Sarava and her feckless neighbour away from the mole, calling to me with an unusual urgency in his voice.

"Get everyone off ... Now!" I looked at him askance, platters of delicious nibbles in each hand.

"Why on earth....?" I asked, unaware of our predicament.

"We have to leave harbour immediately!" he insisted, pointing at the telltale signs of a squall approaching from the south.

Our guests, landlubbers all, failed to see what all the fuss was about as I tried to explain that the party was over. Obliviously they continued with their conversations, throwing the odd disparaging remark my way; it was only a bit of wind, after all. But Jeremy, never off duty, had seen the danger and was already easing the warps and tightening the anchor chain, pulling Sarava a few feet clear of the the mole astern. Realising he meant business, our guests teetered along the swaying passerelle, many still firmly clutching their glasses as they headed for the shelter of nearest bar as the first rain beat down. I thought it rather ungracious that none of them asked if we would be all right setting off into the dark and turbulent sea in a rising gale. We told Rory and Miranda to stay in the village with friends for the night, something they were quite used to doing; their evenings never started before ten and rarely ended until dawn, when the youngsters would all enjoy a breakfast of hot kebabs from a little kiosk by the harbourside.

While I hastily stowed away the debris of food and drink into the galley, Jeremy was helming Sarava out of the harbour, where boats were already crashing their sterns into the unyielding quays. Lightning flashed great silver spears over the mountains of Albania, as crashes of thunder competed with the howling wind; rain was now lashing in horizontal sheets, stinging our eyes and obscuring all signs of land. Sarava felt as if she was attached to the rails of a very large roller-coaster as I threw on an oilskin that had not seen the light of day for years and joined Jeremy in the cockpit; my eyes were streaming with the wind and rain, so I grabbed my sunglasses from the saloon, only for them to be blown straight overboard.

"Come and take the watch!" Jeremy shouted above the screaming wind, setting the autopilot on a safe course to take Sarava through the maelstrom of the open channel, before promptly disappearing astern. Not for the first time I thought he should be wearing a safety line, but I knew he would not hear of it; he had often seen how a safety line could become a greater danger in itself. I hoped against hope that if he fell overboard I would be competent enough to turn Sarava around, find him in the cauldron of black water and throw him a lifebuoy. I wished I had paid more attention to him when he tried to show me how to use one of the ship to shore radios; my brain only retains instructions for anything remotely technical after the fourth or fifth attempt and anyway I had never had an occasion to use the ship's radios. I did have the general emergency number on my mobile phone however. Perhaps that would work, if I could get a signal ...

"I cant' see a thing!" I yelled, my eyes streaming rivers of water down my cheeks. Thinking he had not heard me I looked over my shoulder to see where he was. Searching through the swimming pool in my eyes, my legs turned to jelly as I discerned a dark shape balanced high on the stern's wet and slippery guard rail. Jeremy was grabbing furiously at our madly flapping Royal Dart Yacht Club defaced ensign.

"What on earth are you doing?" I screamed. "Get down at once or you'll be over the side!"

Eventually, after my heart had almost stopped, he managed to untangle the six foot long flag and jumped down onto the aft deck with his prize bundled under one arm. His reply to my admonishments about such reckless and highly dangerous behaviour was typically casual.

"I couldn't let the ensign get torn or carried away; you gave it to me for my birthday and it cost a fortune. Anyway, it was hardly a trip up the mast!"

We battled on for another hour in the teeth of a full gale, through waves and rain all the way back to Gouvia. Dear Sarava had seen far worse and took the storm easily in her stride, but I was never so glad to see the leading lights of the marina.

* * *

We are all Greeks. Our laws, our literature. Our religion, our arts have their roots in Greece.

Percy Bysshe Shelley

Minor repairs and upgrades to Sarava were part of a routine for Jeremy; larger jobs were carried out during the winter, leaving our holidays aboard trouble free. But within days of our arrival all four banks of the ship's batteries failed due to the incompetence of the Englishman who was supposed to regulate them in our absence. We are not talking here of the sort you buy in packets from B&Q; these monsters weighed the best part of half a ton altogether and cost several thousand pounds to replace – a substantial setback at the very beginning of the summer holidays.

We had four folding bicycles on board which were most useful for getting around the large marina, particularly for my weekly trips to the laundry with piles of sheets, pillowcases and towels; all had to be changed each time we were back at the marina after having guests on board for seven days at a time. Of course there was a washing machine on board, but fresh water had to be used sparingly during extended days down the Ionian, despite Sarava's generous tanks which held over a hundred gallons each. Our guests generally could not grasp the technique of turning off the shower between soaping or shampooing; one lady friend, (you know who you are!), managed to empty both tanks on her first night aboard.

So it was particularly trying when my own invaluable bike was stolen just at the start of the Italian holidays, when the marina filled with boats flying the *Tricolore*. We never had this problem at any other time of the year, petty theft never featuring high on the local agenda; a Corfiot might well shoot a wife's lover – fair do's – but would never steal as much as a packet of cigarettes. Shoes and sandals could no longer be kicked off beside the passerelle during the thieving season and anything secured with less than two padlocks would quickly vanish. On such mornings, before dropping one party of friends at the airport and collecting the next ones from the incoming flight, I would cycle over to the laundry with eight double sheets, eight single sheets, sixteen pillowcases all in snow white pure cotton or linen – a nightmare to iron but essential in a hot climate – eight bath sheets, eight hand towels, eight coloured swimming towels, four bath mats, plus a few tea towels and face flannels. The efficient laundry would always deliver the clean, fragrant washing back to Sarava the same afternoon, the bed linen all beautifully ironed and wrapped in crisp cellophane. After an extensive search my bike was eventually found by Andreas the Antifouling, abandoned and damaged beyond repair alongside an Italian motorboat on the far side of the marina. Andreas returned it with abject apologies as if it had all been his fault, or at the very least a slur on the good name of the island.

Not a fortnight passed before another misfortune occurred, this time when I was being collected from a pebble beach in the north east of the island. The bay of Avlaki was a splendid morning anchorage, where I usually booked a table for lunch at *Cavo Barbaro,* swimming ashore from Sarava in the early morning and making a reservation for our party in the shade of the rustling eucalyptus trees. Any excuse for a cappuccino beneath the whispering foliage was a welcome temptation, but in fact I would only need at wave to Kalina or one of the waiters from the aft deck, from where I could signal the time and size of table required by holding up my fingers. There is something very appealing about rolling up a sarong, lipstick and hairbrush into a waterproof belt, then strapping it around your waist and swimming ashore through bath warm water before walking up the beach to a taverna, whimsically imagining yourself as Aphrodite emerging from the sea in Cyprus. From our table Jeremy could always keep a weather eye on Sarava at anchor just fifty yards away, an important consideration when the Maestro could suddenly blow in at any time in the early afternoon.

After lunch that day, for the sake of speed, Rory had ferried our guests back to Sarava in the tender and returned for me, as I had been waylaid by friends at another table. The inevitable onshore wind had sprung up with unusual vigour and we needed to set sail quickly, as we were running down to Paxos for the night. Sarava's anchor was already stowed and Jeremy was edging her slowly out of the bay. I waited at the end of the creaking wooden jetty, but Rory was unable to bring the tender into the shallows in the gathering onshore wind.

"You'll have to wade out Mummy!" he shouted above the roar of outboard engine and wind. I duly went back onto the beach and was just putting on my bathing shoes when Rory shouted again.

"For God's sake Mummy, don't bother with *those*! We're in a hurry; just wade out and jump in."

Against all my instincts, knowing well about the danger of stonefish lurking in the shallows ready to sting me, I waded out. With my first step into the water I thought I had trodden on a nail or a piece of broken glass, the pain like a red hot needle piercing the ball of my left foot. I had hoped to step gracefully from the jetty into the tender as our friends had done; instead, very unlike Aphrodite, I scrambled into the boat most inelegantly and flopped onto the floor like a beached seal, dearly hoping nobody at the restaurant was watching. Aboard Sarava I made for my cabin to inspect my throbbing foot and to change out of my wet swimsuit. There was not much to see on the sole, just a small red spot, so I applied some tea tree cream and joined our guests on the foredeck.

Sailing to Paxos was always fabulous. Sitting on the spacious foredeck, leaning against the tinted windows of the saloon, handily set at an angle to provide the perfect backrest, with a glass of chilled wine in your hand as you scan the sea for dolphins or flying fish, was a pleasure of which we could never tire. A cooling breeze over the decks was so welcome after the fierce heat of the day; to add to our happiness was the prospect of a little souvenir shopping, followed by drinks on board and a delicious supper at one of the harbourside tavernas. The little shops were particularly fascinating, selling an eclectic assortment of clothes, gifts, artisan pottery, paintings and jewellery made on the islands. We ladies on board would often slip away from the taverna during longer meals to shop again, handily leaving husbands to chat and drink. This habit became known by all who came to stay on Sarava as inter-course shopping.

But the enclosed harbour at Gaios often held the heat and by the time we were getting ready to go ashore, our cabins were roasting. As fast as you applied foundation, it would slowly melt and slide down your face in rivulets, while shiny beads of perspiration would turn face powder into a glutinous mess. Any attempt to use a hairdryer would bring yells from the men on board, knowing that the heat in the cabins would be multiplied as the ladies tried in vain to smooth the frizz out of damp hair with a blow-dry. After swimming in a nearby cove, Din and I were trying to put on our make up before going out to dinner. I can still hear Din calling across the saloon from her cabin in one hull, to mine in the other.

"Jani I can't do my make up, as soon as I put it on it's melting!"

The meze of little dishes, home made blush pink taramasalata, cool tzatziki, thick houmous, fiery hitipiti and local black olives with fresh crusty bread, followed by an enormous charcoal grilled sea bream was as memorable as always. But my foot was hurting rather more painfully by the time we left the taverna and, as we walked along the quayside towards the tender I lagged behind, limping awkwardly.

"Hurry up Mummy!" called Rory. I was getting used to this by now.

"I can't hurry, my foot's really hurting."

"Well, you must keep up! We're going to leave for Antipaxos now."

I've learnt from years of experience that schedules are vitally important when sailing anywhere – usually with very good reason; but punctuality has never been my strong point and I know to my cost that time and tide have rarely waited for me. Two of our oldest friends were staying with us that week. Tim had been Jeremy's best man and is Rory's godfather, and Denise, always known as Din, was my friend from childhood; their teenage daughter, my goddaughter Natasha, was also with us. The men and children steamed on ahead but Din was concerned.

"Are you okay, Jani?"

"My foot is agony and I can't put any weight on it."

"Here, lean on me," she said, offering her arm.

Together we made slow progress, I hobbling on one foot, Din trying her best to support me and both weighed down with our bags of inter-course shopping. Walking ahead of us arm in arm, Miranda and Tasha turned around to see where we were.

"Oh my God, look at them!" they chortled to each other. "They're like two old age pensioners on a coach trip to Bognor!"

They collapsed into fits of giggles but carried on regardless, blissfully unaware of my predicament. Din and I suddenly saw the funny side, no doubt enfeebled by the wine at supper. We had to stop in our tracks, bent over double with laughter as we tried in vain to recover our composure; the more everyone told us to hurry, the more we laughed. Soon we were in imminent danger of having an incontinence episode – more so when I reminded Din how Miranda, at the age of seven, had heard something on the evening news about a conference at an Intercontinental Hotel somewhere. 'I thought that was for people who've lost control of their bladders,' she announced with a clinical pragmatism beyond her years.

We tumbled into the dinghy and sped back aboard, where Din came into my cabin to inspect my foot as Sarava made her way southwards through the darkness in search of a cooler anchorage.

"Oh God, it looks awful!" she said.

Sitting on the edge of my bed, I turned my foot upside down and saw something that resembled a fat, protruding, half-chewed blackcurrant fruit pastille.

"It really hurts now. If it doesn't get better I'll have to see a doctor when we get back to Corfu."

I almost wish I hadn't said that. Once back in Kassiopi a couple of days later, I hobbled up the main street to the local surgery and was ushered into the treatment room where Dr. Dinos peered at the even bigger fruit pastille on my foot.

"Aha, ye-es. Is very bad." He was never one to mince his words, possessing the bedside manner of a tax inspector.

"Oh Lord, what is it?"

"Stonefish!" he announced gleefully, splashing on a copious amount of iodine which made me break out in a sweat.

"Why you not wear beach shoes? You been here enough years to know that!"

"Well it wasn't my fault......" I began, then screamed in agony as he sliced off the pastille with a scalpel hitherto carefully concealed about his ample person.

"Ow, ow, OW" I yelled, certain that he had used a red hot poker.

"Why didn't you give me an anaesthetic?" I demanded angrily.

"Just for *that*? Ha!" he answered, lighting a cigarette and walking out to reception to summon his next victim. An elderly woman, purportedly a nurse, applied a bandage so enormous that I could no longer get my left sandal on. I hopped across the road to a little gift shop and bought the largest pair of men's flip-flops before hobbling next door to the bar, where I ordered a large brandy. Sitting on a stool next to me was Dr. Dinos.

"This was your fault," I told him, downing the brandy in one gulp, "You should be paying for it!"

I heard him laughing with his chums at the bar as I hopped out and limped painfully down the street to the harbour. I decided he must be from another country; he most definitely was not Greek, although some mainlanders can lack the social graces. I was delighted to hear the following year that he had left the island quite suddenly, although nobody would tell me the reason.

The wound refused to heal and a specialist in Corfu Town was eventually booked. It is the most wonderfully easy thing to make an appointment with any kind of medical or dental specialist in Greece; a visit to any *pharmakeio* comes first, where one of the assistants will print out a list of the doctors or surgeons in the field you require. You then ring the one you fancy and make an appointment, which is usually confirmed for the next morning, never more than a day later. In my case I very sensibly chose the one whose consulting rooms were in one of the choicest shopping areas in Corfu Town. After a brief telephone call to the specialist's receptionist my appointment was booked for 9 o'clock the following day.

Next morning Jeremy drove me to Corfu Town; winding our way through the narrow streets with their myriad tiny boutiques I was in too much pain even to window shop. The consulting rooms were on the third floor of a large and imposing Venetian building. I hopped up three flights of white marble stairs, which led us to an elegant waiting room filled with pleasantly scented air-conditioning, where we sat for less than a minute before the doctor came out of his surgery. Greeting us warmly and courteously like old friends, the experience was the polar opposite of Dr. Dinos' surgery in Kassiopi, I mused. I took to this specialist at first glance, his gentle manner, neat appearance and spotless starched white coat filling me with confidence; in fact my foot was already beginning to feel better as this silver haired expert delicately examined it, tut-tutting and po-po-po-ing softly as he did.

"Who cut this foot? Your local butcher? It is badly infected, you will need a two week course of strong antibiotics and must change the dressing four times a day. You must keep it dry all of this time," he informed me, gently applying some antiseptic, a clean dressing and a generous helping of sympathy before handing me a prescription and a bill for thirty euros.

Inwardly I groaned, being seriously allergic to most antibiotics known to man; moreover it was the hottest time of the summer, we lived on a boat and it meant I couldn't swim for *two whole weeks*. Fortunately we had a rare week without guests on board and by the second week, when more friends were due, I was sure it would be much better. All I remember of those weeks was the boredom and frustration of being shut inside Sarava at the marina, my bandaged foot up on one of the sofas in the saloon with the air conditioning on full, changing the dressings every few hours and trying to shower while keeping the infected foot precariously balanced on the hand basin. Jeremy, who always had a long list of jobs on board, made the most of his time in port.

For the first few days I watched enviously as the children cycled off for swimming at the nearby Kontokali Bay Hotel, which was handily situated on a bluff overlooking the open sea beyond the marina. It had an excellent infinity swimming pool set elegantly in the pleasant landscaped gardens, which marina residents could use for just a few euros each day. But the hotel also boasted an Austrian chef who made the most delicious cakes, served with tea in the afternoons at small tables in the gardens; the temptation proved too hard to resist and by the fourth day I found myself sitting in the shade of the fragrant pine trees by the pool, cooled by sea breezes and enjoying a pot of Earl Grey and slices of freshly baked Sachertorte and Linzertorte. Needless to say I never went into the sea again without my beach shoes and always insisted on taking our visiting friends to the nearest beach shop to buy pairs for their family as soon as they arrived.

Natural forces within us are the true healers of disease.

Hippocrates

In between our frequent visitors things were finally progressing with our house. Spiro would meet us at Agios Stefanos whenever we moored at the end of Kostas' jetty. Always sporting his tattered shorts and various unflattering singlets he would argue for hours with Jeremy, studying the technical drawings and stroking his luxuriant grey moustaches as he made suggestions in his unique mixture of English, Italian and Greek. As the relationship between us deteriorated, and as Spiro became ever less reliable, the conversations would always descend into a predictably tetchy circle of confusion and misunderstanding.

Spiro: "How many bathrooms you wanting?"

Jeremy: "Two en-suite upstairs including our bedroom, plus one family bathroom, a downstairs loo in the cloakroom by the front door and a loo plus one large bathroom on the lower garden level."

Spiro: "Why so many and why you need a loo by the *brostini porta*? You have many incontinent friends? If they want the bathroom as soon as they arrive they can go *epano,* upstairs."

Jeremy: "Talking of stairs, Spiro, do you think it would be a good idea to include a staircase in the plans of the house?"

Spiro: "Ah ..." Long pause as he searched the plans for the missing staircase. "... I thought we might use an outside staircase to the bedrooms, so don't worry we will add it later."

Jeremy: "Somehow, Spiro, I can't imagine Jani struggling down stairs outside for early morning tea in her dressing gown in the teeth of a winter storm."

Spiro: "But the old *botzos* you see in the mountain villages ... you know those traditional covered balconies with a *volto*, a Venetian arch beneath the stairs? They are *pára polí* handsome!"

Jeremy: "Don't be ridiculous, Spiro. In England that's called a fire escape!"

I tried hard to take these conversations seriously, but more often than not I would sidle off after an hour or so to swim or browse in the little gift shop. Unbeknown to Jeremy, I was making a collection of small and not so small items which The Lion House would need to make it a perfect home. This collection was growing and I was running out of locker space on Sarava. It would be stupid to take these things back to England, only to bring them back to Corfu when the house was finished. My solution came easily one day when a kind English friend, who had built a house in the hills above Kassiopi, mentioned she had a very large basement which was only used for storage. It was secure, dry and until my collection arrived, almost empty.

Jeremy and I always looked forward to any rare week without visitors; as much as we enjoyed their company, these were leisurely times for us. I had been reading and sunbathing contentedly on the foredeck one afternoon in a secluded bay when, quite out of the blue, Jeremy announced that we would have to sort through and reduce all our furniture and possessions during our next visit to Devon, in preparation for our move to The Lion House. Here was a prospect that filled me with unbounded terror; immediately a heavy weight pressed down on my bikini clad chest and I found it painful to breathe. I sat up, had a drink of water and waited until it passed, which it did not. All our furniture, clothes, paintings, ornaments, kitchen equipment and personal effects had been stored in nine huge containers in Cheltenham for three years since we sold our house on Dartmoor. I had always been a hoarder and could not bear to part with anything, whereas Jeremy was casually unsentimental about possessions. Apart from inherited furniture, family silver, valuable old books and paintings, he has kept no more since childhood than would fill a matchbox.

My health problem had surfaced almost a decade ago, just before our first holiday to Corfu. For the very first time in my life I had put on a few pounds that summer, forcing me to buy holiday clothes in a size 12 instead of my usual 10. A few weeks before our flight I began to get heart flutterings, which Jeremy put down to over excitement about our forthcoming trip. I told him that although I was greatly looking forward to our week's holiday in Corfu, my levels of ecstasy had not actually risen high enough to cause palpitations. Once home again in Devon my GP diagnosed an irregular heartbeat brought on by a very underactive thyroid, for which I would have to take a prescription for the rest of my life. Apparently the thyroid gland is what keeps one alive and regulates the metabolism – something I had not known before. He told me to keep an eye on my heart, but I completely dismissed the warning; after all I was only just into my forties, not nearly old enough to suffer from heart problems. Perhaps I should have been more wary as my father and two grandparents had all succumbed to heart failure.

Jeremy was very concerned and immediately took Sarava back to her berth at the marina, insisting I see a heart specialist in Corfu Town. Having made some enquiries I telephoned next morning and was given an appointment the same afternoon with a cardiologist, who greeted us courteously and ushered me into a surgery containing more state of the art equipment than most English hospitals. Various scans and tests were dutifully carried out, interrupted only by the customary tuttings and po-po-po's which all Greek doctors seemed to emit subconsciously whether you were expecting triplets or had grazed a finger; so I wasn't unduly worried when he asked me to wait outside with Jeremy while he compiled his report. Moments later he

joined us, waving the print out from the cardiograph; even to the un-
trained eye it plainly showed a trace flatter than Norfolk that erupted
spasmodically into a cross section of Alps. He had also seen something
rather more disturbing on the heart scan.

"My dears, you must not go home today!" he said gravely.

"What do you mean? We are not planning to go back to England
until December," I replied.

"No, no! I mean you must not even return to the marina! You are
in imminent danger of having a serious heart attack! You must not fly
anywhere either."

Jeremy and I were taken aback but it wasn't until the cardiologist insisted we drive straight to the municipal hospital that my legs began to
shake – if I hadn't been feeling ill until then, I certainly was now. The
very thought of driving past this ghastly place was appalling enough,
let alone any idea of being admitted. I said as much to the doctor.

"But my dears, you must. This is your life we are talking about and
you could die at any minute!"

Jeremy paid the modest consultation fee and agreed to take the
advice very seriously. Walking back to the car in a cold sweat I made
up my mind.

"I would rather die in the road than go anywhere near that hospital," I told Jeremy.

"Are you quite sure about that?" he asked, looking very worried.

"Positive," I said. He knew from experience that once I had made
up my mind about something, there was no use arguing.

"In that case we'd better get you back to Devon for a second opinion as soon as possible."

We stopped at the Minoan Lines office on the way out of town and
Jeremy left me in the Jeep while he went to book tickets on the next
available sailing. Minutes later he came back to the passenger window.

"Do you think you can last until the day after tomorrow?" he asked.
"Because that's the next ferry."

Back on board I packed a few things suitable for several changes in climate, not knowing how long we would have to be away: twenty four hours on the ferry to Venice, then two days drive through Europe, stopping for a night at a favourite hotel in Alsace, an unknown number of nights in Devon, followed optimistically by a more leisurely return to Corfu. In our cabin on the ferry Jeremy spent most of the night studying me to see if I was still breathing; if I as much as sighed he jumped out of bed to ask if I was all right – waking me up in the process – so I tried hard not to make a sound. Then of course he worried that I had expired altogether and would gently prod me, once again waking me up.

From Venice we hared through Italy and France at full tilt. We stopped in Reims for coffee in the square beside the spectacular cathedral, from where I called a rheumatologist friend in Devon to ask if she could recommend a heart specialist, adding that we wanted to stay in England for the shortest possible time. Mary must have pulled several strings and rang back within a few minutes with an appointment to see her chosen cardiologist privately the following afternoon; thankfully we still had full medical insurance. Twenty four hours later we arrived at the Exeter Nuffield, where the cardiologist repeated some tests and compared them with the report from Corfu.

"I can see what he was worried about," he said, "But I don't see it as quite such an issue, although to be absolutely certain you must go to hospital tomorrow to be monitored on a treadmill. I'll make a priority appointment for you first thing in the morning."

This meant an overnight stay nearby, in Devon at the height of the holiday season where, it turned out, only one particularly grim room was available. It was in a modern, soulless hotel that was obviously built specifically for commercial travellers; the trouser press in the corner was the giveaway. Then I realised I couldn't go on a treadmill wearing my trousers and shirt; I was imagining a marathon of an hour or more where I would be drenched in sweat, like the masochists I had often seen exercising at the spa in my local hotel on Dartmoor. (I never went within ten feet of the gym and only ever used the pool for my regular exercise during the wet and windy winter months in Devon). Jeremy simply could not understand why I needed to buy something.

"But you'll only be there for a few minutes. Why can't you wear your underwear?"

Seriously? Men!

"Certainly not!" I exploded. "Goodness knows who'll be in the room with me."

I dragged Jeremy into a sports shop in the main street of Exeter and scanned the unfamiliar rails for something suitable amongst the hideous black lycra. Coming out with a pair of turquoise stretch towelling shorts and matching top, a pair of spotless white gym shoes and short white socks, I felt fully equipped for the daunting challenge ahead; in fact I was confident I could train for the Olympics in such an attractive ensemble. However my first and only session on the treadmill lasted just ten minutes. For the first five minutes I thought I was doing terribly well and wondered what all the fuss was about; this was a doddle! Then the male nurse pushed a button and suddenly I was ascending a one-in-three hill. My legs soon turned wobbly and I was puffing hard as the rubber belt ran ahead without me, leaving me struggling to stay upright as I slid backwards, so the machine was turned off and I sank onto the nearest chair. The test results were faxed over to the specialist and once again we found ourselves being told not to travel under any circumstances. I was given prescriptions for a couple of medications, which we collected before leaving England the same night, gratefully bound for our beloved Corfu. Back on board Sarava eight days after we had left, we felt in need of a holiday to recover; our whirlwind trip of 2,400 miles driven in five days was precisely what the doctor had not ordered.

The following Christmas we finally made the dreaded trip to Cheltenham from our rented cottage in South Devon. We unpacked our nine containers in turn and sifted through every box and piece of furniture, labelling some things for charity shops, some for auction and some for Corfu; the remainder, including our two antique four-poster beds that would not do well in the heat and humidity of the Ionian, was returned to storage for the time being.

The day after this sorting marathon was completed my chest pains mysteriously disappeared and never came back.

Chapter Ten
A Blessing and a Curse

Don't look for big things, just do small things with great love ...
The smaller the thing, the greater must be our love.

Mother Teresa – Saint Teresa of Calcutta

One morning Jeremy and I were sitting at our favourite table at Porto Restaurant, by the harbour in Kassiopi, sipping the ice cold *café frappé me gala kai págoto* (iced coffee with milk and vanilla ice cream). I had taught the kitchen staff to make this delicious concoction during our first visit to Corfu. When Simos joined the staff he had mistaken the ice cream flavour and we all had coffee frappés with banana ice cream floating on the top; they were quite revolting but we never had the heart to tell him. We were approached by Bambas, a giant of a young man whose grin and personality equalled his size; he could easily be descended from the Spartans. He was a waiter at the restaurant and a tremendous, larger than life, fun-loving character, even by Greek standards; like so many of the waiters in Corfu, he had inherited several parcels of prime building land over the years and was actually quite well off. A few years before we met him he had been goalkeeper for the local football team until a fall during a game broke his back. He told us of the miserable six months he spent that summer, flat on his back in a hospital with no air-conditioning, his dreams of representing Corfu in national matches lying in tatters beside him.

"So I decide to become a waiter," he had told us philosophically and with his usual good humour. "At least I can walk, the doctors told me I would never walk again – but here I am!"

"I want you to meet Antonia," he said, as the timid girl behind him stepped forward to shake our hands.

"She is taking the place of Short Spiros," he announced proudly, patting the top of her head and smiling down on her from his great height like a doting and benevolent uncle. We felt he must have conjured her up from his imagination; she looked exactly like the young Julia Roberts, if slightly darker and even prettier.

"You are much prettier than Spiros!" I joked. But she looked a little perturbed, something having been lost in translation and she was thinking, 'Well I should hope so!'

Antonia was tall and very slim, with high cheek bones and a beautiful smile which lit up her large dark brown eyes. She was one of those rare lucky ladies who needs no make-up thanks to perfect skin and eyelashes which were naturally black and lustrous. Her long, curly hair tumbled over her shoulders, gently tinted from its original black to a warm shade of autumn leaves. As soon as they met her, Rory and Miranda were enchanted by Antonia, not only by her looks but her sweet and caring disposition; it was not long before she began to mother us all the way she mothered her own family.

"She is from Albania but it's okay, because she is half Greek," said Bambas, as a flicker of embarrassment crossed Antonia's face.

"How nice," I said, not really understanding why he had said this, or why it even mattered.

Only later did we discover more. Her family had fled from Albania when she was very young. The eldest of five siblings, three sisters and two brothers, her mother had brought them to Corfu as refugees in the hope of better life. Once safely in Corfu, already fluent in Greek and Albanian, Antonia had quickly learnt English, Italian and a smattering of German, which was useful at the restaurant; the proprietor knew what he was doing when he employed Antonia. All the other waiting staff were men and, delightful as they were, Antonia brought a touch of glamour with her natural charm and Hollywood looks. Antonia quickly became our friend, guide and confidante; worrying and fussing over our family like a mother hen with her chicks. Miranda would seek her sound advice about boys, Rory would do the same about girls. I found talking about anything to Antonia was just like talking to my darling Mummy, who I missed every day since her death a dozen years earlier; Antonia had an old and wise head on young shoulders and like my mother, was also born under the sign of Aquarius. This lovely girl was so sensible and practical; I always felt our ages had been switched.

The following year, on a beautiful summer morning, I popped over to Porto for my usual iced coffee after shopping for provisions for Sarava. Antonia was folding paper napkins around cutlery at the back of the restaurant. Most unusually for her she seemed downcast, so I asked her what was wrong.

"It's my boyfriend Angelos," she said, her beautiful brown eyes full of unshed tears.

"What's the matter with him?" I asked.

"Oh not *him*," she said, "But he wants to marry me and I can't get engaged to him."

"Why not? You love each other, don't you?"

"Of course, but I am not allowed to marry in the Greek Orthodox Church."

I was getting nowhere fast.

"Why ever not?" I asked more impatiently, remembering the fresh food in carrier bags at my feet, which needed to be in Sarava's fridges before it spoiled in the early morning heat.

Antonia stopped her work and sighed tragically.

"I am not baptised."

"Well that's easily solved. Get baptised!" I said, not realising the religious complications that lay ahead of her.

"I can't," she wailed, as the tears overflowed and ran freely down her lovely face.

"I have no *Noná*, no godmother!" she wailed. "You must have a godmother to be baptised into the Greek Orthodox Church. We were too poor to get baptised when we were children, so I have *no godmother*".

The emphasis she put on these last two words made me think this must be of far greater importance in Greece than it is in England. Seeing my puzzled expression Antonia continued.

"Here the godmother is more important than the Mother, she must baptise her goddaughter, give her to the husband at the wedding and baptise her goddaughter's children. Nobody I know here in Corfu is worthy of being my godmother; the woman must be a serious and important person. So you see it's impossible for me to marry Angelos because I have no....."

"Ah yes, now I see," I interrupted her for the sake of a speedy resolution to her thorny problem.

"Well that's easy, I'll be your godmother!"

She looked astonished but delighted.

"Would you?"

"Of course! I would be honoured, if you think I'm suitable. I'm not very serious and I'm certainly not important though..."

Antonia stopped me mid-sentence.

"You *are*. Even more because you are *English*!" Again this unbelievable attitude towards my nationality.

"I must ask Papa Makis," she raced off towards the Church of the Panayia Kassopitra which was just a few yards from the restaurant.

My salad vegetables were rapidly wilting at my feet; I could feel them expiring. But she was back in minutes, sobbing, holding her face in her hands.

"Antonia! What happened?"

"He won't do it!" she cried.

"Oh no....Why ever not?"

"He says because all English are Catholics."

I exploded with fury.

"I most certainly am *not* Catholic, I'm Church of England!" I leapt from my seat and before she could blink I was off at a trot down the bougainvillea covered path to the church.

"I'll give him Catholic!" I called over my shoulder to the crumpled girl who was now sitting on my chair, weeping into her apron.

I found Papa Makis lighting candles ready for morning worship.

"I am *not* a Catholic!" I said in as forceful a whisper as I could muster, standing as I was on holy ground.

He looked a little surprised, ever proud to maintain his faith's stance against the Catholic Church that dated from the Great Schism in 1054.

"Oh, but I think all English are Catholic."

"Well you've got that entirely wrong. England has been Protestant since the reign of Henry the Eighth when he broke away from the Church of Rome and appointed himself Head of the Church of England. Moreover our religion has close ties with the Greek Orthodox Church."

"Okay, my mistake," he said simply, blowing out a glowing taper.

"So I *can* be Antonia's godmother?"

"Of course, come." He gestured for me to follow him into the vestry.

'Oh heavens', I thought, meekly following him down the aisle, he's going to start a lecture on how to be a good Greek godmother. I would have to shop all over again as my lettuces would have definitely turned to liquid by now. Instead he reached into a cupboard and pulled out a large jam jar.

"For you," he said, handing it to me. It was a large jar of dark golden honey.

"From my bees," he said. It must have been his very sweet way of apologising.

Antonia's joy knew no bounds when I reported back to her. We hugged and kissed and she rushed to the kitchens to tell her boss, the rest of the staff and presumably to phone Angelo. Next morning I paid a visit to my friend who owned the little jewellery shop on the harbourside. Marietta and I had become friends since I first bought a necklace I had admired in her window for many weeks; it was a Byzantine inspired design featuring replica ancient coins. Marietta's husband was a serious collector of ancient coins and had some very rare examples which I coveted but could never afford. Her delicately scented shop, always decorated with fresh flowers from her garden, was a treasure trove of beautiful and unusual designs; they predominantly included pearls of all shapes, sizes and qualities, but also precious and semi-precious stones set into rings, necklaces and earrings.

Always charming and keen to chat, Marietta picked up her mobile phone and ordered coffee from a nearby café. We sat in air-conditioned comfort on a silk upholstered antique sofa in front of the glass topped coffee table. Sumptuous books on jewellery were displayed on the table alongside an ornate silver bowl containing a collection of pure white pebbles collected from the beach in Kassiopi. Marietta and I often met for a very early morning swim before she opened the shop, usually discussing our passion for pebble collecting. This is something of an obsession in my case, in particular my large collection of perfectly egg shaped stones from a cove near Kassiopi.

"I wanted to ask you what is involved in being a Greek godmother," I asked.

"Are you to be one?" Marietta looked only slightly surprised.

"Yes, I am. To Antonia," I answered.

"Ah, yes, I see." Marietta knew Antonia and her family circumstances well and understood the situation regarding her marriage to Angelo. "That's wonderful! But you must know everything."

Her description of the duties and responsibilities of a Greek godmother sounded rather daunting. Never in Greece would you find the casual attitude to becoming godparents that exists in England. I am godmother to five children and my duties have only consisted of attending the christening, taking them to a ballet or a musical and providing good presents for every birthday and Christmas; one of them lives in Australia and another in Germany, so sending gifts is the only option. Marietta continued her instruction apace. Firstly I had to buy the pure white clothes for the baptism ceremony; a godmother also buys a gold cross which they secure around the baby's chubby neck after the immersion in the font. In England we are accustomed to small babies, dressed in long christening gowns, being held over the font while the vicar daintily sprinkles a few drops of holy water over their tiny foreheads and traces the sign of the Cross with his thumb. Not so in Greece; due to the years before the war when infant mortality was high, children are not given a name until they are over six months old. Hence the larger, bonny seven, eight or nine month-old baby's mother removes all the new clothes until the child is completely naked, even the nappy is whipped off.

The priest pours a generous quantity of blessed olive oil – extra virgin no doubt – over the baby's head, then, holding it under the armpits he submerges it up to the chin in the water filled font. The poor infant usually screams in terror as a heavily bearded and pony-tailed complete stranger, wearing an even stranger ensemble and peculiar hat, seems to be attempting to drown it. How any child ever recovers from this trauma and eventually learns to swim astounds me. I have been told by Greek parents that the more the baby screams the better, as they believe it's the devil escaping from the child. I just can't believe this mumbo-jumbo, no child is born with the devil in them … with the possible exception of those who chase ducks and stamp on beetles of course.

After immersion in the font, babies are then handed back to the godmother, who dries them with a newly purchased towel and removes as much of the oily water as possible. The babies are then dressed in another brand new white outfit, in honour of the fact they are starting their new life as a fully fledged member of the Greek Orthodox Church. Dear heavens, you can never imagine how elaborate and fashionable these outfits are! I have seen many miniature sailors, complete with nautical cap, and diminutive princesses of whom Walt Disney himself would be proud. More prayers are intoned by the priest while the godparents hold enormous white candles decorated with ribbons, lace, charms, frills and furbelows. The godparents, priest and babe in arms process three times around the font. As they leave the church, all guests in the congregation are handed 'favours' of the sort given at weddings. For baptisms these small boxes of sugared almonds are decorated with a childhood theme; boats, cars or dogs in primary colours for the boys; fairies, dolls or cats in pastel shades for the girls.

However Antonia was not a baby; she was a fully grown young woman, so the clothes would not consist of tiny garments covered in frills and lace. It would be my duty as godmother to buy the outfit for my adult goddaughter. The suppliers of these clothes and accessories must make an absolute fortune; each baptism seems to vie to outdo the last, very like Greek weddings. Anyone who has watched the film, *My Big Fat Greek Wedding* will know exactly what I'm talking about; I am still waiting impatiently for *My Big Fat Greek Baptism*, perhaps I could write it....

"The godmother is the most important person at the baptism," Marietta explained, "She must be present at every special occasion during the life of her godchild. As a godmother you too will be reborn."

I asked her what she meant by this last statement.

"As Antonia is being baptised, you will enter another, what is the word? another stage in your life. Everything that has happened to you before will be wiped clean, like a slate, and you will have the chance to begin again. A fresh start I think you say in English?"

I very much approved of this novel concept, having so many things I would like wiped off my slate.

Jeremy and I made a special visit to Corfu Town to buy a cross for Antonia. At Christos and Andreas' jewellery shop on the Espianada, while being treated to the customary glasses of fresh orange juice and Greek coffee, we chose a necklace made by Christos in his workshop. The cross which hung from a sparkling gold chain was in yellow gold, with two thin bands of white gold which criss-crossed the middle section like a kiss. It was a contemporary but elegant design which I knew would suit a modern young woman; babies were given smaller crosses of course.

This was the easy part, the problems began when the time came to help Antonia choose her baptismal outfits. When Bambas had heard the good news he came striding out of the kitchens and sat at my table on the terrace.

"This will be very, very good for Antonia," he said, "The boss will be more respectful to her because you are her godmother and you are English."

I failed to grasp his point so I asked him to explain;

"What do you mean? Why will he have more respect for her?"

He sighed, this English woman was more stupid than he could believe.

"Because you are *English*!" He annunciated the last word slowly and loudly, imitating the way some of the more ignorant tourists spoke to him. "He always say to her, 'You stupid Albanian'. Well he won't ever do that again after you have baptised her."

I gave up and simply nodded sagely, in the way a Good Greek godmother should. As Bambas had predicted, Daniel was only too happy to allow Antonia a rare day off to come with me to buy her baptismal outfits. As the sun rose on a perfect July morning I left Jeremy and the children sleeping soundly in their cabins on Sarava. I collected Antonia from the restaurant in the Jeep; she always came to work from her home in the nearby village of Perithia on a very ancient scooter. We headed off along the coast road towards Corfu Town like a couple of excited schoolgirls. I adore shopping at anytime, anywhere; the more foreign the place the better I like it. Jeremy complains that I can buy shoes in eight different languages including Turkish and Thai. We laughed and chatted all the way, Antonia filling me in on all the village gossip. I swung the Jeep off the main road and pulled into the hamlet of Sinies to buy breakfast: a crusty loaf of fresh bread from Stamos the Baker and some bottles of ice-cold chocolate milk from the little grocery store. The sun shone, the sky was blue, the birds sang, and a day of clothes shopping and chatting stretched before us. In the distance Corfu Town rose like a glowing jewel from the sparkling sea. We were in seventh heaven.

Antonia and I began our search in the freshly washed streets leading from the Espianada, their pale flag stones glinting in the low sun. Between numerous shoe, jewellery and handbag shops were exclusive boutiques selling the latest fashions from mainland Greece and Europe. I noticed none of the clothes in these shops were made in the UK; even in the Marks & Spencer store in Theotoki Georgiou Street, the vast majority were made in the Far East. I led Antonia to one of my favourite boutiques and, ignoring her mutterings about it being too expensive, we chose two outfits in pure white linen which I thought would be perfect for the ceremony.

A groan came from behind the velvet curtains of the changing room.

"Are you all right Antonia?"

Another groan.

"What's the matter? Don't you feel well?"

"I look awful, I am so ugly in this. I hate my body!"

I couldn't believe my ears; this girl had the figure of Helen of Troy.

"Don't be silly; come out here so I can see you," I said.

"Noooo!" she wailed. "No one can see me in this!"

To the disappointment of the attentive sales assistants, we left empty handed. After several more perfectly suitable ensembles had been rejected in the next three shops, I decided I was badly in need of a coffee. Antonia, now with a face like a wet Tuesday in Lent, was in need of a good talking to from her future godmother.

"What on earth do you mean by saying you hate your body?" I asked as I sipped my frothy cappuccino.

"My hips are too big, my legs are too short, my boobs are too small, my stomach is fat ..."

"Stop!" I almost shouted. "You have a perfect figure; you look like Aphrodite. I wish I had your body!"

Right on cue, a handsome young Swedish tourist appeared at our table, clutching a dog-eared notebook.

"Excuse me Miss Roberts, could I please have your autograph?" He put his notebook and a biro on the table in front of Antonia, blushing to the roots of his shiny blonde hair. Antonia removed her large, film star sunglasses and gently explained that she was not Julia Roberts, but her mood improved from that moment and the rest of our expedition was easier. We bought some pretty white sandals and I began to be encouraged that we were getting somewhere. But it was getting uncomfortably hot as we walked the length and breadth of the town, fruitlessly scouring all the shops for an outfit which Antonia considered reasonably priced; she knew I intended to pay for it and didn't want to take advantage. By early afternoon I would have happily paid a king's ransom just to be able to go back to Kassiopi and have a swim. Sweat was trickling down my back, my dress was sticking to me, my sandalled feet were sore and, despite my straw hat, I was beginning to get a headache. We returned to the car with only the new shoes.

"But Antonia, your baptism is the last day of August," I warned her. "It's the end of July now and I doubt if your boss will give you another day off."

"He will, because he is very pleased that you will be my godmother and you are English, although he says he won't come to my baptism because he doesn't like church, " she replied.

"I will come to town again with Angelos," she added, "We can go to the cheaper shops around Sa'Rocco Square and find something."

"Well when you do, remember that I'm going to pay for it."I said, conceding defeat.

Angela and Geoffrey were again staying with us on the boat during the last week in August. I had advised them to bring something fairly smart as they would be joining us for Antonia's baptism on the 31st. Knowing the ropes by now, they usually only brought casual holiday clothes in their luggage. Sweetly and with typical generosity they had also bought a solid silver picture frame as a christening gift for Antonia.

On the appointed day, dressed in our best, we assembled in front of the pretty church. Antonia, Angelos and their families were already there, all chattering excitedly. Antonia's younger sisters, Irini and

Krissa had white flowers in their hair, like bridesmaids. This was a big day and like all Greeks, both families were determined to make the most of it. Antonia looked stunningly beautiful dressed in a simple plain skirt and sleeveless blouse in pure white linen, her long curly hair tumbling loosely over her sun-kissed shoulders almost to her waist. I wondered if she had really found this outfit in a cheap shop; it looked suspiciously like the first one she had tried in the expensive boutique. Perhaps Angelos had been able to persuade her she didn't look ugly in it and had generously bought it for her after all; she would not hear of me paying for it when I offered. After taking some photographs we made our way into the dark interior of the church, where narrow shafts of dusty sunlight shone down from the high windows; the cool air within was pleasantly laden with incense, musty prayer books and lamp oil. On the white altar cloth I placed a silver vase bought from Marietta's shop especially for the occasion. It contained a large bunch of jasmine I had picked from an obliging hedge early that morning; it was Antonia's favourite flower, one of the many things we shared in common. We were not a large party so we filled the first few pews and waited for Papa Makis to make his entrance. A handful of locals wandered through the open doors, keen to join in the occasion, and took their places behind us, chattering like magpies in contrast to the respectfully silent English contingent. In the middle of the floor, directly in front of the altar stood an enormous sky blue plastic tub, wide and deep enough for a small child to swim in, of the sort favoured by Corfiot housewives for soaking their washing.

"What's that doing there?" I whispered to Jeremy, who shrugged his shoulders.

"I think the cleaner must have left it there by mistake," I answered myself as he wasn't forthcoming. 'Don't worry about it' was his standard answer to most things that I was worrying about.

Papa Makis swept open the velvet curtains which divided the interior of the church from the vestry, with the dramatic effect of an actor making his grand entrance onto the stage. He was dressed in his best vestments, over the usual black cassock he wore a white epitracheleon, literally meaning 'around the neck', a kind of silk stole, heavily embroidered with fine gold thread.

I nudged Jeremy's side as we all stood up.

"The tub's still there!" I whispered.

"Sssh!" he hissed.

"Someone should move it!" I insisted, thinking it a disgraceful oversight.

"Don't worry about it," he said.

Papa Makis did not seem to notice the unsightly tub at all as Antonia made her ceremonial entrance and walked down the aisle like a bride on her wedding day. As she reached me she grabbed my arm.

"Look!" She nodded towards the tub.

"Yes, I know, I was sure someone would have moved it by now," I said apologetically, thinking she was offended by the this incongruous item at the service.

"No, you don't understand, he is going to make me stand in it and pour water all over me!"

"Well that's all right," I said, "It's so hot you'll soon dry off."

Her grip on my arm tightened like a vice and she pressed her mouth to my ear;

"But I'm not wearing any underwears and this material will be see through when it's wet!"

Now I understood. I tugged Jeremy close to me and whispered urgently in his ear.

"You must go back to the boat and fetch my white swimsuit!" I said.

He looked at me as if I had finally gone around the bend.

"What on earth for? You're surely not planning on going for a swim now?"

"No time to explain. For once in your life just do as I say and don't ask questions!"

"But I'll miss the service," he complained. "Why could you possibly want your swimsuit?"

"Antonia's not wearing any underwear," I hissed.

He looked at me blankly, his mouth open but unable to think of anything to say. Men can be incredibly dense at times. I shoved him out of the pew and told him to go.

"We'll wait for you," I said, trying to reassure him we would be able to stall Papa Makis.

"It's in the top right drawer of my dressing table – *Hurry*! And don't come back saying you couldn't find it!"

To my amazement, Antonia's boss sauntered into the church, looking even smarter and more dapper than usual, and sat in the pew behind me.

"I thought you weren't coming," I whispered, knowing he was a man of few words;

"I wasn't. I hate church," he said. "But I've come to support Antonia, she wants me as she has no father here. The last time I was in church was to bury my own father."

Antonia whispered something in the priest's ear and they both disappeared behind the velvet curtain. I tried hard not to read anything into this; improper thoughts must be restrained in this sacred place. None of the Greek contingent seemed to notice this delay in proceedings and carried on talking cheerfully. Time is of little importance in Mediterranean countries; *avrio methavrio* has the same meaning in Greek as *manana por la manana* in Spanish, or *domani o dopodimani* in Italian; in Cornwall, the closest equivalent to anything pleasantly Mediterranean in England, *dreckly* conveys the same meaning.

Jeremy must have put on a turn of speed as he was back in a few minutes, the swimsuit discreetly bunched up in his hand. I took it from him, keeping it hidden from the congregation, and gave it to Antonia, who I found in the vestry. Papa Makis returned to take his position at the altar and I stood to one side of the aisle, as he instructed me. Antonia soon appeared and stood beside me, smiled sweetly and winked. The priest beckoned us to step forward and handed each of us a very long white candle. More prayers followed over our bowed heads. With his own candle, lit from one on the altar, Papa Makis lit ours then led us in a sombre procession three times around the baptismal washing tub, melodiously intoning prayers which echoed around the almost empty church as we followed. He then turned to face me and said something in Greek which I couldn't understand. I thought he said; 'Repeat after me,' but I couldn't be sure and didn't want to do or say the wrong thing. I shot a confused glance towards Antonia.

"You must say the words he will say first," she explained quietly.

"You are just saying you believe in God," the Papas assured me.

Oh crumbs, nobody had told me about this. I am sure the Papas tried to speak slowly and clearly, reducing his customary lightening speed for my benefit, but it took all my powers of concentration and mimicry to repeat his words. I thought I was fairly competent at conversational Greek until that moment; this ecclesiastical language was new to me, containing as it did so many religious words and phrases. Trying to avoid catching the astonished eyes of Jeremy and our English friends, I did my best to repeat Papa Makis' words parrot fashion. It seemed to go on for hours but I guess it was only about two minutes. How could the four simple words he had promised I would say have taken all this time? He gave a satisfied nod in my direction as he closed his prayer book with a thud. I think he was as relieved as I was that my ordeal was over. 'Phew', it must have been all right I thought, hoping to goodness I wouldn't have to say anything except Αμήν for the rest of the service.

Papa Makis gestured to Antonia to step into the tub, which she did with confidence and grace after removing her new white sandals. He took the bottle of blessed oil from the altar and poured it over Antonia's bowed head. More prayers were incanted as he proceeded to pour holy water from a huge silver ewer all over her and made the sign of the cross with his free hand. There was a sharp gasp from the English guests as the water cascaded over her hair and ran down her body, mostly into the tub; she looked like a mermaid, less the fish tail. As she had predicted, the white linen outfit became instantly transparent, but all that could be discerned underneath was a demure white swimsuit. As Papa Makis gave Antonia his hand to help her out of the tub, now lethally slippery with oily water, she looked at me and winked again. As I fastened the new gold cross around her neck, the radiant smile on my new goddaughter's lovely face spoke a thousand words. She was no longer an insignificant refugee from Albania; she was now a bona fide member of the Christian Church. Antonia and her children would be welcomed as equals by Orthodox Greeks everywhere and she would command the respect of her employer. Most importantly she could become engaged and eventually married to Angelo. I, on the other hand, was looking forward to inspecting my clean slate.

Antonia asked me to join her and we went into the vestry again leaving Papa Makis to clear away the baptismal accoutrements from the altar and presumably the greasy washing bowl from the aisle. I put her wet clothes and my swimsuit in a plastic bag while Antonia dried herself with her new towel and changed into a pretty summer dress, also bought for the occasion. By the time Antonia was ready, everyone from the church had adjourned to the terrace of the restaurant, including Papa Makis. Several tables had been pushed together so the party could sit together. Antonia's boss bustled backwards and forwards between the long table and the kitchens. On his instructions the waiters brought coffees, orange juice, brandy and whisky; I noticed the priest thoroughly enjoyed a glass of Scotch Mist, although it was only mid-day. The eldest of Antonia's brothers, Iolandis, asked very courteously if I would mind if he took the seat next to me. I was surprised but extremely pleased, as it was the first time I had met him properly; I was certain this handsome Adonis would have much preferred the other end of the table where the younger people were sitting.

"We are all so happy you have honoured Antonia by becoming her godmother," he began earnestly.

His English was as perfect as Antonia's and his genuine appreciation made me want to cry. I muttered something about the honour being all mine, but he wasn't finished.

"What you have done today will change Antonia's life forever." he added, most touchingly. "On behalf of my family I want to thank you most sincerely."

Were those tears in his beautiful almond eyes? I was quite taken aback, not only by his sincerity and obvious love for his sister, but also by the eloquence of such a young man who had enjoyed none of the benefits of a conventional education. Iolandis had left school at sixteen to become an apprentice with a local carpenter, literally learning his trade from the ground up as a floor sweeper.

Jeremy and I led the principals of the ceremony to the harbour where Sarava lay waiting at the quayside. Our guests settled themselves on the comfy French blue and ivory striped cushions in the cockpit and we cast off. This last day of August could not have been more perfect; the water twinkled in the sun and a light sea breeze kept us cool as we raised a toast to Antonia with chilled Champagne and headed down the coast for lunch. Angelo had his arm protectively around Antonia, who was prone to sea sickness; he looked so proud of his soon to be fiancée and thankfully she did not feel sick on the half hour trip. Kostas was waiting on his pontoon to welcome us and take our lines. He gallantly helped the ladies ashore, warmly embracing Antonia and wishing her *Xronia polla,* long life, the twinkle in his eyes at the sight of this beautiful girl cofirming our suspicion that he had been a bit of a lad in his younger days. Several tables had been pushed together and covered in a long white linen cloth. I placed the vase of jasmine used for the ceremony on the middle table and its perfume wafted around us as we ordered. Iolandis sat beside me again and kept up an interesting and intelligent conversation throughout the long lunch, exhibiting all the charm and kindness we had found in Antonia and her siblings. They were such a credit to their mother and to each other.

A delicious meze of dishes appeared, spilling from our table onto another one that had been hastily moved beside us. Eventually our main course was finished and Kostas brought enormous plates of sliced water melon, its icy cool sweetness perfect on this hot afternoon. Once on board Sarava again, sleepiness overtook some of us and we lazed on deck or in the shady cockpit as we motored gently out of the bay on the homeward journey to Kassiopi. Antonia was still not brave enough to venture onto the foredeck and sat enveloped in Angelo's arms next to Jeremy at the helm. Her siblings were enjoying the trip immensely and stood in line on the netting between her twin bows with Angela and Geoffrey, leaning over the high guard rails to watch the waves running under the hulls. This magical day would live in our memories for years to come and we would often reminisce about it afterwards. Antonia told us it was one of the best days of her life and I hope, in some small way, it helped her to face the tragic time that lay ahead.

* * *

Less than a year later Antonia's youngest sister, fifteen year-old Krissa, *Xrisa* in Greek, was sitting her school summer exams when she collapsed and was rushed to the local doctor. Trips to specialists in Corfu Town and subsequently to the mainland confirmed the family's worst fears, when Krissa was diagnosed with a particularly vicious form of leukaemia. I kept in constant touch with Antonia after we returned to England for the Christmas term and soon learnt that Krissa was in hospital in Athens, accompanied by Antonia who was able to stay with a distant relative who lived in the city. Antonia spent every day at Krissa's bedside, caring for her as is the custom in Greece, where families are expected to tend to the patients' needs; this included including washing them, their bedlinen and night clothes, making their beds and even bringing in food from outside. Krissa existed on a very specific diet, everything had to be boiled thoroughly; this was a challenging situation for Antonia, having to buy all the food, using her relative's kitchen to cook it, then carrying it on public transport to the hospital every day. All treatments, medicines and bus fares had to be paid for somehow and Antonia was unable to work during the time she was away from Corfu.

Jeremy and I flew back to Corfu for a brief visit later that autumn; in Athens, instead of making our connection to Corfu, we took a taxi to the hospital to meet Antonia. I had bought a selection of things in England which I thought might add a little comfort to the girls; nice toiletries, slippers, sweets and chocolate, fashion magazines and some of the latest music for Krissa to listen to on her portable CD player – Miranda and Rory had been a great help in advising me what to buy for a teenager; I had also bought some audio books which I thought would be useful to her when she was too tired to read. I chose *Gone With The Wind*, *My Family & Other Animals*, *Sense & Sensibility* and *Rebecca*. We were not allowed to see Krissa for risk of passing her an infection, so Antonia met us in the shabby reception area and stayed for less than half-an-hour, as she was anxious about leaving her sister alone. One glance at the hospital had shocked us to the core. This was not the sort of hospital we were accustomed to in England and certainly not the place for any young girl. Antonia put on her bravest face but we could tell how bad the situation was when we questioned her about the conditions at the hospital. Krissa was in a large, mixed ward that lacked air-conditioning, full of patients that included geriatrics and the insane. Day and night it was impossible for her to sleep because of the moaning, shouting, screaming and wanderings of her fellow patients. She had become weaker by the day and, not wanting to leave her alone at night, Antonia had moved into the ward and was attempting to sleep on two plastic chairs pushed together next to Krissa's bed.

"We've got to do something!" I urged Jeremy in the taxi back to the airport.

"Naturally," he said, "But how to go about it?"

We had asked Antonia if there were any private hospitals in Athens, but none were entirely suitable and all were expensive. To offer money to Antonia would have been considered an insult, although we had slipped several bank notes amongst the toiletries on this occasion. We had to find another way to help the sisters; once back in Corfu I went to see Marietta at her jewellery shop and related the awful conditions in the Athens hospital. Everyone in North East Corfu knew of the girls' horrendous situation and although a collection had been made it was not enough to pay for private treatment. Through her involvement with the national blood transfusion service Marietta knew some influential medical people in Athens, who she offered to call.

For the rest of our winter in England, the two sisters were never out of our thoughts and prayers, as Krissa's health followed the painful pattern of improvement and relapse. Returning to Corfu for the Easter holidays with Rory and Miranda, we heard from Marietta that she had been able to arrange for Krissa to be transferred to a modern, state of the art children's hospital, despite Krissa having turned sixteen.

"However did you manage it?" I asked Marietta.

"I had to pull a few ropes," she answered coyly.

"Strings, Marietta, the English expression is 'pull a few strings', not ropes!"

"Ah yes," she laughed, "But it was so hard that they were definitely ropes!"

The next time we visited Antonia in Athens the situation was so different. Antonia greeted us in the reception area of the children's hospital with a warm smile, dressed like a nurse in white linen trousers, shirt and soft-soled white shoes, with her long hair twisted into a neat bun. In stark contrast to the municipal hospital, this one was like a Nuffield Nursing Home: air-conditioned, decorated with potted plants and tasteful pictures, spotlessly clean and free from the smell of pine scented disinfectant, *chlorini* or worse. Krissa's treatments had been taking their toll; sometimes she was allowed home to Corfu for brief visits but her condition was worsening, despite sessions of chemotherapy which had robbed her of all her beautiful curly hair;

continued doses of antibiotics left her weak and listless. Antonia never left her side except to go outside for an occasional short walk to get some fresh air and exercise. Again we brought a few gifts for the girls but I had also slipped in some cash with a note telling Antonia to buy whatever small treats she thought Krissa would like. Miranda had sent some Champneys white velour slippers for both girls as her contribution and Rory had compiled some popular music onto CDs.

During the early part of the summer holidays Krissa was allowed home once more to Corfu. She seemed to be very much better, although still weak and painfully thin; a bone marrow transplant from one of her brothers had raised hopes for a while. Antonia was still unable to work at the restaurant in Kassiopi as she had to care for Krissa and cook for her as she did in Athens. Their mother and all their siblings were working at two or three jobs each to scrape together enough money to cover Krissa's medical bills and the frequent trips to Athens. Jeremy and I visited Antonia often and suggested that she and Krissa joined us for supper one night at a restaurant in Acharavi. The Lemon Garden was the girls' favourite; rustic tables and chairs were set in the middle of a grove of lemon trees decorated with fairy lights. It was enchanting, like a fairy glade, with the sweet scent of the lemon blossom wafting around us in the warm night air. Antonia had decorated what little was left of Krissa's hair with rows of miniature plastic hair clips, which was so touching it brought tears to my eyes. But we kept up a cheerful demeanour throughout supper and both sisters seemed to be enjoying themselves, although Krissa ate little and occasionally laid her head on Antonia's shoulder, smiling adoringly up at her. After a couple of hours Antonia could see that Krissa was tiring, so we said our fond goodbyes, waving to the girls as they sped off on Antonia's scooter.

"She seems so much better," I said to Jeremy as we drove back to Sarava.

"I do hope so, but I fear she's not out of the woods yet."

As usual, despite my optimism in all things, Jeremy was right of course.

Chapter Eleven
Burberry and Belgravia

Fashion may not be a weapon of the woman, but at least it gives her the ammunition.

Brigitte Bardot

A few days after Antonia's baptism we sailed Sarava to Corfu Town to have supper at *La Cucina*. The anchorage we always used was spectacular and we knew Angela and Geoffrey, with their passion for history, would appreciate seeing the historical the Old Fort, which towered above a sheltered bay. After dark the classical buildings and ancient ramparts were illuminated like a film set; on the very pinnacle of the castle stood a monumental cross outlined with light bulbs, which cast a shimmering reflection on the dark water. One Easter, when Jeremy had first seen this cross glowing eerily against the evening sky, he remarked how dramatically the last rays of the setting sun highlighted the cross. Having studied it at close quarters in daylight I had to shatter his uncustomary romanticism by pointing out that it was lit by electricity and not the sun.

This impressive fortress dates back to the fifth century BC when Corfu was one of the three great naval powers in Greece, along with Athens and Corinth. The original castle was built to defend the island against invasions by marauding pirates; since then it has gone through various metamorphoses over the centuries. Standing on a natural rocky promontory, it offered protection to the Corfiots from numerous invasions; the entire population of Corfu Town and its outskirts would take shelter within the Fort's walls whenever the city came under attack. In the fifth century AD the city of Corfu was installed here, from its previous location on the island, following the destruction of the ancient capital by the Visigoths.

Once Sarava was securely at anchor, we changed out of our swimwear; the ladies into summer dresses, the men into short sleeved shirts and cotton trousers. We climbed into the tender and headed for the NAOK Yacht Club, whose marina housed many local craft, from substantial cabin cruisers to small fishing boats and skiffs. Visiting superyachts lay serenely at anchor stern-to the harbour's outer wall; these leviathans of the sea made Sarava look like a bath toy. Tying up alongside one of the wooden pontoons, we climbed the steps which led from the patch of shingle beach to the club house. This has to be one of the most picturesque and elegant yacht clubs we have visited in the Mediterranean, and we have seen many over the years since sailing to Cyprus from Salcombe on our beloved first catamaran, *Aries*, for our honeymoon in 1980. We lived very happily aboard Aries in Cyprus for two full years, eventually returning home to South Devon for the birth of our son.

The spring before this visit to Sarava, Angela and Geoffrey had been invited to luncheon by Countess Raine Spencer at her country home, not far from their own ancestral castle in South Devon. The other guests included Spiro, a Corfiot born Count and his wife, Milly, a great friend of Raine's since boarding school. Raine Spencer was of course the daughter of Dame Barbara Cartland, doyenne of the romantic novel and step grandmother to Princess Diana.

Spiro and Geoffrey had got on famously with their mutual love of history and Corfu. Angela and Milly had also found interests in common: antiques, architecture, history of art and Corfu. At the end of the luncheon party, Spiro handed Geoffrey his calling card and told him to be sure to look him up when they came to stay with us again in Corfu. Geoffrey was a stickler when it came to keeping details of friends and acquaintances. He kept a little black book with him in his pocket at all times, in which he would write the contact details of every person he met, each noted with the date and place he met them. On arrival in Corfu, Geoffrey had telephoned Spiro, explaining that they were staying with us on Sarava and asked if we could meet somewhere. Spiro suggested the Yacht Club, so this evening found us sitting at a table on the spacious terrace waiting for them to arrive. Our drinks had just been delivered when Angela looked towards the entrance to the balcony.

"I think that's them," she said, squinting against the evening sun as we got up to greet them.

Countess Milly looked cool, calm, collected and elegant in a silk dress with matching court shoes and a small handbag exactly like those highly favoured by Her Majesty The Queen. Amongst the other yachties at the Club that evening, she stood out like a rose amongst daisies. Introductions were made and more drinks ordered. Impeccably groomed and debonair, Spiro was apologetic.

"You could have come to the Cavalieri but we are renovating the rooftop restaurant, so we would have had to sit inside; this is much better," he said agreeably in his cut glass English accent. "Next year you must be our guests on the roof!"

The Cavalieri Hotel had formerly been Spiro's ancestral home in Corfu Town since the days his family were ennobled by the Venetians. The elegant six-storey mansion was originally built in the 17th century, but Spiro and Milly had converted it into a splendid hotel in the late 1960s. The gracious building stands at the more elevated end of the Espianada, from where the views from its rooftop terrace are something to behold as one's gaze settles first on the lush canopy of chestnut trees, out of which the ivory Maltese limestone dome of the Maitland Rotunda* shines like a pearl. Above the park rises the craggy outline of the Old Fort, itself commanding the azure Ionian beyond.

---

* This neoclassical monument – erected in honour of Sir Thomas Maitland, First Lord High Commissioner of the Ionian Islands – carries a local and far less flattering title of 'sterna' or Cistern, as it is built on top of an antiquated Venetian water cistern. Greeks are nothing if not down to earth and have a charming propensity to call a spade a spade and a cess pit a … but I've already mentioned that. The park and the monument can be seen in the 1981 Bond film, *For Your Eyes Only*, a rather more glamorous connection.

Burberry was a fully paid up member of Continental Café Society. Welcomed with open arms and his own chair everywhere we went in Europe, he was enjoying a late snooze when Spiro and Milly joined us. Burberry's mother, Hannah, belonged to Angela and Geoffrey and the children and I had been determined to have one of Hannah's first litter of puppies. Milly was enamoured with Burberry from that first time she saw him snoring contentedly and enjoying the cooler evening air after a hot day on the boat.

"Which is your yacht?" Spiro asked Jeremy. "Is it that white one?" he said, pointing to a very large motor yacht lying at anchor outside the harbour.

"No, she's the catamaran just there," Jeremy replied.

If Spiro was disappointed in the smaller size of Sarava, he didn't show it, not a glimmer crossing his face.

"Ah, yes, how lovely," he commented politely.

Our new friends had plans for dinner that evening so they left after an hour or so. But as they were leaving Milly turned to me.

"You must come to dinner at our villa at Pirghi one evening. I would love to show you *La Serenissima*; I think you would like it."

"But there is one condition," she continued.

Oh crumbs, I thought. Did this mean we would have to sing for our supper, or recite poetry or some such?

"You *must* bring Burberry with you."

With a mischievous smile she kissed me on the cheek and was gone, leaving a waft of delicious and very expensive scent in her graceful wake. The four of us walked through the park just as the Venetian lanterns were lit on the Espianada and the town began to buzz with the sounds of the evening. The Mediterranean swifts had vacated the skies to roost in their nests, made of material caught on the wing, bonded together with the birds' saliva and precariously constructed in the nooks and crannies of the town's weathered buildings. The shrill, piping, daytime cries of the swifts, the soundtrack to a Mediterranean summer, were replaced by the low hubbub of conversation, through which gentle, romantic strains of guitars and mandolins blended with the clinking of ice against glass.

The scent of night-blooming jessamine, mingling with the irresistible aroma of meat grilling over smokey charcoal, filled the air and made our mouths water at the thought of the meal we would soon enjoy. Burberry was in no hurry, he had eaten his supper on board Sarava, followed by a refreshing nap, and was now intent on investigating every canine scent on every lamp post and tree trunk in the town. We headed towards our favourite Italian restaurant, whose speciality was home made fresh pasta and the thinnest, most crispy stone baked pizzas; the dish I always chose was tortellini filled with creamy gorgonzola and walnuts in a delicate white wine sauce. Outside one of the many little shops which line the narrow street leading to La Cucina, an elderly man sat on a wobbly wooden chair, taking the evening air as he watched the world go by.

"*Kalispera sas*, you Germans?" he asked as we approached.

"Good God, no!" Geoffrey almost shouted.

"American?"

"I should say not!" said Jeremy with a smile. "We're English."

The little man leapt from his chair as if he had been stung on the bottom by a hornet.

"Aaah, *Eengleesh*!" he repeated ecstatically, an expression of pure joy spreading across a face that looked like crumpled brown leather.

'Oh no, here we go again!', I thought to myself. This unconditional love of the English was getting embarrassing. He shook each of our hands in turn, effusively bestowing flowery compliments about our nationality, our country, our Queen and all English people.

"Please to wait here a moment," he said, disappearing into the doorway of his dark little shop.

"Oh dear," said my cynical husband. "We could be here for hours and we've booked a table. Perhaps we should just go."

"No, we can't, it would be too rude," I said, "Just wait a minute and see."

Angela and Geoffrey agreed with me and a few seconds later the man came hurrying back, carrying something carefully in his wizened hands.

"I want for you to have this," he pressed a large bottle wrapped in paper into Geoffrey's hands.

"It is *Limoncello*, I made it myself with lemons from my garden," the man said proudly, "I hope you will like it."

This tangy liqueur was a particular favourite and, as with most things, the home made variety was usually the best. We thanked him profusely but Geoffrey was puzzled.

"Why did you want to give us this wonderful gift?" he asked mildly.

" Because you are English," the man answered simply. "You are the best peoples in the world – after the Greeks, of course!"

"But there must be a reason you like the English so much. What is it?" persisted Geoffrey, genuinely intrigued.

"You came to our rescue in the war," he said; there were tears in his rheumy blue eyes. "And you sent wonderful cheese for the starving children."

There it was again, the Cheddar.

"I remember the taste to this day!" he said, smiling and closing his eyes at the memory. We all thanked him for his kind gift and as we walked on to the restaurant Geoffrey was waxing lyrical about this man's generosity and affection for our countrymen.

"Next time we come to Corfu I'm going to bring a whole Cheddar to give him," he announced.

"Well it's not coming in my suitcase," observed Angela. "Imagine the smell!"

* * *

Milly was as good as her word and a couple of weeks after Angela and Geoffrey had gone home, she telephoned.

"Will you come to dinner next Saturday? We have some friends we would like you to meet."

Sitting in the cockpit at anchor off Koyevina when I took the call, I realised I had nothing appropriate to wear to a formal dinner party. Our Corfu was not a dressy place; a simple knee length sleeveless linen frock, of the kind made fashionable by Audrey Hepburn in the film, *Breakfast at Tiffany's*, and later much favoured by the incomparably well dressed Jackie Kennedy, was my dress of choice for shopping or lunching in Corfu Town in the summer; but all mine were distinctly faded and jaded after numerous washes and being dried in full sun. The rest of the time I was hardly out of a swimsuit or bikini; dressing for lunch at a beachside taverna only involved putting a sarong around my lower half as a concession to being suitably and modestly attired. Many modern tourists didn't even bother with sarongs, sitting instead in wet swimming costumes, which is the reason most tavernas had swopped their traditional and comfortable rush seated wooden chairs for the modern white plastic variety.*

A trip to Corfu Town was called for; I knew I would find something suitable and reasonably priced, as the August sales were on. I drove into town very early the next morning, parked easily in the car park by the cricket pitch and headed for the market to buy a few things before the day became too hot for the long walk there and back. I was pulling my trusty basket on wheels, bought in Dartmouth; it was invaluable and could be filled with a few days' worth of fruit and vegetables, a couple of loaves of bread and even some fresh fish in ice, for which I kept an insulated cool bag at the bottom of the basket. I had also invented a wonderful way to keep my cool during shopping expeditions; for perfect personal air-conditioning I would tuck a miniature plastic ice block inside the middle section of my bra. Several of my lady friends in Corfu have copied this ever since. At one of the fruit stalls I found myself standing next to Christos the

---

*I see now that most of the beachside tavernas have thankfully replaced the obligatory white plastic chairs with the traditional and attractive wooden ones. Whenever we ate at Taverna Agni, George would lend me the one wooden chair he had kept for his own use.

Jeweller's mother-in-law. Roma greeted me and we chatted about our families, South Devon and other news. At the age of five I had been at school with the daughter of previous owners of her house; the vast scale of this Queen Anne mansion, with its rather sinister atmosphere, had always terrified me as a child.

"Shall we go for a coffee?" I asked Roma. "I could really do with your advice about something."

We sat at a little metal table in a makeshift café in the shade of a frayed canvas awning, wedged between two stalls in the bustling market beneath the walls of the New Fort. Roma, a lady of my parents' generation, had spent many years in Corfu and knew where to obtain everything. I told her about our invitation and asked what I should take as a present.

"Not chocolates," she said, "Your hostess will be very figure conscious and that might be an unwelcome present."

"Flowers?" I suggested.

"But you live on a yacht and you would have to get them back from town, then keep them until the dinner party; they would be dead within hours in this heat. What does your hostess like?"

"I don't know her well ... we've only met for drinks, but I understand she loves entertaining."

"Okay, go to the little shop in the side street opposite Marks & Spencers; it has lovely things for the home, so you will find something there. They also sell Crabtree & Evelyn, so maybe you could get her some soap and bath gel. I for one would love that!"

I found the little shop easily and had fun choosing a selection of pretty things which all seemed to have co-ordinating colours; some napkins, candles, soap, bubble bath, talcum powder and very lifelike silk flowers which I thought could be useful in a hot climate. The assistant put everything in a smart carrier bag and tied the handles with ribbon matching the colour scheme of the gifts. Job done, I thought, and I don't even have to wrap the present.

My next port of call was a small boutique, almost next door to

St. Spyridon's Church, which was owned by the effervescent aunt of our friend Bambas. Auntie greeted me with a Bambas style bear hug and kisses on both cheeks. I was immediately offered coffee or fresh orange juice and it would have been rude to refuse, despite the fact that I could still taste the strong Greek *metrio* that I had enjoyed in the market, so I opted for orange juice. Auntie was always pleased just to chat, but I was on a mission. I told her about the imminent dinner party and asked her if she had anything suitable for me to wear. She instructed me to sit on a little gilt chair and proceeded to take numerous glitzy, sequinned dresses from her clothes rails, holding them up on their hangers for me to view. Never wanting to hurt her feelings or criticize her flamboyant taste in evening wear, I asked for something a little more casual.

"CASUAL!" she exploded, her face turning the colour of a ripe pomegranate, "A dinner party at La Serenissima will *not* be casual!"

This was slightly worrying; I could not see myself crossing Sarava's passerelle and tottering along the wooden slats of the long pontoons to the Jeep in any of these elaborate dresses.

"I really prefer trousers," I suggested meekly.

"Okay, so you want to be casual. I have the *evening* trousers," she replied with laboured emphasis, delving into another alcove and rummaging in its depths. My heart sank as I tried to conjure up an excuse for leaving Auntie's shop empty handed. I was imagining she was going to produce trousers of the shiny, black, skin-tight variety worn by Olivia Newton-John in *Grease*; Olivia had to be sewn into the trousers and couldn't go to the loo for hours – two prospects that filled me with horror.

But the outfit she eventually extricated from the selection of *Casual and Cruise Wear* quite took my breath away. It consisted of three pieces; silk crêpe de chine palazzo pants, long sleeved shirt in gossamer silk chiffon over a satin camisole, all in a serene aquamarine the exact colour of the sea in Antipaxos. Tiny pearl buttons ran down the front of the overshirt and fastened the deep cuffs, these buttons the only decoration. It fitted as if it had been made for me. I didn't even ask the price but handed over my credit card, hoping Jeremy would never find out how much I had paid. Being made in Greece, it was not that expensive, certainly not the extortionate price of a 'designer' label; but men are peculiar creatures when it comes to clothes or shoes and seem to think everything should cost less than fifty pounds. What a pity I would only get one chance to wear it, as fate later decreed.

"Now, *Kyria* Jani. What about some beautiful costume jewellery to complete your outfit?" suggested Auntie eagerly, throwing open a display cabinet laden with fake diamond and pearl necklaces of the sort adored by Pantomime Dames.

Before she could deck me out like a Christmas tree, I hastily changed back into my own clothes, grabbed my carrier bag, kissed Auntie on both cheeks and rushed out, pretending that a taxi was waiting to deliver me back to the marina.

Burberry, our King Charles Cavalier, was given a thorough shampoo on the afternoon of the dinner party. He scampered madly around the foredeck afterwards, as he always did after being washed, going for a swim, or even if he had been caught in the lightest shower of rain. That evening we drove from the marina along the coast road towards Ipsos as the sun was sinking beyond the Corfu Straits into a rose gold sky. Turning off the road into the long driveway of La Serenissima, Jeremy parked tidily under the trees and I lifted our very fragrant Burberry from the car.

" You can't possibly take him in! Think of all the hair on Milly's carpets, Jani. " Jeremy insisted.

"Oh yes I can!"

"No you really can't! He'll be fine here; the car's in the shade, he's got water and I'll leave all the windows open."

I tried to convince him that Milly had asked me to bring Burberry, but Jeremy was already waiting for me by the large stone lions at either side of the imposing front door. The butler had anticipated our arrival and before we could put a foot inside, Milly was also there to greet us.

Wearing a beautiful, floor length silk evening kaftan, she was never-theless looking somewhat crestfallen and I wondered if our choice of *casual* evening wear was not quite up to muster.

"Where's Burberry?" she asked, rather wistfully.

I explained that Jeremy thought he should stay in the car, but she stopped me in mid flow.

"But he *must* come in, everyone's dying to meet him! Go and get him, Jeremy!"

Jeremy would never dream of arguing with our hostess and I was quietly delighted. I hated leaving Burberry alone at any time of day or night and the joy of finding he was welcome anywhere in Europe meant we never had to worry about him after crossing the English Channel. It always strikes me as very odd that the British are supposed to be a nation of dog lovers, yet it is only in Britain that dogs are so often banned.

A particular memory still niggles of a bitterly cold December day spent Christmas shopping in Burford, the picturesque village in West Oxfordshire. Burberry was with me as usual and by about 4pm it was already dark; I was in desperate need of a hot cup of tea and a sit down. I went to the door of every café on the main street and was abruptly turned away because of my little dog. I couldn't believe it, having just made the four day journey by car from Corfu to England to spend Christmas with our children, during which he had been warmly welcomed in every country along the way.

Having struggled almost to the top the hill, a waiter at the last café reluctantly agreed I could sit at a table on the pavement. I relented and sat down, placing Burberry on another cold metal chair next to me. The sky was black and forbidding and the air bitter with the damp, frosty chill that is so common in that area of the landlocked Cotswolds. As I shivered I was reminded of the saying, *Even the Devil gets cold in Stow-on-the-Wold.*

Burberry was so pleased to be invited into La Serenissima that he almost pulled me off my feet in his hurry to join the assembled

company on one of the terraces. My evening sandals slipped dangerously on the polished marble floors of the entrance hall until they
found foothold on the deep softness of a plush carpet in the drawing
room.

"I had this carpet specially woven to match the wall paintings," said
Milly modestly, unaware I knew her to be an artist of great renown.
Looking around the walls, trying to ignore Burberry's impatient
whining, I could see what she meant. A frieze of delicate hand painted
designs of flowers and foliage in pastel colours decorated the walls of
the room and were reflected in the pattern of the carpet. It was like
being in a fairy ring; *A Midsummer Night's Dream* come to life, only
lacking Titania. Milly led us through the drawing room and the tall
French doors which opened onto a terrace, where Spiro was handing
cocktails to the other guests.

"I love your trouser suit," Milly remarked. "Did you buy it in Italy?"
This was a generous compliment, although many of Corfu's boutiques sold fashions made in France, Italy and Germany, as well as
Greece. Much as I adore Austrian clothes, the Italian flair for style,
originality and flamboyance is unparalleled. Jeremy used to complain
about me buying clothes from the Austrian fashion house Geiger
whenever we were skiing in the Tirol and joked relentlessly about my
dangerous attraction to the 'Geiger Counter'. However this shopping
habit led to the discovery of a blatant breach of my copyright, so he
had to admit the expense was most worthwhile in the end. My designs for a collection of bespoke greeting cards for The Scotch House,
then owned by Burberry (the fashion house, not my dog) had been
copied by Geiger, who eventually agreed to pay me a considerable
sum in compensation; over a thousand pure wool skirts featuring my
'Highland Birds' had been sold all over the world, from the USA to
Korea. The best moment of the legal process came when I was instructed by my German lawyers to buy one of the skirts as evidence,
should the case ever reach court. I was able to buy one over the phone
from Simpsons of Piccadilly; naturally I ordered one in my size, which

I still wear and love today, although Jeremy nearly fainted when he discovered it had cost the equivalent of a year's private nursery school fees for Miranda.

The view from the terrace of La Serenissima was spectacular; above the vast expanse of glassy sea Corfu Town rose in all its honey coloured glory. The water was streaked with the pastel shades of Neapolitan ice cream – 'Nollipum', as Miranda used to call it when she was little. Spiro introduced us to the other guests and Burberry was thrilled to shake paws with everyone in turn, much to the delight of Milly.

"I told you how clever he was!" she said.

Jeremy and I need not have been there; Burberry was the star of the evening. One guest was particularly fond of dogs and had recently lost a much cherished pet, as Milly must have known; he was a portly and elderly man, a distinguished former Greek government minister as I recall, who owned homes in Eaton Square and in Athens.

"Show him how Burberry can do tricks," Milly said.

Burberry had a little party piece which he would cheerfully perform in anticipation of the treat I always gave him. I can't remember teaching him these actions as a puppy, but I think it must have been a combination of the children's patience and Burberry imitating his older Cavalier cousins, Bramble and Briar.

Everyone's eyes were on Burberry as I asked him in turn to 'sit, give me your paw, lie down, roll over, get up, turn around, sit and give me your paw again.' At this point he received a small treat. Everyone laughed and applauded, Burberry was delighted at this reaction and wagged his tail madly, hoping to be asked to repeat the trick. I told the guests that he could also speak Greek.

"No, it is not possible!" said the elderly guest, "Please show me," he said, leaning forward in his cane armchair to get a closer look at Burberry who was sitting at his feet enjoying having his ears tickled by this admirer.

"Burberry," I said, holding out my hand. "*Dóse mou to pódi sou*" – give me your paw. Burberry obliged immediately, much to the astonishment of the assembled company, but honesty compelled me to explain that my son had recently shattered my illusions of our little dog's great intellect. Rory had held out his hand in front of Burberry while uttering a sentence of complete gobbledegook that sounded vaguely Chinese; of course Burberry had obediently given his paw.

The Minister was enchanted and bade me sit and tell him all about Burberry. With tears in his eyes, which he dabbed at intervals with a large silk handkerchief, he told me about his own beloved dog and the many adventures they had enjoyed together. It seemed incongruous that such a man, larger than life in every sense of the word, had chosen a miniature white poodle as his constant canine companion. I recited one of my favourite quotes from Mark Twain which I was sure he would like: *The dog is a gentleman, I hope to go to his heaven, not man's.*

"Dinner is served, Madame," announced the butler from the doorway.

We followed Milly into the dining room and took our seats around the long glass topped table on which were tiny place cards; written in a refined hand on mine was *Jani and Burberry.* I sat next to Spiro at the far end of the table with the Minister to my other side; Milly sat at the other end with Jeremy to one side and – equally to my husband's delight – a renowned authority on Edward Burne-Jones on the other. When we had finished our delicious first course our hostess rang a little hand bell and the butler appeared from the door to the kitchens, followed by a couple of uniformed waitresses who removed our plates. Milly summoned the butler before he could leave.

"Take Burberry to the kitchens and give him some fillet steak," she asked. "But make sure it is cut up into small pieces."

With great dignity the butler gingerly took Burberry's lead and off they went into the kitchen. A few minutes later Mr. B was brought back, licking his chops and reluctant to sit obediently at my feet as he looked longingly after his new best friend every time he disappeared through the door as each course was finished. Finally coffee was served on the terrace, where ornate candle lanterns flickered on the coffee tables and low turquoise faiance balustrades; below the terrace tiny white fairy lights twinkled amongst the olive trees where a winding path led through the gardens to a small private beach. Across the dark water of the bay Corfu Town looked like Tolkien's ethereal *Rivendell*, pinpricks of light from a thousand elfin windows shimmering over the water. On the end of the high promontory, the Old Fort stood guard over the Straits, softly illuminated by an apricot glow against the star spangled night sky.

As the hand made chocolates were passed around, Burberry looked longingly at the silver dish. In his opinion this would have been the perfect finale to the evening; of course he could not know that chocolate is extremely poisonous to dogs. Nor did his cousin Briar, who several years before had found the large chocolate cake I had made for Miranda's twelfth birthday cooling on a high windowsill; somehow he had pulled it down to the floor and eaten the whole thing, leaving just a few crumbs on the tiles to testify to his crime. He could hardly move afterwards and lay panting in his basket, resembling an amply stuffed Chesterfield sofa, with his long pink tongue lolling out of his mouth like a piece of cooked ham. He suffered no ill effects whatsoever but, much to his disappointment, he was allowed no food for two long days.

As we drove back to the marina, with Burberry snoring contentedly on the back seat, we talked about our time at La Serenissima.

"The entire evening was a glorious little taste of Belgravia, transported perfectly to Corfu," mused Jeremy, eager nevertheless to change out of his linen suit back into well worn shorts and faded tee shirt at the first opportunity.

Milly and Spiro were no strangers to that exclusive area of London and came to their villa in Corfu for the month of August each year, with occasional shorter visits at other times. They were leaving for England soon, so I wrote our thanks on one of the cards I had designed for Scone Palace and dropped it into their letterbox the following morning; naturally enough Burberry tried to get out of the car too, convinced we had been invited back for breakfast. Thereafter, whenever the car approached the bend on the coast road above La Serenissima, Burberry would rouse from the soundest sleep to stare out of the window, tail wagging furiously in hope of more fillet steak at his favourite venue on the island.

At the time of that dinner party, Spiro and Milly Flamburiari* had recently produced a beautiful 'coffee table' book, *Corfu the Garden Isle*. In 2000 Spiro founded the Corfu Heritage Foundation, of which he is Chairman, for the purpose of promoting Anglo-Hellenic relations and supporting the cultural and architectural heritage between Corfu and Britain. Since then he has also co-founded the Edward Lear Society to commemorate the wonderful artist and poet who represents one of the many important links between Britain and Corfu. Many of Edward Lear's distinctive watercolour paintings of Corfu, from the years he lived on the island, are reproduced in Spiro's book; one such adorns the cover.

My favourite nonsense rhyme by Lear is *The Owl and The Pussycat*, which always reminds me of the day Jeremy and I set sail from Salcombe, bound for Cyprus on our extended honeymoon – not in a pea green boat but in our cream and brown catamaran. I can still recite it by heart. Many of Lear's limericks are also world famous; for no particular reason this one seems appropriate:

> *There was an old man of Corfu,*
> *Who never knew what he should do;*
> *So he rushed up and down,*
> *'Til the sun made him brown,*
> *That bewildered old man of Corfu.*

---

*Spiro and Milly appear in episode 2 of Joanna Lumley's fabulous travel series, *A Greek Odyssey*, meeting her on their beach and welcoming her to La Serenissima.

Chapter Twelve

A Girl's Best Friend

The best things in life are free.
The second best things are very, very expensive.

Coco Chanel

We had driven across three countries in Europe a week or so before-hand, the Jeep full to the roof with a large portable, folding massage couch, boxes of cosmetics, aromatherapy oils, specialist equipment for facials, manicures, pedicures, waxing and other paraphernalia needed by beauticians the world over. Beauty treatments were scarce in North East Corfu and the ladies of the area were forced to make the tiresome journey to Corfu Town; being attired for nine months of the year in swimwear and revealing summer clothes, with much of the body exposed for all to see, regular waxing and pedicures were an essential part of island living.

In Fiskardo I had discovered a charming young beautician from South Africa, who had a small salon in her Greek husband's family hotel overlooking the sea. Apart from holidaymakers and locals, most of her clientele came from the superyachts which put into Fiskardo during the summer season. All the rich and famous seemed to favour Kefalonia, particularly since the release of *Captain Corelli's Mandolin* which was based and filmed on the island. From Abramovich to Jobs and Gates to Spielberg, they all found their way to this corner of the Ionian in their floating palaces. Merilda would be ferried out to the yachts by crew members in a tender, complete her treatments and be brought back to shore afterwards. She told me how her husband would usually accompany her for security reasons, as a yacht full of men might well want something more than she was offering, or could even kidnap her; the white slave trade was still very much alive and kicking, she insisted.

The good ladies of North East Corfu, whether Greek, English, Italian, American or Dutch, eagerly awaited Miranda's arrival that summer and many had pre-booked appointments at their villas. Legs were getting hairier, nails growing longer and sun baked skin was getting drier and more damaged as each day passed without any available treatments. Miranda's first professional appointment was executed on board Sarava; a simple back massage with aromatherapy oils. Luckily the cockpit was easily large enough to accommodate her portable couch and was comfortably shaded by the bimini hood. The lady client was thrilled to be treated on board in Agios Stefanos, her villa being situated just a stone's throw away above the hamlet. Word soon spread in such a small community and the mobile phone constantly rang with ladies wanting to book appointments.

Miranda had not taken her driving test before coming to Corfu that year, so I was suddenly deployed as chauffeur as well as receptionist and secretary. The appointments came thick and fast, so I did what all Mummies seem to get landed with – lots of washing. Each day there were piles of fluffy white towels in varying sizes and Miranda's white uniforms to be washed and ironed. Bottles needed refilling, her beauty boxes had to be replenished and reorganised and her equipment sterilised after each treatment; Miranda's afternoons off were usually spent swimming or sleeping. Thank heavens I was doing all this in the heat of the summer when washing dried within minutes of being pegged on the line. Sarava took on the appearance of a Chinese laundry, but Miranda couldn't complain as it was for her benefit. Wherever Sarava was at anchor, onlookers must have thought I was the most vigilant boatwife who did her washing at least twice every single day. As the two Champneys dresses needed ironing I soon got fed up with that chore; it was my summer too and ironing on Sarava made me very hot and bothered, even when I took the ironing board into the open cockpit. So Miranda and I made an expedition to Corfu Town very early one morning. In the air-conditioned comfort of Marks & Spencer, we bought three pairs of white linen trousers with wide legs and an elasticated waistband, a few white camisole tops and some white leather flip-flops. At a nearby accessories shop we found some white hair 'scrunchies' which would look lovely around her bun or ponytail. I soon discovered that the trousers could be 'pressed' easily by folding them carefully, while still slightly damp, and putting them under one of the long cushions in the cockpit. The weight of our bodies sitting on them each evening brought them out looking as if they had been dry cleaned. With her glowing natural tan, Miranda looked stunning in this ensemble; it was cool, comfortable and casually elegant, her shiny Champneys badge adding a nice professional touch.

It was not long before Miranda's expertise came to the attention of the managers of Lord Rothschild's estate, which straddled two capes to the south of Agios Stefanos. Most mornings in high season I would drive Miranda to Kanonas and drop her off by the gates. She would complete her treatments for the family or their high profile guests in a designated treatment room, or sometimes beside one of the swimming pools in the exquisitely landscaped grounds that ran down to the sea. For these appointments Miranda did not need many towels as there was always an abundance of fresh, neatly rolled towels in baskets all around the pool area. There were also very large Ali-Baba baskets into which all the used towels were left. After one morning's treatments she came back giggling, telling us very touchingly how Lord R had hidden inside one of these empty baskets while his small grandchildren were sent to find him. Another of Miranda's clients at that time was Lord Sainsbury; unlike some of the celebrity and supermodel guests who didn't possess the manners or breeding to utter as much as a grunt, he was most agreeably avuncular towards her. She was particularly tickled to see he was wearing the very same, very inexpensive Swatch wristwatch as Jeremy – funny the things a girl notices.

After her morning treatments at Kanonas, Miranda was often given lunch in the kitchens; I would collect her afterwards and she would describe in mouthwatering detail the gourmet recipes she had gleaned from the resident chefs. Miranda has always loved cooking; she must have inherited this passion from her grandmothers, both ladies being excellent home cooks. This talent obviously skipped a generation, as I loathe cooking or handling anything hotter than a cup of coffee. Miranda usually gave my number to prospective clients as she was often out at night with friends and slept much later; I was acting as her full time secretary and receptionist, keeping a little notebook with me at all times to write down her bookings.

A year or so later Jeremy and I were swimming in a quiet bay along the coast when my phone rang. I climbed out of the water, wiped my hands on a towel and answered the phone.

"Hello, is that Miranda?" a man's voice asked.

"No, this is her mother, I take appointments for her. Can I help you?"

"Oh super, yes. I'm Captain of the yacht *Elisabeth F.* Is she available for an appointment near Agios Stefanos tomorrow?"

"I'm sure she would love to. What time would you like her to come?"

"The treatment is for the lady who owns the yacht. It's her fortieth birthday and a party is being given for her by the Rothschilds; her yacht will be at anchor in the bay below. The crew want to give her this treatment as their birthday gift. Could you ask Miranda to be on the jetty at Agios Stefanos at 5pm, where she will be collected by one of the tenders. She will be doing a full body massage, manicure and pedicure."

My mothering instinct was already in overdrive. Should I go with her as chaperone? What if they kidnapped both of us? Should Jeremy go with her instead? Who was this mystery lady and what if the whole thing was a ruse to get Miranda alone on the yacht? My fertile imagination had been further stimulated by Merilda in Fiskardo; Miranda was not quite 18 years-old and very inexperienced in the ways of this world of the rich and famous. But after some hurried research Jeremy assured me that Miranda would be safe enough, as the yacht belonged to Elisabeth Murdoch – the one next to her belonging to Rupert

Murdoch, her father. Nevertheless the following day we deposited Miranda and all her equipment on the appointed jetty then hovered nearby in the dinghy to keep an eye on things. Miranda looked so vulnerable standing alone on the end of the wooden jetty in her white uniform, her waist length blond hair swept up into a tidy bun. She held her white sandals in her hand, leaving her perfectly pedicured, suntanned feet bare, in deference to the decks and carpets of the very smart yacht she would soon be ushered aboard.

At precisely 5pm a large white tender pulled up to the jetty, driven by a dashing young crew member in navy blue uniform. Beside him sat another, equally good looking young man wearing the same livery. Miranda had banished us to a discreet distance from where I could just see her smiling demurely at these two chaps. The second crewman leapt out and loaded all her bags and the folding couch into the tender, before gallantly helping Miranda into one of the white leather passenger seats at the stern. They roared off at speed, leaving a frothy wake which sent all the boats at anchor bobbing and rolling on their moorings; had I been at the helm of our dinghy I would have been right behind them, but to my intense frustration Jeremy insisted on keeping a more innocent distance between us.

"Get a move on, Jeremy, or we'll lose them!" I shouted above the roar of our outboard engine. "They're going even faster now!"

They were completely out of range of my little camera, so I resigned myself to the inevitability that we would have no lasting record of Miranda's first appointment on a superyacht.

"I'm not going any closer," he replied firmly, keeping pace behind them.

"Quick!" I shouted, as the tender swung to starboard and accelerated, a wall of spray flying up behind them. We slowed down and hovered opposite the northern promontory of the Kanonas estate, dominated by the castellated structure which our children had nicknamed 'The Sandcastle'. The bay resembled Monaco on Grand Prix weekend; a line of vast yachts lay at anchor in row abreast, their sterns to the shore beneath the simple, faux castle that has settled so well into Corfu's landscape. A couple were of the usual motor cruiser variety that always remind me of white steam irons; these always look as if their sterns have been chopped off, square as the back of a bus. I much prefer the aesthetic of staid motor cruisers of the 1930s, or of traditional schooners, or even the modern sailing superyachts – a colossal example of which was alongside the yacht belonging to Miranda's client. The tender carrying Miranda and her mobile beauty salon pulled up alongside one of the larger craft in the line up, a sleek white motor yacht from the 1980s. Miranda stepped with practised ease out of the tender onto the boarding ladder to the aft deck and disappeared from my viewfinder; all I got was a grainy view of her back. I would have stayed until I saw my young daughter returning to the tender, but as Jeremy pointed out, she would be on board the yacht for at least three hours. In fact he had not factored in extra time taken when the crew had given Miranda a glass of ice cold champagne at the end of the session to toast her client's birthday. That evening Miranda told us all about her experience, hugely impressed above all that the bubbly was served in Swarovski crystal flutes.

"That's what I'll have at my wedding," she announced, leaving Jeremy to reach for the oxygen bottle.

"You've got champagne tastes on a beer income," I reminded her.

But in that first summer Miranda was earning substantially more than a beer income and only needed to take appointments for the mornings, before the heat was too intense. In fact, with the generous tips she received on top of her considerable fees, she earned more in those two months of high season in Corfu than she would have made in a year in a top salon in England.

"Some famous singer has been flown over from America to perform at tonight's party," she added nonchalantly. She was becoming very blasé during these halcyon days of rubbing the shoulders of the super rich.

"Who is it?" I asked.

"Not sure," replied Miranda, busily looking at text messages on her phone. "I've never heard of him ... I think he was called Billy something."

"Billy Fury?" I suggested.

"Don't be daft," Jeremy interrupted. "He must be on a zimmer frame by now! Was it Billy Joel?"

"That's the one," said Miranda, totally unimpressed.

The following day Miranda had already been booked for a whole session of appointments when she was asked to give treatments aboard another megayacht visiting Corfu that summer. We had watched the *Queen K* arrive off Kanonas a few days earlier. Slightly sinister in appearance with her gleaming gunmetal grey hull, she boasted a couple of dozen crew and security guards, nine guest suites, one with a private terrace and pool. This seventy million pound megayacht was then owned by the young Russian oligarch, Oleg Deripaska, who made his billions from aluminium. That must represent an awful lot of tin foil. One of this plutocrat's chums was Nat Rothschild – hence his presence in Corfiot waters. Guests on board the *Queen K* that week included George Osborne, at the time our Shadow Chancellor, and Peter Mandelson, European Union Commissioner for Trade and Britain's Secretary of State for Business. No coincidence perhaps, as Jeremy later observed, that aluminium tariffs into Europe were eased shortly after this gathering of the clans.

I had tried to persuade Jeremy to take us within shooting distance so I could take some photographs of this unusual yacht at close quarters. But even from a respectful fifty yards we could clearly see a line of black uniformed security guards glaring at us from the port side. They were each brandishing one of those powerful assault weapons I always call Baryshnikovs, like the Russian ballet dancer – better known, as Jeremy later corrected me, as Kalashnikovs. We didn't venture any closer.

On the previous day Messrs Mandelson and Osborne had notoriously shared a table at Taverna Agni, where all conversation had been caught on the taverna's webcam; a live feed had been installed in the rafters for the amusement of customers, who could wave to their friends and relations back in Blighty as they dined at the tables. Within a few hours the paparazzi had flown in and converged on the quaint little taverna, offering very substantial sums of money to release the webcam footage. The taverna turned down all offers, recognising that customers' privacy and trust trumped the temptations of a bagful of quick bucks.

Miranda's reaction to hearing she had missed the chance to see the *Queen K* at close quarters was typically down to earth. She didn't mind at all: she couldn't stand caviar, which was what she would probably have been given for lunch, and anyway she had far nicer people waiting for her treatments.

* * *

We too eventually got our invitation onto a superyacht, and moreover one we actually liked. We were having morning coffee at one of the bars in Agios Stefanos when I recognised someone I had last seen at his newly purchased hotel on Dartmoor. The famous entrepreneur Peter de Savary had completely refurbished the lovely Manor House Hotel near Moretonhampstead and changed the name to Bovey Castle. Despite my private opinion that the new name made the grand old building sound like a steam train, the hotel definitely benefited from some considerable and costly TLC. Peter and his beautiful daughter were alone at a table so I went to say hello. We chatted about Devon, mutual friends, sailing and dressage. One of his other daughters, Amber, was a talented dressage rider who had represented Great Britain on numerous occasions. Adonis and I had represented Devon and been placed in the National Dressage Championships when I was seventeen, so we had a lot in common. As we said goodbye, Peter invited Jeremy and me to join him for drinks aboard his gorgeous yacht, *Gloria*, the following evening. The fabulous forty metre schooner was a replica of one built for the King of Siam in the 1930s. We were expecting a large party of guests to be on board, but as we approached in the tender it soon became apparent we might be the only ones. Two handsome young crew members dressed in the yacht's tropical livery took our line as we boarded. Jeremy gave them the keys and asked if they would like to secure the tender on the other side of the yacht, away from the boarding ladder.

Jeremy and I were Peter's only guests on board *Gloria* that particular evening, during which we discovered several mutual interests and connections, including a Devonshire property for which he and Jeremy had both bid. As we waited for the steward to replenish the nibbles PdS and his charming daughter took an informed delight in showing us around the yacht's sumptuous staterooms.

Lovely as *Gloria* was and fortunate as her owner seemed, we envied only the schooner's French crew, for they had the yacht entirely to themselves for many months of the year; evidently PdS came to the same conclusion a while later, selling *Gloria* to Pete Townsend of *The Who*. Much later that evening Jeremy and I eventually struggled back on board our tender, each clutching an armful of branded gifts promoting our host's many business ventures; with sun hats advertising a holiday village in the Grenadines, tee-shirts from Rhode Island and fountain pens from Scotland, we felt like victorious Crackerjack contestants.

* * *

Paint the flying spirit of the bird rather than its feathers.

Robert Henri

One of my greatest pleasures during our summers on Sarava was my early morning swim around the boat as she lay at anchor in some secluded cove; before dawn the sea was always flat calm and lukewarm in the comparatively cool air. You could not describe the colour of the surface; it was at once pearlescent, translucent and opalescent until the upper rim of the fiery, rising sun cast its crimson rays over the water. It was like swimming in tepid milk. Leaving the others sleeping peacefully in their cabins, I would pull on my bikini and tiptoe out of the saloon into the cockpit to welcome the new day; the scent of cypress trees and salty air was a tonic after a night spent in our cabin. We always slept with the deck hatch over our double bed and the smaller ports in the cabin wide open, their custom made nylon netting screens keeping away any unwelcome night time visitors. But there was little breeze at night and Sarava held the heat collected during the hottest days, so the fresh cool air of morning was doubly welcome. Barely awake, I would climb down the boarding ladder and slip quietly into the water, suddenly aware that the small ripples I was making on the mirror like sea were fanning out into deeper water to make my own microscopic imprint on this watery world. As Alphonse Daudet said: *One becomes part of the foam that drifts, of the wind that blows, and of the pines that answer.*

Once I had scanned the immediate area for any other craft, I would return to the ladder and, with my body submerged, strip off completely, hanging my bikini over the top step of the ladder where I could discreetly put it on again before climbing on board. It was the most glorious feeling of freedom, strongly to be recommended to anyone who has not tried it before. Swimming *au naturel* early one morning at Agni I was some considerable distance from the boat, heading towards the neighbouring deserted cove, when I spotted something skimming over the water in my direction. I trod water to try to make out what it was and as it got closer I saw it was a kingfisher, brilliant as the gas flame of a Bunsen burner, its iridescent plumage sparkling in the morning light. I was mesmerised. These little birds have always been my favourite and, if one were to believe in reincarnation, I would wish to come back as a kingfisher; that way I could swim, fly and eat fish – three of my most favourite things, although kingfishers can't actually swim, which is why they only dive in calm water. I of course can only fly in my dreams.

This tiny creature's long, sharp bill was aiming straight at my head and he was only inches away when he spotted me and swerved sharply to my left and alighted seconds later on a rock beneath the cliff face. If I had blinked I would have missed it. As I watched, he peered down into the crystal clear water below, then dived into the sea as swiftly and cleanly as a dart. He emerged a couple of seconds later and flew to his perch grasping a small silver fish in his beak. Tilting up his head he swallowed the fish, shook himself, did a quick preen of his gleaming feathers and stared down into the water again. I watched him for several minutes, he repeated the process a few times until he had satisfied his appetite, then shot off towards the other side of the bay. Only as I swam away did I realise that if he had not seen me in the nick of time, his sharp dagger of a beak could have impaled itself in my forehead, given the speed of his flight. I imagined the headlines in the newspapers:

NAKED ENGLISHWOMAN FOUND DEAD IN SEA,
HARPOONED BY GREEK KINGFISHER.

I nearly always saw kingfishers during these early morning swims, sometimes flying, their distinctive piercing, peeping call echoing over the water, at other times perched on rocks or low hanging branches as they searched for their breakfast. On one sad occasion I saw a dead kingfisher hanging stiffly outside a shop in Mourtos; the owner told me it was to ward off lightning strikes, which struck me as a rather backward superstition. Further research showed that medieval doctors and alchemists hung dried kingfishers in their treatment rooms, believing them to have magical properties; a more general belief was held of their power to deter hungry moths. English and French seafarers and fishermen would hang a stuffed or dried kingfisher, wings stretched akimbo, from a string where it could freely rotate into the wind – a rather morbid weathervane.

But how stands the wind? In what corner peers my halcyon's bill?

Christopher Marlowe – *The Jew of Malta*

As everyone knows, the expression 'Halcyon Days' refers to a rare period of calm in winter. The Greek name for the common kingfisher is *Alkyon*, which became 'halcyon' in modern times. The Halcyon of legend nested upon the sea during the two weeks either side of the winter solstice. With the ability to calm the waves, the mythical bird kept her intricate floating nest of fish bones safe while incubating her eggs. In Greek mythology, as is so often the case, the bird started life as a human being. Alkyone, daughter of the wind god, Aelous, was inconsolable in her grief for Ceyex, her dead husband who had been lost at sea. The gods were full of compassion for her and they turned the pair of humans into kingfishers so they could be together for eternity. I hope Jeremy will likewise join me in my reincarnation ...

The shallow promontory between Agni and Yialiskari, where Sarava often lay at anchor with a long line astern to the shore, was a favoured spot for these morning dips. I could easily swim across to the adjacent cove of Yialiskari, a tiny horseshoe-shaped bay fronted by a spit of smooth white pebbles, which was separated from the vegetation inland by a row of majestic Agave plants. With their enormous stems and long curved, serrated and dangerously thorned leaves, they looked utterly prehistoric; you could easily imagine huge dinosaurs lumbering between them. Only flowering once in two decades, the plant pushes up a single stem about twenty feet high, adorned at the top with pale yellow blooms; having done so, it then dies. Visiting hoopoes often stopped off for a little rest and relaxation in Corfu during their annual migration from northern Asia to breed in the milder climates of Europe. These flamboyant birds would perch on the topmost tip of an agave and call, "Hoop hoop hoop", their distinctive cry would echo around the bay and far out to sea. As they called they would lower their heads and erect their black and white tipped, pinky-brown crests, reminding me of flamenco dancers wearing particularly fetching, feathery mantillas.

During the time we lived in our 200 year-old *finca* in Spain, a hoopoe would arrive at precisely seven every morning and call from the very top of one of our agaves near the swimming pool. We never had to set an alarm clock to get five year-old Rory up in time for school in Javea; our wake-up call was a beautiful *abubilla,* a hoopoe after which the property had been named. Rory named the resident bird Abu-Dhabi. When Jeremy's mother came to visit from England she spent most of her holiday with nail scissors in hand, patiently snipping off all the sharp thorns on the fleshy leaves of the agaves that were at Rory's head height, so anxious was she that he would lose an eye if he bumped into them whilst playing in the garden.

Yialiskari was being used as a location for the filming of another television adaptation of *My Family & Other Animals,* starring Imelda Staunton as Mrs. Durrell. Our friends Angela and Geoffrey's arrival for their annual holiday with us in Corfu happily coincided with the filming and I was determined to see some of the action first hand. Angela came with me as I drove the Jeep up the east coast before turning down the narrow, bumpy track from Loustri to the cove below; meanwhile Jeremy and Geoffrey were sailing Sarava from Gouvia to the north of the island, where we would meet them later. We were stopped by a young man wearing a security tag around his neck; he politely informed us we couldn't drive any further because of the filming. We could see the bay below and a group of actors, film crew and props, including the unmistakeably stripey 'Bootle Bum-Trinket', assembled on the beach. I explained that we lived on the island and would like to watch a bit of the filming.

"I'll just pop down to the beach and ask the director," he said.

We watched him as he approached a man who was talking to Imelda. A few seconds later he came back up the stony path to us.

"He says you are very welcome to watch and you can use these two chairs," he said, pointing to a couple of canvas directors' chairs perched on the grassy clifftop, giving a perfect view of the beach below.

"We are filming the scene where the Durrells have breakfast in the water," he explained helpfully. We could clearly see a table and some wooden chairs in the shallows.

"We've had to weigh down the table and chair legs with big stones ... they kept floating away!" he laughed.

"Have you read the book?" he asked.

"We both have, it's my all time favourite and I can recite many of the passages by heart," I said. "It's the reason my family and I came to live in Corfu!"

"That's amazing," he replied, "I'm ashamed to say I haven't; I meant to before we flew here, but somehow I never got round to it. I wish I'd brought a copy with me. Can you say a bit for me now?" He looked so interested and hopeful that I launched into one of my favourite pieces.

> *"Gradually the magic of the island settled over us, as gently and clingingly as pollen. Each day had a tranquillity, a timelessness about it, so that you wished it would never end. But then the dark skin of night would peel off and there would be a fresh day waiting for us, glossy and colourful as a child's transfer and with the same tinge of unreality."*

"Golly, that's brilliant!" he said, "I must go and tell the director, he'll be amazed!"

Angela and I, feeling just a little self-conscious, (and not a little unlike a couple of pampered Hollywood film stars) settled ourselves comfortably in the chairs and I rummaged in my handbag for my camera.

"You may not be allowed to take photographs," Angela warned me. Her daughter Arabella had just been working on the latest *Harry Potter* film that year and Angela knew how cagey the production companies could be about unofficial photos.

"It would be too far away anyway," I said, "Let's ask that nice young man to take one of us with the bay in the background; they can't object to that."

Fortunately our polite young friend managed to take a picture of Angela and me with the actors, cameras, film crew and other paraphernalia clearly visible on the beach below; even the Bootle Bum-Trinket was in shot.

As we watched the proceedings and the actors had taken their places in the thigh deep water for the breakfast scene, we were puzzled to hear the director shout 'CUT!' We wondered why the filming had stopped so suddenly.

"Oh God, look!" exclaimed Angela, pointing towards the bay.

I looked out to sea and there, right in shot as she glided serenely past, was Sarava, close enough for us to see Geoffrey enthusiastically waving a beach towel at us from the foredeck. Later that day when we were in Kassiopi, I went to the little supermarket by the harbour, owned by dear Mr. Kiros, and chose a paperback book from the spinners outside the shop. I drove the couple of miles back to Yialiskari and handed the young security man the book in a paper bag. He looked astonished.

"For your kindness," I said and walked back to the car, hoping he found time to read his new copy of *My Family and Other Animals* while he was still on Gerry's idyllic island.

* * *

We had a delightful chum who worked at the marina in Gouvia. Thanassis spoke English with a strong accent and a pronounced lisp which he rather enjoyed and often accentuated, even if understanding him could sometimes be difficult. Of the many Thanassis on Corfu, we knew when this particular one was on the telephone. 'Yiathath, thith ith Thanathith,' he would always begin.

Thanassis had been a charter yacht skipper for many years and knew the Ionian most intimately. Often he would suggest fresh anchorages for Sarava, unspoilt bays, little known beachside tavernas, or perhaps an inlet sheltered from a strong *maistro*. One day, finding me in the little supermarket at the marina, he recommended a tranquil anchorage on Kalamos as a good place to escape the summer flotillas; on the way we could stop at Frikes or Kioni, tiny anchorages on Ithaca – an island that was his particular favourite because of its abundant pumice stone. We had visited other parts of the island before, but had never looked for pumice on the beaches; this was a mouthwateringly tempting prospect for me as I had always used pumice stone to smooth the hard skin on my heels, yet I had no idea it could be found so locally. Jeremy on the other hand was always complaining how my lifelong obsession for collecting pebbles, rocks and fossilised sponges was lowering Sarava's Plimsoll line with every new addition; but at least, I retaliated, pumice was light enough to float.

"Indeed, you would love the north of Ithca," Thanassis told me. "They therve the betht thordfith in the Ionian."

Jeremy agreed it would make a pleasant little diversion from our usual itineraries when we set sail a few days later. As the island rose sheer out of the early morning mist like a floating mirage, I scanned the coastline and hills for flame trees. The trees I could see were dense and varied; with the binoculars I could identify olive, oak, eucalyptus, cypress, orange, lemon, pear and fig trees, but no 'flames' at all. As we hovered by the breakwater at the entrance to Frikes harbour I suddenly noticed the water on our port side swirling like a whirlpool. I pointed it out to Jeremy, who left the helm to take a better look. We wondered if it was an unusual eddy caused by an earth tremor – of which there were several every day in the area – or perhaps some massive bath plug pulled out by Poseidon. Then suddenly we saw the glint of small silver fish leaping out of the water at the centre of the vortex.

"It must be a swordfish!" exclaimed Jeremy, peering down into the water. "Look! You can see him thrashing his sword about!"

We knew that the favoured method for any self respecting swordfish was to surround its chosen prey and corral them by swimming fast in ever decreasing circles, flailing his sword to and fro until the fish were so compacted and damaged that it was easy to pick off the choicest specimens. The technique reminded me of those old Western films I used to watch with my father, when the red indians used to circle a wagon train; my mother always called these virtually dialogue-free productions the 'Yep/Nope' films. We watched in absolute fascination and wished our video recorder was to hand; by the time I retrieved it from the saloon the action was over and the sea was calm again. It was highly unusual to witness such an event, especially so very close to shore. Later we sat at a harbourside taverna in the tiny hamlet, eating swordfish caught that morning, fervently hoping it was not the one we had seen hunting; either way, the thick melt-in-the-mouth steaks, grilled over charcoal and accompanied by a crisp Greek salad and chunky hand made chips, were absolutely delicious. Across a patch of water dotted with the tufty islets of the inland sea, the Greek mainland above Astakos shone briefly in the last glow of sunset until pinpricks of light gradually appeared amongst the folds of the virtually empty, dark velvet mountains.

"I'm very disappointed not to have seen any flame trees yet," I remarked to Jeremy as we walked along the breakwater. "Where do you think we could find some?"

"What exactly are you talking about?" he asked, looking rather puzzled.

"You know, *flame trees,* like the book *The Flame Trees of Thika,*" I annunciated slowly, as if the heat of the day had affected his head.

"But we are in *Ithaca* the legendary home of Odysseus, not in *Thika,* which is possibly somewhere in Kenya!" he explained.

I was nonplussed until the penny dropped; I had mentally translated Thanassis's slushy pronunciation of *Ithaca* to *Thika*. Jeremy found it amusing, but I was disappointed to have misplaced the famous Flame Trees. After all, I consoled myself, I had not looked at the charts and, moreover, there was no sign as one sailed into Frikes harbour announcing *Welcome to Ithaca,* as might be seen on arrival at Torquay or Brighton. Jeremy spent the rest of our visit to Ithaca stalking me mercilessly with comments such as 'The ithmuth on Ithaca ith where Odytheuth lived' and 'What'th thith? Ith it pumith?' whenever I picked up little pieces of pale pink pumice stone on the beaches.

* * *

There was an old man whose remorse,
Induced him to drink caper sauce,
For they said, 'If mixed up,
With some cold claret-cup,
It will certainly soothe your remorse!
Edward Lear

In high summer when barely a drop of rain ever fell, most of the wild plants that thrived on all Greek Islands were those with tough, dessicated, spiky stems and thistle-like flowers, clumps of herbs such as thyme, sage and oregano, or succulents such as prickly pear which could store water in their fleshy leaves; the horned poppy with pale, frilly, eucalyptus coloured leaves and lemon yellow papery flowers was also an attractive feature on the edges of the white pebble beaches. One July morning I picked a caper stem, bearing several flowers in different stages of development, from the cove around the headland from Kassiopi where I swam each morning whenever Sarava was in the harbour. I took it back to the boat and sat at the cockpit table, under the shade of the bimini, to capture it in watercolour. Painting from life is the very best way and the only way for me to make an accurate portrayal, but I always had to work fast, even in a vase of water, these sensitive flowers do not live long once picked. The ephemeral flowering plants, like the Sea Daffodil, are the exception; once the flower you have been painting shrivels and dies, there will be a new one on the same stem to replace it the next day.

My study of the caper instigated my passion for painting some of the wild flora and fauna of the Greek Islands, as well as any interesting natural objects I found during our years sailing the Ionian. Once, as I swam ashore from Sarava to a tiny beach on an islet near Astakos, I found a beautiful fossil right at my feet, exactly where I stepped out of the sea. Thereafter any heart-shaped stones, colourful pebbles, shells, fossilised sponges, insects, live birds and animals, skeleton leaves, birds' eggshells, nuts and seeds became grist to my mill and I felt compelled to record them in my sketchbook, wherever the winds and waves took us.

Free time to paint was scarce however; during the summer months Sarava was always full to the gunwales with friends of ours and our children's coming to stay for a week at a time. We loved having their company – well, most of them – and showing them a few of our favourite haunts on the islands. But by the end of the summer Jeremy and I often felt that our floating home was, as our manor house had become, Butlins and we were once again the Redcoats. The majority of our visitors were accustomed to life afloat and would happily muck in with chores, both nautical and domestic; but one or two would treat their week as a free private charter and allow us, the crew, to wait on them hand, foot and finger, from the moment we collected them from the airport to the day they left Corfu.

Vanessa, Stefan and their daughter Sara, another of my goddaughters – extraordinarily born on the same day as Miranda – were welcome annual visitors; they lived in an exclusive area of Munich where we would often stay with them on our regular car journeys between Corfu and England. Vanessa and I were both born in Devon and had met in the late 1970's at a fashion show in which I was modelling; we hit it off immediately, although at that time I was working in Cyprus and had only come home for a couple of weeks.

In those days only British servicemen were allowed to stay on the island for longer than three months at a time without a special resident permit, which was very hard to obtain in those early years just after the Turkish invasion. There were numerous tented settlements around the southern side of the island, wretched camps for Greek Cypriot refugees who had fled from the sudden invasion in 1974 by the Turks in the north of the island; they had been forced to leave behind their homes, possessions, professions and, most tragically for me, their pets. The new border, erected by the United Nations, consisted of a barbed wire fence dotted with occasional wooden sentry boxes; it traversed the island from coast to coast, running through the centre of Nicosia.

Sadly it is still there to this day, a grim monument to yet another red line so handily ignored by the western powers; to our eternal shame, the British forces based in Cyprus did not lift a finger to help the Greek Cypriots. Theodore Stephanides, the Durrell's friend and Gerry's mentor in Corfu, wrote of this episode in 1974 :

> *We stood by Britain in her wars*
> *And followed where she gave the lead;*
> *She used us when the need was hers,*
> *But failed us in our hour of need!*

It had always embarrassed me when my Greek Cypriot friends talked nostalgically about the best beach on the island. Named by the British, 'Governor's Beach', it was unashamedly reserved for members of the British forces serving in Cyprus and British nationals. Cypriots were not allowed to go there, although my Greek friends told me I would be allowed to go there. I never had the heart.

When Vanessa came to stay I was usually working somewhere and food was always provided. My day would start with a visit to my hair-dresser in Limassol, who opened early for me when I was modelling in catwalk shows in Nicosia, for a shampoo and blow-dry. I would be there by 7am and he would have already ordered me a delicious break-fast consisting of a chargrilled halloumi and tomato toasted sandwich and a Greek coffee from the cafe next to the salon.

Vanessa and I had rashly invited a young Cypriot dress designer and her husband to dinner, but having only met them through a fash-ion shoot I decided it might be easier to eat out; restaurants were so reasonable in Cyprus in the 1970's, a full blown meze costing the equivalent of two Cyprus pounds. However, Vanessa bravely insisted on taking charge of the cooking. On the appointed day we shopped at Limassol's wonderful indoor market; everything looked so colourful and attractive, apart from the very dead, naked, pimply, pale-skinned chickens, their butter yellow feet stiffly clenched and their heads lolling on long scrawny necks. I had only ever seen them in butchers' shops in England, legs tucked up neatly, minus their heads, and resembling new-born babies. A couple of years later, when I was just two months pregnant with Rory, I had fainted at the sight of a whole cow's head, perched on a wooden tree stump at the entrance to this gory department of the local market. Suddenly turning a corner and coming face to face with this monstrous spectacle, blood dripping, tongue lolling and covered with flies, my legs buckled underneath me. Luckily, as I was gently sinking towards the floor, Jeremy caught me and carried me out of the market into the fresh air.

I let Vanessa choose the chicken and we returned home with our bags and deposited them in the kitchen. I flung open the window as the house had no air-conditioning and it was mid-summer. Vanessa put the chicken, wrapped in greaseproof paper, on the windowsill where it would keep relatively cool until she was ready to stuff it. We both went to change out of our shopping clothes into shorts and tee shirts for our culinary activities. Coming back into the kitchen, Vanessa asked me what I had done with the chicken.

"Nothing, I'm not touching it! It's on the windowsill where you left it," I replied.

"No it's not!" said Vanessa. We both stared in dumb amazement at the empty windowsill. To our horror we realised it must have been taken by one of the many feral cats who lived in the neighbourhood.

"What are we going to give them for supper?" I asked in a panic, it was too late to go back to the town again to buy another one as the market closed for the day at lunchtime.

"Don't panic," said the unflappable Vanessa. "We'll give them the roast vegetables with some lountza, there's still some in the fridge." I was worried; cold smoked pork fillet with hot roast vegetables seemed an unlikely combination, but our guests were most forgiving about the incident.

Fashions fade, style is eternal

Yves Saint Laurent

Vanessa had obviously taken this quotation to heart, for wherever she went she was always dressed in the latest stylish fashions. Skiing in Austria would see her decked out like a film star; glamorous fur trimmed ski suits with matching accessories. At home in Munich or on visits to any European city she would don chic suits and killer heels. For her holidays with us on Sarava she would wear very expensive Italian swimwear with matching sarongs and exquisite, sparkly, kitten-heeled sandals. A memory that will always stay with me is a morning when we were all swimming off the boat at Agni. The children were having a wonderful time jumping and diving off the foredeck into the crystal clear water. Vanessa and I were trying to keep our faces and hair dry as we were going ashore for lunch, so we were doing what Miranda and Sara called 'mummy-swimming' – sunglasses on and treading water energetically enough to keep our heads well above the water. Suddenly Rory leapt off the bows and dive bombed into the water, rather too close to Vanessa for comfort.

"Don't splash me!" she squealed indignantly. "I'm wearing my Guccis!"

* * *

To plant a garden is to believe in tomorrow.

Audrey Hepburn

In fact a rare opportunity for me to dress up in Corfu and attempt to emulate Vanessa was only just over the horizon. We had been invited to a wedding – a full-on Society Wedding by Corfiot standards – the following June.

I first bumped into 'Leafy' early one morning as I was taking Burberry for a comfort stop on shore at Yialiskari We were making slow progress along the ribbon narrow, twisting goat path that winds its way along the cliff top between Yialiskari and Agni Bay. Burberry was intent on sniffing every prickly holm oak, sweet scented myrtle and stately cypress tree on the path. I heard a rustling in the bushes ahead of me and there, crouching on the ground beneath a high wire fence on the landward side of the path, was a diminutive blonde lady, clipboard and tape measure in hand; her fair young skin was toasted a delicate shade of gold by the Corfiot sun. She got up as I approached and we greeted each other in Greek, neither of us knowing the nationality of the other. I asked her what she was doing on this fine morning and she answered that she was a landscape gardener, measuring the boundaries of the land above the path, for which she had been commissioned to design a garden.

"We must introduce ourselves," I said, holding out the hand that wasn't holding Burberry's lead.

"I'm Alithea, " she said, shaking my hand and looking at me with big china blue eyes. Alithea means 'truth' in Greek, after the mythological Greek goddess.

"That's a Greek name," I said, "But you look so English."

"I am English but my father has spent years in Corfu and loved the name."

"Oh good!" I replied in my native tongue, having reached the limit of my conversational Greek.

We shook hands and she told me to call her Leafy, which I thought was the perfect name for a gardener. I suppose it could have been a derivation of the abbreviation, 'Lithy', misheard by someone, and the name was so appropriate it had stuck. By coincidence we knew Leafy's father and there was also a connection between him and our Duke through one of the London fine art houses. A few years earlier he had shown us a small village in the hills which he had bought in its entirety; he would occasionally sell one of the abandoned houses for sympathetic conversion, but he chose each potential buyer carefully, determined the houses should belong to like minded people. I suppose it had been a compliment to us, but we decided against a village house, mainly because we wanted the sea closer and the neighbours further away.

Leafy and I fell deep into conversation about Mediterranean plants and trees, the differences in soils around the island and the sources for her exotic plants. I asked her which gardens she had already designed and she told me a few; one name I recognised was at Mongonisi, an islet on the southern tip of Paxos, which had been bought by one of the Benetton family as the location for a spectacular house. We had witnessed the stages of house building as we sailed past the land on our way to Antipaxos; as the house grew, we had admired the empathetic colouring of its sandy pink stone and low rise, which blended perfectly into the surrounding arid hillside. With binoculars pressed to my eyes I had been intrigued to see the gardens developing each time we passed by. Within a year of the house being built, swathes of what I took to be trailing rosemary, *dendrolivano* in Greek, cascaded from the top of the walls, convincingly emulating the Hanging Gardens of Babylon. Other imaginative features graced the gardens; gargantuan earthenware pots, some upright, others lying on their sides, spilling out profusions of magenta bougainvillea, powder blue plumbago and frost white jasmine. I longed to walk around the gardens to get a close look at everything and wished I had known Leafy then.

A few days later I telephoned Leafy and asked her to meet me at the site that would one day be The Lion House. We wandered between the ancient olive trees, as she made notes of the inclines, the soil composition and the position of the swimming pool. I had a picture in my mind of how I wanted the garden to look, preserving and incorporating as many of the older olive trees as possible into the design. Favourite plants and trees I had written on a list for her incuded cypress, orange, lemon, mandarin and qumquat trees, gardenia bushes, lavender, rosemary, thyme, cystus, hibiscus, wisteria, plumbago, myrtle and jasmine. On the terrace between pool and house I had marked out a spot to plant an Albizia julibrissin 'Rosea', a Persian or Pink Silk tree. With its abundant but delicate feathery leaves, through which even the most delicate breezes could circulate, it would eventually provide welcome shade over a large seating area; better still, the tree was deciduous, allowing sun and light into the house during the winter months. I had long admired these beautiful acacia trees with their pale pink powder puff flowers; there was a fine example in the little square in Kassiopi. Under the spreading umbrella of its branches the old men would congregate in the summer months, sitting for hours on rather wobbly rush seated wooden chairs, gossiping and playing cards to the background clicking and rattling of their worry beads.

Leafy sourced her stocks of plants and trees from wholesale nurseries in Italy, who regularly shipped containers to her in Corfu. It all sounded beyond my budget, but she assured me my order would be transported together with hundreds of plants for much larger clients and therefore she would only charge me what she had paid for them. In February the following year we unloaded our order with great delight, amazed at the size of every single plant; amongst the ten foot high cypress trees at the bottom of the load was my treasured Albizia. Jeremy was extremely disappointed that my precious tree, as he callously put it, was just a very large twig, albeit about two metres high; it was completely devoid of a single bud or leaf and looked very dejected. I assured him that all acacias looked like that during their dormant period, but I had my fingers crossed behind my back, as I really didn't have a clue if it was supposed to look so miserably barren. However, with guffaws of muffled laughter from our motley crew of builders, Jeremy placed the tree in the very large hole I had insisted the builders left in the paved area around the swimming pool.

Our builder in chief was certain it would only grow other bare twigs, calling it 'Jani's Twig Tree' and telling Jeremy it was an expensive waste of money. I had the last laugh though, as by April the young branches had spread out in an umbrella shape, were covered in emerald green feathery leaves and by June there were at least thirty perfect pink powder puffs on the topmost fronds. Each morning of that very hot early summer, before construction work stopped for the height of the tourist season, I would arrive at Liondari to find the builders huddled under the shade of the Twig Tree, eating their breakfast as they gazed over over the sparkling sea beyond. By the end of the summer the umbrella had doubled in size, spreading its branches into a perfect shape without any help from us. When we eventually sold The Lion House the new owners immediately cut down my beautiful tree and put up a modern canvas awning instead; at the same time the delicate mottling of paint on the house – the product of five subtle layers of variegated pinks, yellows and peaches which changed with the light at different times of the day – was replaced with a colour most easily described as wet cement. Both these acts of vandalism remain a constant sadness to me.

Leafy had asked me if I would write the addresses on her wedding invitation envelopes, saying she loved my handwriting which she had noticed on the list of plants I had given her. The guest list was something to behold – a veritable Who's Who of England, Greece and further afield. Jeremy and I were very touched to see our names on the guest list; Miranda's was there too, having become friendly with Leafy over the years in the younger social scene.

The wedding was to be on the first of June, especially to coincide with the *pansélinos*, the full moon. The evening reception on the very top terrace of the Old Fort would command a spectacular view of the rising moon over the sea and the distant mountains of Epirus. Naturally Miranda and I had to go shopping in Corfu Town for new outfits; even Jeremy agreed to buy a new Italian linen suit. I designed a sleeveless fitted dress and short jacket, which was exquisitely made up in coral Shantung silk by a young local dressmaker who had trained at a famous New York fashion house. At hip level I added a wide cream silk sash over the dress, tied in a very large bow on one side, an idea directly copied from the suit the Baroness wears in *The Sound of Music* when she visits Captain Von Trapp's home to meet his seven children. Miranda and I found a gorgeous dress for her, with matching micro shoulder bag in the same fabric; a delicate black filigree design embroidered on white cotton piqué, the dress echoed the 1950's style with a full skirt over layers of stiff net petticoat. A boned, strapless bodice showed off her natural tan and sun-bleached hair which fell to her waist.

There was just one thing missing: good jewellery. Neither of us had anything with us in Corfu, other than our rings and watches.

"I'd love a diamond necklace and earrings. Wouldn't you?" I asked Miranda as we carried our new dresses back towards the car.

"In your dreams!" she answered.

"Well, I've had a great idea!" I said, grabbing her hand and pulling her after me towards the Espianada.

"Oh no Mummy, you can't!" she exploded, as Christos and Andreas' shop came into view.

Once inside we were greeted as always with open arms and chilled orange juice. After the usual pleasantries had been exchanged, I told the twins about our invitation to Leafy's wedding. They knew Leafy and her father by reputation and realised this would by any standards be an *important* wedding. They asked to see our outfits and at once, without any prompting from me, Christos did exactly what I had known he would.

"Then you will need some diamonds!"

His eyes sparkled with glee as he ferreted in the safe and produced a fabulous single strand diamond necklace with matching earrings and bracelet. He fastened the necklace around my neck. It looked stunning, glittering and twinkling under the shop lights.

"Now, Miranda!" he grinned at her, "Something more modern and fun for you, I think."

From the window he removed another set of diamonds from their display stand. This necklace was longer than mine, with a cluster of diamonds at the bottom. Christos put the earrings and bracelet on my blushing daughter and stood back to see the effect on us both.

"Perfect!" he said, glowing with pride as if we were his own family.

"But Christos, dear, we can't *buy* these, much as we'd like to!" I said.

He waved a hand in the air, dismissing my words with a wink and a grin.

"Of course not, you will borrow them for the wedding! It will be a marvellous advertisement for our shop; in fact you will be modelling them for me at no charge! All those rich guys at the wedding will see them and maybe come to our shop. I will give you some business cards in case anyone asks you where you bought them – don't say you borrowed them – then it will be just like Cinderbloodyrella!"

"Do we have to get them back before midnight?" I asked.

"Aha! You worried you will turn into the pumpkins?" he laughed. "Of course not! The party will go on until dawn, so just bring them back next time you are in town." There was no arguing with Christos, so we arranged to collect the jewellery on the day, just before the church service.

There are a few occasions in life when one is showered with their radiance; they are fleeting, short lived golden moments where you find yourself walking on air, yet the glow stays with you for years each time you remember them.

Thus it was that Miranda and I literally felt like a million dollars at the wedding. We noticed many admiring glances as we walked in procession to the little Greek church of Panayia Kremasti in Corfu Town, where the early evening sun was still strong and Christos' spectacular diamonds shone like cold fire against our tanned skin. Some of the guests we knew well asked where they had come from, so naturally we told them the Espianada Jewellers; we omitted any mention of the loan, just as Christos had instructed. One young acquaintance of Miranda's took her to one side outside the church and tried to pump her for information. Who had given her the diamonds? Were they a birthday present from her parents? Were they from her handsome Greek boyfriend of the time? I kept quiet and watched my daughter, quite the actress, from a discreet distance.

"Can you keep a secret?" whispered Miranda with a perfectly straight face as the girl's eyes widened with rapt anticipation.

"Yes of course!" she replied.

"Good. So can I," said Miranda, walking away to leave her interrogator speechless.

Chapter Thirteen
The Three Fates

It is during our darkest moments that we must focus to see the light.

Aristotle

In September that year, true to the pattern of the summer's incidents and mishaps, one of Sarava's twin engines started misbehaving after taking on some polluted fuel in Levkas. Jeremy did nearly all the maintenance on Sarava, having learnt his skills from the labourers on the farm during his childhood. In his late twenties, Jeremy had rebuilt the colossal engine on *Valdora*, an elegant seventy foot ketch from the classic era of the 1930s. He and close friends from Devon had bought her in partnership and had spent two years refitting her for a cruise across the Atlantic to the Caribbean. The three young bachelors were away for eight months before returning somewhat reluctantly to Dartmouth. When Jeremy proposed to me shortly after his return, my mother asked him why on earth he wanted to get married and settle down. How little did she know. In our forty years of wedded bliss we have never really felt any urge to put down anything but the shallowest of roots. Somehow we have always managed to lead a nomadic life, often on the tightest of budgets.

An acquaintance of ours had written to say she was holidaying in Paxos while her son was working in Fiskardo during his summer break from university. As it fitted in with our plans, we offered to take her to Kefalonia to visit him. It was the third week in September and the weather was perfect; a stiff breeze from the open seas to the west gave us a wonderfully exhilarating sail to Fiskardo. We had no idea that Jean was a very nervous sailor; in fact Jean herself probably hadn't known she was a very nervous sailor. Once on board she glued herself to a corner in the cockpit with her nose in a book and her back to the wonderful panorama unfolding before our bows. At the helm, Jeremy spotted two pilot whales swimming languorously beside us, keeping pace with us for several minutes; but even this rare sight could not move Jean, stuck as she was to the cushioned seats like a limpet to a rock. Jeremy had noticed her green shorts with some alarm and complained to me in barely concealed whispers that he thought her a 'Jonah'.

"Well we can't do anything about it now, you can't exactly throw her overboard," I said.

"I don't like it. Can't we leave her in Fiskardo to make her own way back to Paxos?" he asked.

I was surprised to see Jeremy, normally so sceptical about superstitions, becoming more and more unnerved as our voyage progressed, but some of the sorcery must have rubbed off from his mother. Liz had been a principal dancer with the Ballet Rambert, a star from her youth having been selected first by Balanchine and then Rambert between the wars. Like the notorious Windmill Theatre, but fully costumed, the Rambert company had continued dancing throughout the London Blitz in which two of Liz' homes in succession had been destroyed by bombs. She had also been on tour to Australia with Rambert, travelling on a flying boat as far as South Africa and stopping to refuel at various places *en route* including, strangely enough, Gouvia; like all those connected with the stage, Liz was incredibly superstitious. She had gone into overdrive during the time I was expecting Rory and would never let me pour from any teapot she had herself used for our first cups, as she firmly believed such action would produce ginger twins. No whistling was ever allowed at sea, green clothes were most awful bad luck and 'Bexhill donkey' had always to be substituted for 'rabbit'. There were literally hundreds of these superstitions, including never passing a sharp object directly from one person to another – to this day we always have to put down a knife or a pair of scissors before the next person can pick it up. My mother was also extremely superstitious, partly due to her time singing and dancing with the Torquay Operatic Society in the last years of peace before the second world war. When Mummy and Pop came to stay in Cyprus on Aries I was expecting Rory; we were swimming in the shallows off Nissi Beach as a shoal of inquisitive little fish surrounded us. I squeaked with surprise.

"DON'T TOUCH YOURSELF!" shouted Mummy in alarm.

"Why?" I asked.

"Because if you do, the baby will be born with a birth mark where you touch!"

I was so incensed by such hocus pocus that I slapped myself on my shoulders with bravado. Rory was born six months later with a small birthmark on his shoulder – a perfect map of Cyprus!

In her later years as a renowned choreographer on stages from New York to Leningrad, Liz had broken a bone in her ankle whilst rehearsing Nureyev at the Paris Opera for Yves Saint Laurent's launch of the men's cologne '*Kouros*'. Despite the great man famously saying *For me, perfume must be adapted to fashion, not the other way around,* the new cologne was nicknamed Eau de Pong by the corps de ballet. Liz remained implacably convinced The Phantom himself was to blame for her misfortune. Returning home to England with her ankle in plaster Liz was only mildly pleased by the arrival of an enormous basket of blue and white flowers with an expansive handwritten message of thanks from Yves Saint Laurent himself. I saw the flowers when we went to stay a few days later and asked her what she had done with the card, only to be horrified to hear she had thrown it away. Jeremy had to literally drag me away from the dustbins.

It was typically hot and airless in the shelter of Fiskardo harbour when we collected Jean's son Peter from the dock, but gamely we took mother and son to Antisamos, where many of the beach scenes in *Captain Corelli's Mandolin* were filmed. We anchored Sarava beside a deserted cove, only accessible by swimming ashore and well away from the crowds. But Jean was not keen to explore, even though the alluring strip of sand was only a fifty yard swim through warm water as clear as turquoise jelly. Jeremy offered to lower the tender from the davits and run her closer, but she was determined not to leave the cockpit. Peter was contentedly jumping and diving off the boat, so I left Jean reading her novel and snorkelled to the beach, occasionally sinking down in the water to be completely surrounded and gently nuzzled by shoals of tiny, iridescent fish; it was just like being in a giant aquarium and I felt immensely privileged to share their under-water world for as long as I could hold my breath.

Ashore on the beach I strolled inland, whimsically imagining myself an intrepid naturalist, following in the footsteps of Sir David Attenborough, to see what fascinating flora and fauna I might find. The heat was intense amongst the bushes and scrub, wafting up in waves around me with its aromatic scents of wild herbs and baked earth. The cicadas were scraping out their signals to each other so loudly that the noise reverberated within your skull, almost drown-ing out other sounds until your ears grew accustomed to it. Bright green, sunbathing lizards scuttled away at my approach; a hypnotic undertone, the soporific humming of bees, surrounded me as they sucked nectar from the dainty blue flowers of wild thyme, in sharp contrast to the shrill, rasping of the cicadas. A small tortoise dozed peacefully under a myrtle bush, looking as if his brown and cream patchwork shell been recently gloss painted. Then a large yellow but-terfly fluttered in front of me, disturbed from its perch on a nearby Monks' Pepper flower. A shrub highly favoured by butterflies, the Monk's Pepper or Chaste Tree* grows all over the Greek Islands, its

---

* Monk's Pepper has been well known to the Greeks for thousands of years and was used by the Ancients as an anaphrodisiac, being given to men in holy orders to divert mind and body from lust – hence the name Monk's Pepper. John Trevisa, a Cornishman (1342–1402), wrote: '*The herb is always grene, and the flore therof is namely callyd Agnus-Castus, for wyth smell and vse it maketh men chaste as a lambe*'.

The tree was sacred to the virginal Greek goddess Hestia, the Roman deity Vesta. Pliny the Elder, in *Historia Naturalis,* describes Athenian women using Monk's Pepper stems and leaves as a bedding to subdue the passions during the *Thesmophoria,* when they left their homes and husbands for three days each year to remain chaste. But whether the special bedding was used

delicate blue-violet flower spears very similar to those of the common buddleia, but much smaller. The attractively seven-lobed leaves are almost identical to those of Marijuana sativa, the cannabis plant – not that I would know of course...

Within minutes I realised there were hundreds of butterflies of numerous varieties and colours amongst the bushes; one settled on a leaf, so close to me that I could see the veins in its wings; this butterfly was the biggest I had seen since the weeks I had spent in Thailand as a teenager. It was vibrant orange-red and black, with elongated wings of a span which would not have looked out of place in the hothouse of a zoological garden. Lacking a butterfly net I had to be content with trying to capture the images of these butterflies in my mind; I do have a photographic memory, but it could not do full justice to these gorgeous creatures. I wonder if it could have been the Giant African Swallowtail, holidaying out of Africa in the more temperate climate of Kefalonia before returning home for the winter months.

Late in the afternoon we plugged our way back to Fiskardo through short seas whipped up by a strengthening headwind. Safely moored in the calm of the harbour, Jean eventually prized herself out of her seat in the cockpit and dashed across our passerelle with a surprising turn of speed onto the quay where, by this time somewhat greener than her shorts, she announced that she would take the cargo ferry back to

---

by the women to subdue their passions, or to pacify their lonely husbands while they were away, he doesn't make clear.

Adult women of high birth would assemble for this festival dressed in virginal white to honour Demeter, goddess of the harvest and fertility, and her daughter Persephone. Men were not allowed within kissing distance of the women at this time, or to know any of the secret and grisly rituals performed.

The festival occurred during seed planting time, usually in the second week of October, to commemorate Persephone's kidnapping by Hades and her subsequent half-yearly return from the Underworld to her mother Demeter. To this very day Monk's Pepper is still used as a natural, homeopathic remedy to support hormonal behaviour in humans and animals; for pre-menstrual relief and fascinatingly but not surprisingly – given its history – for regulating the behaviour of stallions!

Paxos. That night we ate a simple meal of pasta and salad on board; this was so unusual as we loved the various tavernas by the harbour with their gaily painted wooden chairs and coordinating checked tablecloths, but most unusually Jeremy was distracted and did not feel like going out for supper. Early next morning we set out for Corfu; I made coffee and brought it out into the cockpit with some crispy *milopita*, bought from Theodora's while they were still warm and fresh from the oven. This would cheer him up I felt sure.

"It's that bloody woman!" snapped Jeremy. "I told you she was a Jonah! There wasn't any dew on the decks this morning and the barometer has plummeted like a stone, so some serious wind's on the way."

The first gale of the autumnal equinox was soon upon us, bringing with it lashing rain and spray that brought our horizon down to yards. Even I was a little spooked, the disorientating lack of visibility was unnerving to say the least. I have never been frightened at sea, despite losing my brother by drowning, but I do like to be able to see where I am going. I was reminded of the time something similar had happened during our honeymoon voyage to Cyprus. We were in a very busy shipping lane off the west coast of Portugal, a nautical equivalent of the M25, sailing from Lisbon towards Cape St. Vincent; I had slept for a few hours during Jeremy's watch until I was awoken by the sound of our foghorn. Almost becalmed, Aries had been enveloped by thick fog in the blackness of the night; it was suddenly very cold and damp, even in the middle of July. Unlike Sarava we had no radar on board, but we could hear the powerful throb of supertankers as they passed all too close for comfort; their wash a few moments later often showed how very near they had passed. It was terrifying, as was the sight of Jeremy running to the bow every few seconds to listen, before blasting our pathetically small foghorn into the darkness.

As I sat there shivering I detected a very fishy smell surrounding Aries on all sides, stronger than I could ever have imagined. It was accompanied by occasional strange sounds like someone blowing water out of a snorkel, but much louder; a snorting bull about to charge a matador could sound similar, but bulls were quite a rarity at sea. Was I hallucinating? Jeremy heard it and shone his torch beam into the black sea. I ran over to join him and stared at the inky water below. All around the boat was a school of silvery dolphins, just moving their tails gently to keep pace with our drifting, like humans treading water. We were completely surrounded by circles of dolphins, roughly three deep, forming a dense barrier. They stayed there for a couple of hours until the fog lifted, exhaling noisily from their breathing holes at intervals, generously sharing their fishy breath with us. It might have seemed fanciful but we liked to believe the dolphins were trying in their own way to protect us.

In Sarava's cockpit I sat perched astride the starboard coaming beside Jeremy at the helm, pulling my sweatshirt sleeves over my hands to keep them warm as I peered into the chilly murk; on Sarava we did have radar, but it could often give a false sense of security. We were sailing up the west coast of Levkas, some fifteen miles off the lee shores of its sheer and inhospitable cliffs – near the southern end of which is the spot known as Sappho's Leap, whence she is supposed to have plunged, heartbroken, to her death. Any boat in trouble here would have to fend for itself, which only added to my anxiety.

Our passage back to Kassiopi, where we had arranged to meet Miranda and Rory, was distinctly unpleasant by Ionian standards, but Sarava behaved beautifully as always. She surfed over the steep seas as we ran northwards; nevertheless the muck in her fuel tanks was shaken and stirred by the unruly conditions, further clogging the fuel filters. Consequently one of the engines spluttered and died just as Sarava motored into the safety of the harbour. Early next morning I was getting ready to return to Gouvia in the car. The gale had spent itself during the night, leaving clean skies and a gentle breeze in its wake.

"Do you want to come with me or stay with Daddy to bring Sarava back?" I asked Miranda. "I'm taking the Jeep back to the marina."

"I'll stay with Daddy as it's the last trip of the summer before we go home," she answered. "Anyway he might need some help." Out of the mouths of babes....

Tears come from the heart and not from the brain.

Leonardo da Vinci

As I drove out of Kassiopi I noticed Angelo Kiros sitting on the pavement outside his scuba diving shop; it was closed and I wondered why he was sitting there by himself, most uncharacteristically hunched over and holding his head in his hands. I stopped the car beside him and gave my usual greeting.

"Hello handsome!"

As soon as he looked up at me I saw something was dreadfully wrong. Angelo had to be one of the most exuberant and extrovert characters in Kassiopi, if not the whole island. Tears streamed from his eyes and ran down his suntanned face.

"Angelo, what on earth's the matter?" I asked, jumping out of the car.

He sobbed into my shoulder as I sat beside him and put my arms around him.

"Scuba has been killed, he's dead!" sobs shook his strong body as he spoke.

"No! How? What happened?"

"He was hit by a car or lorry and was found dead on the road by one of my friends passing by. Now I am having to bury him in my garden."

It was useless trying to console him; Scuba was like an adored brother. I told him I understood his grief completely, having lost many pets over the years, but I had to leave him as I knew Jeremy would worry if I wasn't at the marina when he and Miranda arrived. I stopped just outside the village to pick a large bunch of wild jasmine; I immediately took the flowers back to Angelo and pressed them into his hand.

"For Scuba," I said, with tears in my eyes and a lump in my throat, "Put them on his grave with our love."

Scuba had been a friend to all who had known him, an unofficial mascot of the village who stood two metres tall on his hind legs, a gentle giant who Angelo had bought as a fluffy black puppy from Canada. Jeremy and I had rescued him from the harbour early one morning when he had evidently gone in for a swim and couldn't find his way out again. Like all Newfoundlands, he adored swimming, frequently going to the 'rescue' of bathers at the local beach and trying to round them up back to the safety of the shore. But on this occasion his thick, woolly adult coat, once sodden with water, was weighing him down and he was becoming exhausted. We called him to the only spit of sand on the opposite side of the harbour, where it had taken all our strength to haul him out. From that day he always came to Sarava to pay a courtesy call and scrounge a biscuit whenever we were moored in Kassiopi, waiting politely on the jetty with two gigantic front paws on the end of our passarelle. Burberry would tolerate him on our walks around the village, where he trotted along happily behind Scuba's bulk, but would growl disapprovingly from the safety of the cockpit whenever this lion sized giant came close to Sarava. I called Miranda to tell her the sad news, not wanting her to hear about it by text from one of her Greek friends.

I arrived at Gouvia an hour later and waited at the little marina cafe. It usually took Sarava slightly longer to get back to her berth, so I ordered a coffee and sat back, relishing the peace and quiet of my own company, thinking my own thoughts after such a hectic summer. Half an hour later my mobile phone rang, I expected it to be Jeremy telling me they were going to be later than expected, but it was a Greek friend from Acharavi.

"Mrs. Jani?" the woman's voice sounded very distressed.

"Yes, who is this?"

"It's Athena, I'm afraid I have some terrible news for you." Athena was a close friend of my lovely goddaughter Antonia.

"Is it about Scuba?" I asked.

"Who? No, it's about Krissa, Antonia's sister."

Krissa had recently been brought back from the hospice in Athens, as it was feared she was losing her brave battle against Leukaemia. I feared the worst.

"I'm afraid Krissa died at home this morning."

Although the terrible news had been expected for some while, it was the most premature end to this beautiful girl's short life. She was only seventeen years old.

I put the phone down on the table in front of me and gazed out to sea, once again that day through a veil of tears. I knew I should call Antonia, but in the Greek tradition her family would have already shut themselves away in their homes incommunicado until the day of the funeral. I decided I would try anyway; at least she would recognise my number and know I had tried to call her. In my fevered mind I heard my mother's voice saying 'Bad things always come in threes'; and before I could dial Antonia's number my phone rang again. I picked it up quickly with some trepidation.

It was the 24th September, a day none of us will ever forget. The third tragic event had played out. As I was not on board Sarava at the time, I am adding Jeremy's own account here ...

I let go the stern lines and secured the anchor as Miranda, still with tears for Scuba in her eyes, deftly helmed Sarava between the breakwaters while I gathered the fenders and lashed them to the pulpit. We headed down channel on a languid sea which still breathed fitfully after the recent gales, heaving its unruffled surface into a random pattern of unseen hillocks and valleys. Rounding the point opposite Kaparelli Island the starboard engine once more faltered and fell silent as yet more dirt found its way into the new fuel filter. Sarava could easily continue under her other engine, but that was not the issue. Her berth at the marina was at the head of a narrow channel between two long rows of moored yachts; there was always a prevailing crosswind that required a fast approach towards this dead end, followed by deft use of both engines to manoeuver her. Normally Sarava could perform a pirouette on a pinhead, but with one engine out of action she was about as handy as a bull with a blunderbuss; accordingly I asked Miranda to set course towards a sheltered bay where I could work on the fuel system at leisure.

After an early lunch we set off once more, but with the starboard engine still faltering I decided to radio ahead, asking the marineros to shepherd us into our berth when we eventually arrived at the marina. Sarava's engines were buried beneath the landings on the small staircases at either side of the main saloon; the soundproof hatch of the reluctant starboard engine was open as I worked on the fuel system. Finally admitting defeat with the engine I threw my handful of tools and rags back onto the bench in Sarava's workshop, located just for'ard of the starboard stairs, and gratefully joined Miranda on deck. As the wind over Sarava's decks gradually cooled my head and blew away the smell of raw diesel on my hands, a wider perspective soon prevailed. Cloudless and calm it was still a day for the Queen, even by the high standards of an Ionian summer; our dirty fuel was a nuisance easily forgotten on such a glorious afternoon. We had struck out from the coast in search of some breeze, which set in regularly after lunch; from that distance the island's man-made scars all but disappeared into the heat haze as we motored lazily under autopilot towards the indistinct outline of Corfu Town.

I can still recall the doppler shift of stretched and compressed images that recorded the next minutes of our lives; a nightmare relived over and over again, second by second and frame by frame as the oncoming express train of events hurtled towards us, overwhelmed us as it clattered past, then receded ever more slowly into the distance.

"I think I can smell smoke, daddy," exclaimed Miranda, only slightly concerned as she peered into the saloon from the bright sunlight.

"There's smoke coming from the workshop door ... And flames too!" she screamed as I joined her at the doorway to see for myself.

"Go to the davits and lower the tender!" I shouted, already halfway into the saloon. "Get in and follow at a safe distance, just in case ... quick as you can! You may need to whizz over to the land for help."

At that particular frame on the film I was certain the fire could be contained, nevertheless my priority was to get Miranda safely away from Sarava as a precaution; any idea of launching the liferaft at that stage seemed a ridiculous overreaction. Curiously enough I already had a healthy respect for fire, so I decided to make for one of Sarava's larger fire extinguishers, which hung on a bracket at the bottom of the stairs on the port side, twenty feet across the saloon from the flames. Ripping the safety toggle from the cumbersome cylinder I ran back across the saloon, aiming the nozzle in front of me like a bayonet. At that instant my world suddenly turned to darkness as a deep, muffled detonation sent a shock wave through the entire boat, knocking me off my feet; searing heat and thick black smoke instantly enveloped me. The extinguisher was gone from my hands as I groped about for anything familiar within the confines of a space I knew so intimately.

Somewhere within those particular fractions of a second, as the hardened soles of my feet struggled for grip on the soft carpet, I sensed a sheet of flame tearing across the headlining of the saloon above me. Utterly disorientated, my eyelids tightly screwed shut against the heat and smoke, I cannoned painfully off furniture and bulkheads before finally barreling through the companionway. Desperate for oxygen I tried to inhale, but the air in the cockpit was no clearer; some primitive reflex refused to allow a single molecule of those hot, noxious gases into my lungs. Amid the panic I had forgotten to ask Miranda to close the throttle of the port engine; as a result Sarava was still making good speed through the water, funneling smoke over the cockpit and aft decks. The heat and roar of crackling flames drove me further aft to the davits, where Miranda had singlehandedly managed to lower the cumbersome tender halfway towards the water.

"Cut the aft fall and jump in, then I'll cut away for'ard!" I croaked with the last remaining puff in my lungs, pointing to the emergency knife in its sheath lashed to the taffrail. But her considerable efforts to crank the heavy tender slowly into the water had exhausted her own supply of oxygen; unable to breathe she summoned the presence of mind to dash up the side deck to the bows, where the air was still clean. Yet all my willpower was still focused on the happier image of Miranda speeding clear of danger in Sarava's tender, while I remained on board to salvage whatever I could from the flames. I lunged for the knife and began hacking feebly at the heavy webbing of the davit falls, but the razor sharp blade was about as effective as a dock leaf in my limp hands. My lungs desperately strained for air, but my head might as well have been vacuum packed in a freezer bag. A veil of red spots before my eyes warned me I was about to lose consciousness ... Another violent shudder inside Sarava redoubled the intense heat and smoke billowing aft from every hatch. On the cockpit table a crystal vase of wild flowers shattered in the heat before my eyes.

Miranda and I were by now separated by some sixty feet of deck, the full span of Sarava's diagonal; now we could only catch an occasional glimpse of each other through the wall of smoke and flame erupting between us. Then, as her lungs at last recovered from their contortions and drew in a deep draught of vital oxygen, a shrill primordial scream of unearthly despair and terror finally shook me from my stupor. Scrambling along the starboard deck I contemplated a final, desperate lunge towards the helm station where my man-bag, as always stuffed at the ready with the mundane wherewithal of daily existence, lay enticingly out of reach. Such a precipitate grab, as it happened, would have cost me my life. Instead, just as I staggered through the smoke towards the bows, a fireball erupted from the saloon door and enveloped the cockpit beside me, sending angry tongues of flame over the aft deck where the pair of us had been standing just moments earlier. Instantly Sarava's large bimini awning evaporated in a staccato crackle, quicker than a pile of dry autumn leaves; a second later the furled mainsail above it was likewise vaporized.

Finally on the foredeck I drank in the pure air with painful gulps as the desperate finality of our situation gradually revealed itself. Miranda and I stared transfixed for a second or two at the inferno raging within Sarava's cabins; through the large tinted windows surrounding the saloon we could see a solid wall of hungry fire, now rumbling like an express train in a tunnel and shaking the deck beneath our feet, as combustion greedily sucked in oxygen from the open port holes below. It could only be moments before the flames shattered the plexiglass and broke out onto the deck. For a split second I eyed the large hatches above the forecabins. Could I dive through them and retrieve our cash and jewellery from one cabin, or Miranda's eighteenth birthday presents – only six days old – from the other? But at that moment smoke began billowing from these hatches too as the cabin doors below were breached; the fire was spreading throughout Sarava's elegant interior with unimaginable speed. Suddenly I realised to my horror we were standing directly above the boat's twin fifty-gallon fuel tanks, just feet from a locker containing two hefty gas supply bottles.

"You must jump, my darling. I'm so sorry, jump for your life!"

Miranda had never been fond of deep water and the horror of leaping prone from a moving boat was etched on her face; but, as on most yachts, every single item of Sarava's lifesaving equipment was located astern. Fifteen lifejackets were in a lazarette, just inches away from the pair of six-man liferafts stowed in lockers beside the aft deck; two horseshoe buoys sat at the ready in their brackets on the stern rails and our RIB tender with its powerful engine was still swinging lamely on the davits. Thus all our emergency equipment, bought at great expense for just such an unimaginable eventuality, was inaccessible if not already consumed by the flames.

"Jump with me, daddy! Look! The fenders!"

She was already standing on the port trampoline beyond the foredeck, her fingers clawing desperately at the running clove hitches securing a couple of the metre-high balloons to Sarava's balcony-sized pulpit.

"Throw them in first and jump beside them!", I urged, fearful that a buoyant fender could break her neck if she clutched it to herself as she hit the water. "And jump out as far as you can!"

Climbing over the high rail Miranda hesitated for an instant before following the two fenders into the blue; I waited for her head to bob up near the stern and then jumped from the rail on the port bow, three metres above the water. My tall, rather skinny frame plummeted deep into the sea like a tern after sardines. Beneath the waves I could see Sarava's keels, rudders and one churning propeller slip past high above me. An eternity seemed to drift by as my body absorbed the tremors of dull explosions amidst lighter tickles from the incessant snap and crackle of flames within the hulls; in that state of weightlessness my mind began torturing me with images of Sarava's furnishings and our belongings that would be disintegrating with each of these resonances. For a moment the soft warmth of the sea enfolded me above its infinite blue darkness, until residual buoyancy finally expelled me into the unwelcoming world above. I surfaced a surprising distance from Miranda, who was already swimming frantically towards me with the spare fender in tow. Holding onto our makeshift lifebuoys, legs kicking out instinctively towards the land as tears streamed from disbelieving eyes, it was difficult to tell which of us was in deeper shock.

Less than two minutes earlier Miranda and I had been surrounded by the familiar comforts of our beautiful floating home; now, from sea level several hundred yards behind her, only the tip of Sarava's mast was constantly visible above the procession of small crests slapping over the backs of our heads. As she tracked away from us, steered relentlessly onwards by her faithful autopilot, Sarava resembled a fire-ship bearing down upon an unseen enemy fleet. A thick pall of smoke was already rising in her wake as we watched the flames grow ever higher. For a moment I wanted to swim after her, forgetting she was moving at six knots and that my sedate breaststroke had never at its most frantic covered ten feet per second.

Flickering like the frames of a silent movie, a distant memory of a foolhardy swim taken in mid-Atlantic, provoked a further shiver:

the incautious leap into two mile-deep seas, the unexpected height of the ocean's swell and the hull already vanished from sight; the grab for the bitter end of a trailing safety line as it snaked by and the long haul back to the rope ladder dangling over the stern of our lonely yacht, a thousand miles from the nearest pinnacle of land ... A violent explosion jolted me back to an infinitely worse reality as the petrol tank in Sarava's tender erupted like brandy in a flambé pan, the ignited vapour sweeping over Sarava's decks like a flamethrower. Moments later further reports followed as her main fuel tanks and gas cylinders exploded, sending deck hatches and debris scything high into the air. Surely this couldn't be happening to us ... We had already lost so much to fire.

"They'll soon pick us up, darling. Don't worry!" I reassured Miranda, whose breathing between racking shudders of grief was still alarmingly fast and shallow.

Yet I knew the dark blue fenders to which we clung would be virtually invisible on the distant sea; rescue would not necessarily be that speedy. We both began to shout and wave frantically at the skies above, suddenly so vast from the inch-high level of our isolation, just like idiotic characters in some cheesy disaster movie; we even waved at a passing airliner, still two thousand feet above us on its final approach to Corfu airport.

"Look!" Miranda suddenly cried through her deep sobs, pointing at the coast a mile or so away. "Boats! Masses of them!"

Sure enough a swarm of craft had appeared like bees from a disturbed hive, trailing thin wisps of foaming wake as they howled at full speed out of a dozen coves and anchorages along the coast. But the armada of boats was speeding off towards Sarava, while Miranda and I were already more than a mile behind her in the water. Then, as if in answer to our unspoken prayers I noticed one boat peeling away from the pack, not quite towards us, but I could tell that her skipper had the good sense to search along Sarava's track. An age seemed to pass as the boat zigzagged this way and that, but eventually the crewman raised a steady arm in our direction and the powerful launch was soon beside us. Miranda and I struggled up the boarding ladder with feeble, shuddering limbs and collapsed into each other's arms at the stern. The Greek skipper, a wise man of the sea who now ran a diving school, quickly established that we were uninjured and that nobody else remained on board Sarava.

"I will take you back to the beats now," he insisted, his English so endearingly laced with the closest Greek consonants available to him. "You sould not wats the end of suts a beautiful yacht; my eyes have followed her many times."

Our final glimpse of Sarava before she was obscured by a headland showed her dead in the water, surrounded at a safe distance by a fleet of onlookers; a billowing column of jet black smoke rose hundreds of feet into the clean afternoon sky from a cauldron of flame, still supported like a funeral pyre by the half awash outline of her hulls. Miranda and I stumbled awkwardly up the unfamiliar beach, arms protectively around each other as our bare feet painfully carried us over the pebbles towards the privacy of our rescuers' beach shack. Roused from the serried ranks of hotel sunbeds and umbrellas, a silent avenue of curious tourists observed our wretched progress agape. Beneath a bamboo awning at the top of the beach we fell onto the hot sand, shivering in unfettered grief; we had probably been in the warm water for less than twenty minutes, yet our teeth chattered and our bodies shook uncontrollably in the heat of the afternoon.

"Here, you must put these sirts on," said Andreas, our barrel-chested diving instructor, handing us a pair of smart new tee shirts branded with the logo of his business.

"You are in sock, my dears; you must keep warm. It was lucky for you the sea was not too tsoppy today, or you would not have been found for many hours."

Indeed, I considered, the sea had not been too choppy, unlike the conditions Sarava had encountered the day before. Fate would not have been so forgiving if such a disaster had struck in the thick weather and empty seas to the west of Levkas.

A waiter from a nearby beach bar came over with two large tumblers of Metaxa; it was probably the wrong medicine entirely, but we accepted the brandy gratefully. Then as the various parts of my brain began to reconnect I remembered that Jani would be waiting for us at the marina. My hand automatically searched for the phone in my pocket; only then did it strike home that all I had to my name was a pair of shorts and my sea duty plastic Swatch. Miranda had fared even worse, possessing just a bikini. I asked to borrow a phone and instantly half a dozen mobiles were thrust towards me by the little group of Greek well-wishers gathered around us; accepting the nearest phone my finger hovered over the dial as I tried in vain to remember Jani's number, which I surely knew as well as my own birthday. Staring blankly at my hesitant left hand, which only minutes earlier had held the nozzle of the fire extinguisher, I vaguely registered that all the hair had been singed off. After a moment or two Miranda's more agile memory kicked in and I dialled the number ...

"Hello darling," said a man's voice.

"Who is this?" I asked.

"It's me, of course." Jeremy's voice sounded completely different, tremulous and hoarse.

"What's wrong? You sound queer."

"Well, there's been a bit of a fire on Sarava and we're at Nissaki. Can you come and pick us up?"

"Oh God, are you all right? Is Miranda all right?" I couldn't ask these questions fast enough, but Jeremy's reply was slow and deliberate; he was always the master of understatement, but I could tell he was weighing and considering each word particularly carefully.

"We're both fine, so don't rush, but come when you can please. You'll find us on the beach."

Forgetting to pay for my coffee, I grabbed my handbag and ran into the cool, air-conditioned marina office.

"There's a fire on Sarava!" I shouted from the doorway. "She's at Nissaki somewhere ... Call the coastguards!"

I ran out to the car without waiting for a reaction from the staff. In my mind I could plainly see Sarava riding safely at anchor off Nissaki, with a small fire in her galley or in one of her engines; I imagined Jeremy and a few local fishermen throwing water to put out the flames; Miranda would be trying to help too by calmly organising a conveyor belt of buckets.

I drove smartly out of the marina along the dual carriageway which led to the coast road. As I passed the last of the buildings which bordered the marina, the first view of the sea opened before me. To my horror I could see an enormous column of jet black smoke erupting from the distant sea high into the blue sky above. Automatically I turned on the headlights, pressed the accelerator to the floor and sounded the horn in a continuous blast with one hand while wrenching the wheel round the hairpin bends of the coast road with the other. I was surprised how all the traffic in front of me immediately pulled over to let me pass; even a huge articulated fuel tanker made way for me on the narrow road. At every bend I caught another glimpse of the sea and the ever increasing smoke column; then the next second my view would be obscured by trees or houses, until the next corner, or the next, or the next again. Within about ten minutes I was close enough to make out Sarava's cream hulls with blood red flames engulfing her decks, sucking the life out of her. Tears poured unnoticed down my cheeks, my foot shaking so much that it took all my strength to keep it on the accelerator. The Jeep swerved and the tyres squealed, the car just inches from the edge of the precipitous road above deep valleys of olive trees.

I tried to control my driving and slowed a little, taking deep breaths as I did so and telling myself that Jeremy and Miranda were safe; this was just a boat after all. But to us Sarava was so much more than just a boat, she was our cherished floating home affording our family the idyllic way of life we had so fortunately enjoyed for nearly a decade.

All this was disappearing before my eyes and in the most horrible way imaginable; this gorgeous, much loved catamaran, who had looked after us so well and given so much joy, was being cruelly consumed by the flames of hell. At the next bend my heart almost stopped as I slammed on the brakes. Through a gap in the trees I saw Sarava's bows turn upwards towards the sky, as if she was taking her last look at the sun which had warmed her decks and her crew for so long. With the dignity and grace that was always hers, she gently sank beneath the surface, leaving only a raft of debris to mark the spot. The column of smoke gradually dissolved into the sky as she slipped down to her watery grave.

I drove down the little track that led to the beach at Nissaki and abandoned the Jeep where the pebbles gave way to sand. Running as if through treacle, stumbling on the stones with legs that felt like jelly, I saw Jeremy and Miranda coming towards me. We fell into each others' arms and sobbed together. It was at that moment I realised how close I had come to losing two thirds of my family. Raised Greek voices brought us back to the present; the locals who had been looking after Jeremy and Miranda, along with the owner of the diving school who had rescued them, were remonstrating forcefully with a team of reporters and cameramen from a Corfu television station. They had easily spotted the column of smoke from Corfu Town and had headed to Nissaki, like vultures hovering near a corpse, determined to film this little English family in their despair as they were reunited on the beach. A brawl broke out and the crew quickly retreated without any footage. Leading us back to the welcome shade of the thatched awning over his beach shack, our benefactor handed me a glass of brandy, as it dawned on me that we had lost everything. My phone rang as I was downing my third brandy.

"Jani? It's Nathan. Are you all right? Have you got Jeremy, Rory and Miranda with you?" he inquired, barely pausing for breath. "You won't have anywhere to stay, so I've got an apartment for you in Stefanos. One of the girls is making sure it's all ready for you; the beds are made up and I told her to leave some supplies in the fridge. You can pick up the key from the supermarket. Stay as long as you like, with my compliments. And come to Agni for supper as soon as you feel up to it."

"How did you know?" I asked, almost choking on the lump in my throat at the thought of such generosity, practicality and understanding.

"Everyone on the island knows. We saw Sarava on fire out at sea; the boys raced after her in the speedboat and a whole flotilla of small boats soon followed. We just prayed you had all jumped to safety ... Eleni, Yiaya, Papou and the waitresses were all hysterical as they feared the worst ... Nobody on board could have been alive at that point, so the boys came back and we phoned the Coastguard, who told us where you were. Thank God you're all safe."

Rory had arrived on the beach moments after me, having driven from the opposite side of the island, where he had taken a brief holiday job as DJ and events manager at a large hotel.

"Do you want to come and stay at the hotel?" Rory suggested gently, "I'm sure they could find room for you, although it's pretty full of tourists; you would probably have to share a double." Although he was in shock, Rory had inherited calmness and practicality from his father and his maternal grandfather.

"No thank you, darling; Nathan has lent us an apartment in Agios Stefanos for as long as we want it. I think we need to be nearby."

I didn't know exactly why, but instinctively wanted to stay where we were known and in familiar surroundings; we had only ever visited Agios Giordis and the west of the island a couple of times by car. Rory stayed with us while the Coastguard officers took some preliminary details, asking Jeremy to file a statement at the Port Authority the next day; tomorrow seemed a lifetime away so I agreed and said we would be there as soon as we could make it. Rory hugged us all and left for the other side of the island; he was on duty in a couple of hours' time and there were rehearsals to be organised. It was only as we climbed into the car that I realised we didn't even have as much as a toothbrush between us.

Until this moment my only thoughts had been for Jeremy and Miranda; yet everything we owned had been on Sarava: passports, driving licences, credit cards and, more pressingly, clothes, shoes and cash. How were we to buy anything, or feed ourselves, pay for fuel or air tickets to get back to England to obtain replacement documents? I had my handbag with me in the car and the clothes I stood up in. Jeremy and Miranda had nothing except swimwear and a tee shirt apiece. I asked Miranda to look in my purse and see what was inside.

"Twenty euros and a few coins, Mummy," she replied despondently.

"Whatever are we going to do?" croaked Jeremy, his voice still hoarse from the fumes.

It occurred to me that I would have to grab the reins and take charge, for a while at least. I don't remember the drive back to Stefanos at all, my brain already composing a mental shopping list. Starting from scratch for the second time in our married life, I tried to recall how we had managed the first time. Fire had totally destroyed our first home on the Salcombe Estuary when Rory was just one year old. Thank heavens we had been out that night at a Guy Fawkes party in Dartmouth and Rory had been staying with my parents in Torbay, or the outcome could have been very different.

* * *

In the small hours of 6th November 1983 a telephone call to my parents' house from Kingsbridge police informed Jeremy that there had been a fire at our home; they assured him it was mostly smoke damage, but wanted him to drive down straight away. It was nearly three o'clock in the morning and we were both the worse for wear after our night out, so a flask of very strong coffee was prepared for the hour's drive through the South Hams. Eventually we arrived at the bottom of the steep, narrow lane that led uphill to our remote home; but the way was blocked by a line of five fire engines, their blue lights still flashing wildly. The firemen manning the nearest engine immediately came over to our car and spoke to Jeremy.

"There's no water hydrant anywhere near your property, sir," puffed one of the firemen. "We've had to pump water all the way up the hill from one fire engine to the next, so I'm afraid you'll have to walk on up from here"

We hurried up the narrow lane, squeezing between the fire engines over a tangle of throbbing hoses, sickeningly aware that our fire was far more serious than a bit of smoke damage; after all it was now nearly two hours since we had taken the phone call and the water was still being pumped up the lane. Eventually we reached our land at the top of the hill, where the Fire Chief came to meet us.

"Watch your language lads," he shouted over his shoulder "The lady of the house is here!".

His words seem laughable now, as there was no house. Arms tightly around each other Jeremy and I stared in horror and disbelief at the piles of charred beams and smoking rubble before us, above which two crumbling chimney stacks pointed gauntly into the darkness beyond the stark pool of halogen. I burst into tears, feeling Jeremy's muffled sobs through my coat.

"Here, drink this," coaxed the Chief, handing us two tin mugs of steaming tea.

Neither of us wanted to swallow anything but somehow the strong builders' tea laced with several generous spoonfuls of sugar was surprisingly fortifying, despite our preference for weak Earl Grey without sugar. There was nothing we could do of course, everything had been destroyed. It had been the night of November 5th and our home and land could only be seen from a handful of houses on the far side of the estuary. Nobody had reported the fire as they had mistaken it for an extravagant Guy Fawkes party; only after midnight had somebody bothered to look through their binoculars and alerted the fire brigade.

"We're so relieved you weren't at home," continued the Chief, "We never know if the occupants are inside when we get to the scene. The fire would have swept through this old place within minutes, leaving no time to escape. The first room we broke into was the nursery, as the lads had spotted a cot through the window; you can imagine how we dreaded the thought of discovering a baby in there. We always try to save babies and children first." This statement made our blood run cold.

A young policeman came over to us and introduced himself. His duty watch was finishing and invited us to his home for some sandwiches and coffee.

"That's awfully kind, but I think we'd rather go back to my wife's parents," Jeremy replied.

"I think you'd better stick around," said the policeman, "You see there will be looters as soon as it's light."

"Looters?" I cried, "But there's nothing left to steal!"

"You'd be surprised madam," he said, "They'll go through the ash and take anything valuable that's survived. Gold and silver doesn't usually melt."

Dawn eventually broke into a particularly gloomy morning, revealing curtains of misty drizzle, through which the kindly policeman escorted us back to the site of our home. It looked worse in the cold grey light of day; a smoking scrapheap of rubble surrounded by the charred and sodden remains of furniture scattered on the singed grass. The firemen had thrown whatever they could into the garden, in hope it might be salvaged later.

"What are all those holes?" I asked Jeremy, staring at the lawns and flower beds.

"Good God, someone's dug up half our young trees and shrubs," he gasped in disbelief.

"And all my rose bushes have gone from the beds too!" I sobbed, surveying the pretty garden we had worked so hard to create, which now resembled a war zone. "I had no idea such people existed."

With the help of my father and two friends from Salcombe, while Mummy stayed at home with Rory, we spent the day sifting through the warm ashes with borrowed garden sieves, like prospectors panning for gold. Unbelievably by the end of the day we had found some of the family silver which hadn't been distorted into Dali-esque shapes by the intense heat. Amazingly we recovered every single piece of a silver canteen of Edwardian cutlery, inherited by my parents and given to us as a wedding present; the canteen had been to India and back during the glory days of the Raj and I was determined to salvage it. Each piece of the set was covered in thick black coating of tar which took over a year to clean, although the wonderful walnut case was burned to a cinder. I was particularly desperate to find a BSJA show jumping medal which I had won as a teenager on my gorgeous Palomino, Adonis. With his practical and methodical mind, Pop asked me where it had been in the cottage and I told him it had been on the Welsh dresser. Eventually finding the blackened fragments of the dresser on the front lawn, he called to me a few minutes later; pointing to what appeared to be a lump of tar, he picked it off the charred oak and presented me with the medal, now welded to its plastic stand.

Predictably my mother-in-law put the fire down to the painting of a gypsy encampment which had hung over the fireplace in the sitting room. Typically, calling upon the superstitions from her stage days, she told me one should never have anything relating to gypsies in a house as they hated being shut in. Strangely the painting had mysteriously fallen off the wall into the fireplace a few months earlier, the hardened steel nail on which it hung cleanly sheered. But during the following months there were four more unexplained fires in the same area; a father and son both perished in the final blaze, which the police discovered had been started by the son, who turned out to be the pyromaniac assumed to be responsible for our fire too. Massively underinsured, Jeremy took two years to build a fine new home for us on the site, much of it with his own bare hands and the help of books on building borrowed from the local Library.

* * *

Man marks the earth with ruin; his control stops with the sea.

Lord Byron

The ripples from a vessel sinking are like those of a rock dropped from a great height into a lake; they spread to the very edges before rebounding to the centre in further confusion.

"Look again darling," I asked Miranda as we drove away from the beach. "Are there any credit cards in there?"

"This one says Harrods on it," she said, pulling out a card in familiar green livery. "Any good?"

My mother and I had both had accounts at Harrods for years, in Mummy's case since before the war.

"Does it say Mastercard?"

"Yes. Why?"

"That's the new credit card they issued recently. I never thought I would need it, but that could just save the day!" I told her.

"It won't work," croaked Jeremy from the passenger seat, "It's probably only for use in Harrods."

"I don't think so, it's not the account card. I'll call them and find out," I said, feeling a bit more optimistic.

As Jeremy had often bemoaned, I must have committed Harrods' telephone number to memory when I was little more than a toddler – hardly a challenge as it ended with 1234! Sure enough the assistant at Harrods accounts department assured me it was a valid credit card with a generous limit.

We pulled up in Agios Stefanos and I parked the Jeep outside the apartment. As I collected the key from the lady who owned the little supermarket she patted my hand, telling me how very sorry they all were and handing me a bottle of Greek brandy as a gift. Walking up the steps to the door of our temporary refuge I thought the previous occupant must have left their rubbish outside; heaps of plastic bags were bundled in front of the door, some with little notes taped to them. Miranda read one as I opened the door.

"It's from Marjorie … She says she hopes these few things will come in useful and to let her know if we need anything else."

"How very kind," I said, taking the bag as I went inside. Miranda and Jeremy followed with more bags.

"This one's from Dave and Alex … another one from Fotis and Maria … they're all for us!" Miranda exclaimed in amazement.

The floor of the apartment soon looked like the stock room of a particularly well supported Oxfam shop. As we unpacked them we found clothes, pyjamas, blankets, bottles of water, packets and cans of all kinds of food and drink, bottles of wine, a few toiletries – even new ladies' pants from thoughtful Alex in their unopened Marks & Spencer packaging. Our Greek and English friends had all heard about our misfortune and had rallied to our aid in our hour of need, realising that late on a Saturday afternoon on the North East coast of Corfu we would be unable to get any clothing except beachwear until Monday.

The apartment was delightful, spotlessly clean and even boasted a vase of fresh flowers on the table. I ran a bath for Miranda and added lots of bubbles, finding her some pre-loved floral print pyjamas which would fit; the late September evenings were just beginning to feel cooler as autumn drew closer. I took some hot tea onto the terrace where Jeremy was sitting, still wearing his damp swimming shorts and the tee shirt he had been given. He was staring out to sea over the anchorage and shivering slightly, more from delayed shock than from cold.

"It's so strange looking at the sea from the land isn't it?" he said quietly. "I feel I've been trapped on the wrong side of a mirror."

I threw a blanket around him and handed him a mug of tea.

"We've never spent a night ashore in Corfu since our very first holiday here all those years ago. I don't think we're going to like it."

How right he was.

As soon as Miranda was out of the bath I told her to try to have a little nap before we went out to supper. I persuaded Jeremy to have a soak in the bath while I rummaged in the bags until I found some mens' jeans, a long sleeved shirt and a sweater. There were no shoes or socks in the bags, so I went out to the village beach shop and chose two pairs of flip-flops, blue for Jeremy and pink for Miranda. They came to under ten euros but the owner wouldn't take my money.

"These are for me," she said, patting my arm gently and handing them over.

It was the same story at the supermarket; they all knew us well of course, as we always shopped there whenever Sarava was moored in the bay. I took a wire basket and filled it with tooth brushes and toiletries, tissues, paracetamol, hair brushes for Miranda and me and a comb for Jeremy. Once again I explained that I didn't have any cash and asked if I might pay them on Monday, after we had been to the bank.

"It doesn't matter," said the lady at the till. "Take whatever you need; you can pay me anytime, next year if you like."

Back at the apartment Jeremy looked strange in his borrowed clothes, but at least he was dressed and warm.

"You didn't see any mens' pants in the bags, I suppose?" he asked hopefully.

"I'm afraid not; I'll buy some for you in town on Monday. Alex has very kindly given me a pack of brand new M&S ones, so Miranda and I can share them for the time being; she hasn't even complained that they're slightly Bridget Jones style!"

"I'm wearing my swimming shorts underneath these trousers of Dave's," he said, "They're really rather splendid, far better than any of mine."

He twisted himself around in front of the mirror to admire the rather trendy khaki cotton cargo pants he didn't even know the name of. I smiled at his endearing lack of interest in fashion.

"Alex says Dave doesn't want them back because he's grown out of them, so you're in luck," I told Jeremy, already suspecting he would wear those trousers for years until they eventually fell apart.

"How extraordinarily considerate everyone is," he remarked, with a distinct catch in his croaky voice, echoing my own thoughts.

"Come on, we all need a good hot meal." I said.

Miranda had put together an extraordinary outfit made up out of the contents of different bags; a sarong, some leggings, a tee-shirt and a cardigan that was several sizes too big for her. For the only time in her life she didn't seem to care what she looked like. I had found a cardigan too, as I only had the tee-shirt and cotton trousers I stood up in, which was all I had left in Corfu, and there was a definite autumnal nip in the evening air. I bustled them both out of the apartment and we walked the few yards to Kostas' taverna, where he rushed to greet us with tears in his spaniel eyes.

" Thank-a God you all alive! Yous all okay?" he enquired, crossing himself rapidly several times. "But where is the Rory?"

We explained that Rory hadn't been on the boat and was now back at the hotel where he was working. Putting his strong arms around me and Miranda he propelled us to his private table in a back corner of the waterside restaurant.

"You will be best-a here," he said, "Nice-a quiet-a table with no peoples to bothering."

We took our seats and before we had even picked up the menus Kostas was back with a bottle of chilled local rose and a large bottle of Perrier water; he could easily have ordered our food for us too as he knew our tastes better than we did. An empty jetty stretched out into the dark water beyond the taverna, reminding us that Sarava was missing and would never grace the little bay again. It was hard to swallow our food and even to converse, none of us willing to talk about what had happened. A group of Bulgarian travelling minstrels arrived at about nine o'clock; they toured the coastal tavernas mercilessly throughout the holiday season, repeatedly playing a scant repertoire that included an excruciating version of *Zorba the Greek* in a minor key. We noticed Kostas speaking to them as they approached, waving his arms in the direction of the neighbouring restaurant; to our surprise, they turned on their heels and walked off. We had never seen our friend do this before, but we realised he had dismissed them out of respect for our feelings and our misfortune. There was no bill that night and Jeremy's assurances to Kostas that he would pay him on Monday were rejected with the now customary; 'It's for me,' response. Jeremy remarked that he wondered if this would ever happen in our own native land. It never had thus far.

It felt surreal to be climbing into strange beds, wearing someone else's nightclothes, in a strange apartment and on land, but we were exhausted. Jeremy was tossing and turning all night, interspersed with the moans and yells of nightmares. Fifteen years on, he hasn't slept through the night once since losing Sarava, explaining to me since that it was the memory of Miranda's screams as the flames engulfed Sarava that haunt him. He was obviously suffering from what we now term Post Traumatic Stress Disorder, but flatly refused to seek any help or counselling – having been brought up with the belief that an Englishman must wear a stiff upper lip, pull himself together and just get on with it – paying no attention whatever to some modern acronym. No doubt the shock of being sent to boarding school at the age of six-and-a-half, where sadistic punishment was the norm, had scarred him for life. Thankfully his mother had removed him after two terms, but it was several years before the school was eventually closed down by the authorities.

In fact Jeremy had spent much of the night retracing the previous day's events. No matter how many times he relived every step and detail of those final moments aboard Sarava, he could not account for more than fifty seconds between the first wisp of smoke and the leap into the sea. If the phenomenal speed of the fire gave him some sense of absolution, his other recollection did not; for he had also come to the devastating conclusion that he had probably caused the fire himself. The chain of events had begun the night before, when a soldering iron was inadvertently left switched on; then, moments before the disaster Jeremy had carelessly thrown his tools and rags into the workshop, where the hot iron would very likely have ignited the oily rags. Despite his concerns, our insurance company would eventually take this confession in their stride: insurance, after all, was there to cover such mistakes.

I awoke with a start at five that morning and took a cup of tea out onto the balcony to watch the sunrise over a bay so strangely empty without Sarava at anchor. I made breakfast and laid the table, trying to add a semblance of normality to our situation. The vase of flowers was such a comfort to me; the thoughtfulness of the lady who had prepared the apartment at Nathan's instructions, someone who hardly knew us, was truly heart warming. It was Sunday and I needed to buy us some clothes and other necessities, but I wondered what shops would be open on this Greek Orthodox day of rest. Then I had a brilliant idea: the duty free shop at the Port was always open for business. I would be able to pop over there while Jeremy and Miranda were with the Chief of Port Police; they would not need me there after all.

The familiar surroundings of the duty free shop soothed me a little; I tried hard to concentrate on the job in hand but could hardly remember everything we had lost and what needed replacing. I managed to find several essentials; a hair drier and make up for Miranda and me; socks, a razor and after shave for Jeremy, as well as some other bits and pieces. I chose a very dainty Swarovski crystal seahorse necklace for Miranda; she had lost all her jewellery and 18th birthday presents, received just six days before, on Sarava and I thought this extravagance might cheer her up a bit. I have absolutely no idea why I picked up a disposable camera and some plastic luggage labels, as we had no suitcases. At the checkout I tentatively handed my Harrods credit card to the girl at the till. She called her superior over and I felt a hot flush creeping up my neck and turning my face into a beetroot, so certain was I that the card would be refused.

"How lovely Madame," the manageress exclaimed. "We have never seen a Harrods card!"

"I do hope it works," I said, "I haven't used it before."

She looked down at it again;

"Mrs. Tsaplin?" she enquired.

"Yes, that's me," I answered, now convinced my name was on some black list.

"Did you not have an accident on the sea yesterday?" she asked with some concern.

"Well, my husband and daughter did. Our boat caught fire and sank; we lost everything ..." my words sticking in my throat.

"We know, we heard about it on the television news last night; we could also see the smoke in the sky in the afternoon from this shop. I am so sorry for you all."

As she rang up the total and took my card, which thankfully worked, she whispered something to her young assistant. The girl went towards the perfume section and returned with two large boxes of expensive designer scent.

"These are for you and your daughter, a gift from us. Is there anything else we can do for you?"

Jeremy and Miranda had finished giving their statements to the Port Police, but they would have to go through everything again next day with the local Lloyd's agent. By the time we got back to Agios Stefanos the apartment had been visited by many more of our friends; word had spread and yet more bags had been left outside. With her usual obsession for tidiness, Miranda got busy; this time however I could tell the ritual was therapeutic. We had left that morning in a hurry, but within an hour the apartment was immaculate; the beds were made, wet towels hung outside on the washing line, well out of sight behind the apartment; all the bags from the day before were sorted and the donated clothes put away in wardrobes and cupboards. The bathroom cupboard groaned with the toiletries we had been given, along with the new ones I had just bought; the kitchen was well stocked and organised. So passed our first day on land, my phone ringing constantly as shocked friends and concerned well wishers got in touch from far and wide. One call was from Nathan.

"How are you? Do you have everything you need?" I assured him that we had enough things to open our own shop and that the apartment was lovely.

"Come to Agni for supper tonight; we all want to see you and we'll keep your usual table for you. I'll send a water taxi to collect you at eight."

It was a bittersweet evening. There we were at one of our favourite places in the world, sitting at our usual table, looking at the same view of the straits and the coast and mountains of Albania beyond; but there was no elegant catamaran in the frame. The little paper sign on the table, which had always read *Reserved for Sarava,* now read *Reserved for Chaplin* for the first time. Everyone hugged and kissed us and offered their sympathy, Yiaya and Eleni in tears and wiping their eyes with hankies. Our usual bottles of wine and Perrier were waiting on the table for us, with a Passion Flower bloom floating in a small finger bowl of water at my place – George's signature gesture whenever we ate there. At the end of the meal I offered my Harrods card to Nathan.

"Don't be stupid Jani, put it away. This is on the house."

Nathan's brother-in-law Theo came over to us as we said our goodbyes; he produced some folded banknotes and stuffed them into the breast pocket of Jeremy's secondhand shirt.

"You will be needing this," he said. "You can pay me back anytime, no hurry."

As the taverna's little motor boat chugged out of the bay, Jeremy took the wad of crisp notes from his pocket and, to his astonishment, counted four thousand euros.

In stark contrast our treatment at the British Vice Consulate next morning came as an unpleasant shock, particularly after the cordial, considerate welcome we had received at the consulate in Lille almost exactly a year earlier. I had telephoned the Consulate in Corfu Town on Saturday evening, leaving a message to explain what had happened to us and adding that we would be there first thing on Monday morning, unless they called back with a specific appointment. I knew that the Consulate was often inundated with queues of people wanting travel visas; I had hoped in the circumstances that we might jump the queue as none of us was in a fit state to line up beyond the gates in the sun. We had left our apartment in good time to arrive by 8.30 when they opened, but my mobile rang when we were halfway along the twisting coast road to Corfu Town.

"Mrs. Chaplin?" a lady's voice asked rather imperiously. "This is the Vice Consul of Corfu. We got your message."

"Oh good, perhaps you could give us the first appointment this morning please, We're on our way."

"No, I'm just ringing to say you should come next week, as we're particularly busy until the weekend. We don't make appointments, so you'll have to queue like everyone else and take pot luck."

I could hardly speak, I was so flabbergasted. I put my hand over the phone as Jeremy, who was driving without his actual licence as he felt I was not up to it, asked me what she was saying.

"Tell her we need emergency passports and they'll have to see us!"

I repeated this as politely and calmly as I could, apparently to no avail.

"Losing your passports is a very serious matter. We don't just hand out new ones willy-nilly." Then before I could answer, she put down the phone.

I was shaking and began to feel sick. Perhaps it was the woman's response that had upset me, or the hairpin bends of the road, or the delayed shock of the fire. In fact my nausea was most probably caused by the lack of medication for my underactive thyroid and heart condition; the pills had been in my cabin and I had been without them for two days.

Jeremy parked on the seafront directly in front of the elegant mansion housing the British Consulate at that time. The Union Jack hung limply on its pole in the beautifully manicured garden; it was going to be a hot day. The wrought iron gates were padlocked, although it was now officially opening time, so I rang the number and listened again to a recorded message, which mainly advised the caller not to bother them. The queue on the pavement was already forming and the temperature was rising by the time the gates were finally unlocked. We dashed in ahead of the crowd to find a receptionist sitting at a desk behind a thick pane of reinforced glass, at the bottom of which was a small gap through which one was expected to speak; in fact the whole interior of the building had been tastefully modelled on a British Rail ticket office from the 1960's. I went first; I was desperate for the loo and was afraid of being sick all over the marble floor.

"Good morning, I'm Jani Chaplin, I rang earlier," I said quietly. "Please could I use your lavatory? I'm not feeling very well and it's been ages since we left Agios Stefanos."

"No," said the woman curtly. "Read the sign," she pointed to a scruffy, faded piece of paper stuck with yellowing sellotape above her protective window: *For security reasons visitors are not allowed to use the toilet.*

"But I'm hardly a security risk am I?" I pleaded, "I have only my small handbag and I can leave that with my husband."

"Rules are rules," she answered without eye contact. "No exceptions."

I could feel my Arian ram's horns rising.

"Do you *know* what's happened to us?" I asked with barely suppressed fury.

"Oh yes," she replied, still rearranging some paperwork. "The Port Authority faxed a report to us earlier. You can walk to the public conveniences in the park, or the ones at the end of Garitsa Bay."

I ran outside, sat down on the marble steps and burst into tears. Jeremy followed me a couple of moments later and handed me a glass of water.

"Drink this, darling, while I give her a piece of my mind."

The options for a comfort stop were highly uninviting, both conveniences being an inconvenient fifteen minute walk. If I had been thinking clearly I could have walked to the Corfu Palace Hotel, a short distance away, where I would have been welcome to use their luxurious facilities; instead I chose the slightly nearer option in the park. As I sat on the loo I looked at my only remaining pair of shoes, lovely soft Italian leather sandals; but they were black instead of tan. The floor was sopping wet and it was only when I registered the sharp smell of bleach that I realised the floors had been recently doused with a vast quantity of *chlorini* – the favoured cleaning fluid of all Greeks. The sandals quickly dried on the walk back, the leather losing all its tan colouring as it hardened and cracked apart like fallen autumn leaves. It really was the last straw – that is until I re-entered the hallowed portals of the Vice Consulate once more.

Jeremy, never at his best with any kind of officialdom, was struggling to explain calmly that we needed temporary passports to enable us to buy plane tickets home. I could feel his exasperation and anger building in the face of such belligerence and I knew he was about to explode into what would be officially logged as an aggressive outburst.

"Could you please tell us what you *can* do to help?" I inquired with a sweetness as artificial as saccharine.

Her response was to point towards a shabby pile of papers stapled together and hanging from a drawing pin on the wall behind the chairs in the depressingly English-looking waiting room. We skimmed through the first page, entitled *What the British Consulate will not do*, quickly learning they would not provide any money, clothing, food, drink, clothing, transport, accommodation, plane or ferry tickets etc, etc. My mind jumped to a fictitious elderly lady of limited means who had come to Corfu alone, not knowing anyone on the island, with no family in England to send funds, and too embarrassed to ask for help from the Corfiots who would have rallied to her assistance in a heartbeat. She would have been on a cheap package holiday, staying in a self-catering apartment when her handbag had been lost. Assuming she would have hitch-hiked to Corfu Town, what would the Consul have done for her I wondered? Would they have given her money for food or water until her flight back to Blighty? Would she have been allowed to use their precious loo?

Evidently we had to go into the town, find a photographer and have triplicate passport photographs taken of each of us, return with them to the Consulate, then wait until they could get hold of someone at the Home Office in London – a full two hours behind Greek time – to verify we were who we said we were. Only then, as the woman informed us with a flicker of smug satisfaction, might we be issued with temporary passports; however this was not guaranteed, she warned, before they closed promptly at twelve o'clock. We hurried into the town and returned with the required photos an hour later, only to be told that we were very unlikely to be granted temporary passports any time soon; the Home Office had replied in the interim with news that Jeremy and I had lost our passports almost exactly a year earlier. Her attitude turned even more hostile, insinuating that we might even have sold them for profit. Jeremy explained that his 'man bag' had in fact been stolen from our Jeep at a service station just outside Venice, but it cut no ice. If only Jeremy had known then that a parcel from the Consul in Padua had arrived at his father's house in Devon the week before; it contained his stolen man-bag, empty apart from a few photographs and keepsakes rejected by the thieves.

We sat and waited on hard chairs in the stuffy waiting room as the clock ticked ever nearer to midday, all of us dreading the drive back to Stefanos and repeat the trip again the next day. Worryingly the woman behind the desk was already clearing away piles of documents and replacing them in box files on the shelves behind her, obviously preparing to leave. Jeremy approached the desk again.

"Any luck?" he asked, as she stared at him coldly.

"Perhaps ..." she broke off, glancing through the window behind her before picking up her phone. Surely this call would confirm the news we had so desperately expected.

"Oh hello Maria, can you bring in my washing? I think a shower is coming," she said in Greek, unaware we could understand her perfectly.

Now we had her measure, Jeremy decided to speak rather more frankly with her. At the very last minute the temporary passports were handed over, the harridan reminding us they were only valid for a direct flight home. We grabbed the documents and returned to the town, sinking into comfortable chairs under the shade of ample white umbrellas and ordering a light lunch. It almost felt like a normal day again.

"Why don't you pop over to the bank before our food arrives," I suggested. "You can draw out the money to settle up with the builders."

"What's wrong?" I asked, noticing how Jeremy was staring away into the distance. "I know we've got at least forty thousand euros in the account; you had it transferred from England last week to pay the builders' latest instalment."

"The bank card's at the bottom of the Ionian now, so I couldn't withdraw anything. But in any case I drew it all out in cash last week, ready to pay the builders today," he murmured.

"Oh God, don't tell me..." I couldn't finish the sentence, the words dried up.

"Yes, it was all on Sarava".

The money Theo had lent us was enough to pay for our extortionate, last minute flights and to settle our shopping accounts, but our twelve builders were still expecting to be paid. The following morning we drove to The Lion House to tell them the bad news; to our surprise they knew all about the accident and were uncomplaining as we explained that we could not pay until we returned to Corfu in ten days' time. There was not as much as a frown from any of them as they lined up in turn to shake our hands and offer their commiserations, although we knew full well this was the worst time of year for them to be laid off. They had been unable to do any building work during the summer months when construction always came to a stop until the end of August. The building of The Lion House would have provided continuous employment for them and a good income for their families until the following June; but now, surrounded by a whirlwind of confusion, we were unsure when construction would resume in earnest.

There was no guarantee that we would receive any insurance payment for the loss of Sarava, which had been insured for far less than her purchase price – let alone her replacement cost. Moreover the cover on our personal effects would not stretch beyond some everyday clothes and new underwear for the three of us. Cameras, laptops, watches and so on topped a long list of lost possessions that ran to a fifteen pages; Sarava, after all, had been a fully equipped home. The week before the accident I had taken my great, great grandmother's and my mother's diamond rings to our friendly jewellers in Corfu Town to have them enlarged; in the heat of Corfu my fingers had swollen and they had become uncomfortably tight. Christos had enlarged them in a couple of days and as the altered rings were rather loose I had put them under my pillow for safekeeping, but they too were now at the bottom of the Ionian and would never be passed down to the next generations.

During the summer I had begun to make a collection of young trees and flowering shrubs for our new gardens; some larger specimens of these orange, lemon, mandarin, wisteria, gardenia and cypress had already been planted, but many of the smaller trees and shrubs would not survive a week in their plastic pots without twice daily watering. I walked down the lane to offer these as a gift to our nearest neighbours, an English couple who we had never really come across before. The door of their bungalow was opened by the singlet clad husband, his wife peering at me over his hairy shoulder. I introduced myself and was about to explain my reason for calling, but he stopped me in mid flow.

"Oh yeah, we know who you are." he scowled. "So you won't be swanning around on yer yacht no more now, will you."

I was so taken aback that I was lost for words, instead turning on my heel to run back to Jeremy, choking back the tears. What had we done to deserve this? We had always kept a low profile on the islands, never 'swanning around' or throwing our weight about as some of our fellow countrymen and boat owners were inclined to do. Sarava was the perfect size to accommodate our family and friends in some comfort, but she was a dinghy in comparison with the super, mega and giga yachts that visited Corfu every summer. As Jeremy later surmised, it was purely a class thing, a chip on the shoulder grudge, much as it had been with the bitter women at the Consulate.

There was one last thing I wanted to do before we left Corfu for England. The day before we were due to leave I drove the Jeep into Corfu Town, stopping to pick a large bunch of wild jasmine from a roadside hedge. I made straight for the church of St. Spyridon and entered the small candlelit crypt where the ornate silver sarcophagus, containing his mummified remains, lay in shining splendour. Suspended from the ceiling and walls by coloured ribbons were hundreds of the tiny silver votive offerings to the saint, glinting in the candle light. The relief images beaten on each of the silver votives represented a different part of the human body, as well as boats and houses, which their supplicants believed needed saintly assistance. I knelt on the cold stone step in front of the sarcophagus and placed the jasmine beside it. I am not overly religious, but on this day I offered my heartfelt thanks to this venerable patron saint of Corfu and sailors for saving the lives of my husband and daughter.

On the way back to Agios Stefanos, rounding the sharp bend that descends to Ipsos, I decided to call in on a fellow mariner who owned a large catamaran he used during the summer months to take tourists on day trips around the island; we had often chatted to him over the years whenever we found ourselves sharing an anchorage. I pulled the Jeep off the main road and parked under the eucalyptus trees beside the little fishing harbour where his boat was moored. George appeared from below at my call; he knew from the Coastguard we were all safe and welcomed me warmly.

"I have some photos for you which could be useful, but prepare yourself, they're pretty harrowing," he warned, handing me a large brown envelope. "You may need to show them to your insurers."

Inside were two graphic colour photographs he had taken of Sarava being consumed by fire.

"I didn't dare get any closer," he explained. "I was horrified at the sight of Sarava, as were all my passengers that day. I called the Coastguard as soon as I saw her and prayed you had all jumped overboard."

George explained he had been a firefighter in his naval days, adding that the protocol for anyone dealing with a serious fire on a fibreglass boat amounted to one single word: *Jump*! It was pure chance that I was given these pictures, having visited him on a whim. Perhaps St. Spyridon had guided me. I had no idea at the time, but the photographic evidence certainly helped persuade the insurance company to settle our claim.

With a heavy weight on our shoulders and sadness in our hearts, it was time to leave the island and its people we had come to love. Before dawn on the morning of our departure I left the apartment on my own to wander through the village and pick some wild flowers. Back on the balcony I fashioned foliage and flowers into a garland, intertwining some jasmine sprays around the other plants; its scent would always remind me of Corfu. Miranda and Jeremy were busy packing our few possessions into two new holdalls and giving the apartment a final clean. Oblivious to what I was doing, I left them to it and walked down to Kostas' jetty. The only other person around was an elderly *yiaya*, swathed in widow's black; although we had never spoken she was a familiar figure on the waterfront. I didn't think she had seen me and I didn't much feel like talking. I knelt down at the end of the wooden jetty where Sarava had so often rested and placed the floral garland gently on the water. In my head I heard lines from the poem, *Santa Decca* by Oscar Wilde, written about the village of Agioi Deka in Corfu.

> *And yet – perchance in this sea-tranced isle,*
> *Chewing the bitter fruit of memory,*
> *Some God lies hidden in the asphodel.*

I took a photograph of the wreath as it floated serenely away from the beach. When I turned away I found Miranda was standing quietly behind me; she put her arms around me without saying a word. As we hugged I could feel her muffled sobs echoing mine.

"Come on, time to say goodbye now," I said bravely, as mothers do.

Jeremy pulled alongside in the Jeep, which we would leave at the airport. I took Miranda's hand and as we walked back up the jetty I glanced towards the old lady, just in time to see her making the sign of the cross in our direction and blowing us a kiss.

At that precise moment I knew we would come back to Corfu; this magical island and its people, like Peter Pan's Never Never Land, were under my skin, in my heart, my blood, my bones and in my soul. We had no idea how long we would be forced to stay in England, it could be weeks or even months, depending how quickly we could replace our documents and set our affairs in order. In the enforced separation to come we would remember the colours of Corfu, the sea's blues and greens, the moon's gold and silver. But would Corfu remember us? Would the Ionian Islands remember us?

We would always remember how extraordinarily fortunate we had been, for we had always known precisely what we had got – long before it was gone. What you have loved will always be with you.

Like Scarce Swallowtail butterflies we seemed suddenly to be flying backwards, nevertheless hoping to return soon, armed with new passports, new clothes and the stubborn determination of two Arians not to be defeated. We would come back fighting with all guns blazing to carry on where we had left off. We still had The Lion House to finish and in the words of another famous Arian, Scarlett O'Hara, 'Tomorrow is another day.'

But that is altogether another story ...

JANI'S 'SARAVA KLEFERTI' RECIPE

Take 10 fresh ripe Italian plum tomatoes, wash and cut in half lengthwise. Lay the tomatoes, insides upwards and not overlapping, on a shallow dish or baking tray covered with tin foil – shiny side up. Dribble extra virgin olive oil over the tomatoes, lay some fresh rosemary sprigs between them and sprinkle liberally with oregano.

Place in hot sun on deck for a couple of hours; if no boat and sun available, bake slowly in warming oven of Aga, or at 140°C/gas mark 1, in a conventional oven for 2 hours. Make a simple batter by beating 4 large free range eggs and folding in 2oz/50g plain flour. Whizz together with electric whisk. Stir in a quarter of a pint/150ml double cream and season with salt & freshly ground black pepper.

Leave to stand until tomatoes are ready.

Butter a shallow gratin dish and arrange the baked tomatoes neatly, insides up. Place small chunks of Greek feta cheese, or goats' cheese, between tomato halves. Stir the batter again and pour over the tomatoes. Bake in medium oven for about 20 minutes until it looks golden and crusty. Before serving finely grate some Parmesan over the top. This can be eaten hot or cold, served with crusty bread, crisp salad and torn basil leaves.

durrell

Durrell Wildlife Conservation Trust

is an international charity working to save species from extinction.
Headquartered at Jersey Zoo in the Channel Islands, Durrell's vision
is for a wilder, healthier more colourful world.
Established by author and conservationist, Gerald Durrell, in 1959,
Durrell's overall aim is for more diverse, beautiful and resilient
natural landscapes in which species can thrive and people can enjoy
a deeper connection with nature.
Their approach concentrates on the rewilding of animals, the
rewilding of ecosystems and the rewilding of people.

www.durrell.org

*Photographs of Gerry as a boy in Corfu and in later life at Jersey Zoo
reproduced by courtesy of the estate of Gerald Durrell*

The author contributes voluntarily to Durrell

Save Erimitis

Today the north-east coast of Corfu between Agios Stefanos and Avlaki, so gloriously blessed with its horseshoe bays, pristine coves, wooded headlands, wetlands and rocky promontories, remains utterly unspoilt. Admired from the decks of passing cruise ships, ferries, yachts and caiques as they ply the narrow straits separating the Ionian from the Adriatic, this unique vista has for many years beckoned holidaymakers and more permanent settlers alike to the island.
Indeed it was a caique trip along this coastline in 1997 that persuaded my family to base our catamaran in Corfu.
Since then we have come to know every inch of its beauty.

More recently, however, the Greek government granted permission to a consortium for the development of Erimitis, a tract of virgin coastline at the very heart of this exceptional stretch of littoral. The area is a haven for wildlife, especially rich in rare flora and fauna and is home to several endangered species.

The proposed multi-million pound development of luxury villas, a hotel, a marina and requisite infrastructure will be about as sympathetic and environmentally sustainable as a skyscraper on Skorpios.
And that is before additional permission is sought for further expansion – as it surely will.
The land has already been acquired for an unrealistically low figure by the developers. However it is not too late.

I implore you to consider lending your support to the campaign to prevent the outrageous desecration of this perfect place.
You can find out much more by visiting:

www.erimitis.gr/en/erimitis-eng
info@erimitis.gr
Save Erimitis on Facebook

Jani Tully Chaplin   October 2020